Jane Austen, Sex, and Romance

Jane Austen, Sex, and Romance

Engaging with Desire in the Novels and Beyond

Edited by Nora Nachumi and
Stephanie Oppenheim

UNIVERSITY OF ROCHESTER PRESS

First published 2022

University of Rochester Press
668 Mt. Hope Avenue, Rochester, NY 14620, USA
www.urpress.com
and Boydell & Brewer Limited
PO Box 9, Woodbridge, Suffolk IP12 3DF, UK
www.boydellandbrewer.com

ISBN-13: 978-1-64825-007-1

The publisher has no responsibility for the continued existence or accuracy of URLs for external or third-party internet websites referred to in this book and does not guarantee that any content on such websites is, or will remain, accurate or appropriate.

Cataloging-in-Publication data is available from the Library of Congress.

A catalogue record for this title is available from the British Library.

Contents

Part Three: Austen on Stage, on Screen, and Online

Part Four: Austen in Conversations and Contexts

Acknowledgments

First and foremost, we want to thank our contributors, who enthusiastically embraced the concept of a book that bridges such varied approaches to engaging with sex and romance in Austen's novels, adaptations, and communities. Their interest in the topic and the diversity of their perspectives and expertise made our work on this collection as eye-opening as it was pleasurable. We warmly thank Sonia Kane, editorial director, University of Rochester Press, for her belief in the book, and her involvement and support from its earliest stages. We also want to thank the Jane Austen Society of North America, which enabled conversations with diverse lovers of Austen.

As many of our colleagues and friends are aware, we have been thinking about this book since we met in graduate school. We want to thank everyone who helped us along the way for encouraging our fascination with Austen and sex. Finally, our deepest gratitude goes to our families, who gave us the space, time, and support that allowed us to make this book real.

Introduction

Nora Nachumi and Stephanie Oppenheim

In perhaps the most famous scene in Andrew Davies's 1995 adaptation of *Pride and Prejudice*, Colin Firth emerges from a pond clad in only a clinging white shirt and a pair of wet breeches. In the 2020 adaptation of *Sanditon*, Sidney Parker walks out of the sea buck naked and dripping before a bedazzled Charlotte Heywood. Despite the intentional lack of breeches, Parker's moment—a direct homage to Darcy by Davies, who wrote the screenplay—raised far fewer eyebrows than the original. Apparently, the idea that adaptations of Austen's novels are not only romantic but sexy has become something of a commonplace in popular culture. The success of *Sanditon*, and of Austenesque fiction, which includes titles like *Mr. Darcy Takes a Wife* and *Seducing Mr. Darcy*, as well as discussions on fan-based internet sites, confirms the idea that Jane Austen's novels have become a potent aphrodisiac for many of her admirers.[1] Even *New York Times* notable book *Longbourn*, the first Austen spin-off to be lauded as serious literary fiction, pulses with sensual detail.[2] Clearly, Austen's novels turn people on.

Jane Austen, Sex, and Romance: Engaging with Desire in the Novels and Beyond explores this phenomenon. If Austen's popular appeal springs largely from her ability to convey her characters' romantic and sexual desires—and to tap into those of her readers—then an understanding of this dimension of her work is crucial to appreciating not only the novels, but the countless works of fiction, film, and other media that they have generated in our time. As scholars like Devoney Looser and Juliette Wells, among others, have argued, those of us who write about and teach Austen in the academy can no longer ignore the dynamic relationship between Austen's work and the majority of her readers—no longer, that is, separate a static idea of Austen from what readers *do* with Austen.[3] As members of a diverse and ever-expanding audience, we need to stop fighting over who is "right" about Austen in order to see what we can learn from one another. This requires confronting the conflicting ways we talk—or avoid talking—about sex and romance in Austen. For this reason, *Jane Austen, Sex, and Romance* zeroes in not just on the erotics of Austen's novels and their adaptations, but on the discourse that surrounds this divisive topic.

Fifty years ago (or perhaps even thirty), the assertion that Austen's novels were sexy would have been met with considerable skepticism by a general readership with very different ideas about Austen and her novels. Beginning with her family's biographical endeavors, she has been constructed as a cheerful, pious sister and aunt, as a chronicler of a bygone era, as a prose Shakespeare, as England's Jane, as a keen observer of manners and morals, as a writer of genteel Regency romance, and as a gentle satirist.[4] Each view of Austen and her novels has had its defenders, and often differing views overlap. Until the 1990s, however, Austen's nonacademic readers had comparatively little to say—at least publicly—about the erotic dimensions of Austen's own work.

Obviously, the situation has changed a great deal. Although interest in other aspects of Jane Austen's novels continues unabated, the erotic charge of her fiction has been widely addressed by filmmakers, novelists, and everyday readers, not only in person, but also through discussion boards and fan fiction posted online. Austen fandom, as Sheenagh Pugh notes, has evolved into a "multimedia fandom; fiction is as likely to be based on the Ang Lee film of *Sense and Sensibility* (1995) or Andrew Davies' TV adaptation of *Pride and Prejudice* (1995)" as on Austen's originals.[5] Although the most popular subgenres concern heterosexual relationships between Austen's protagonists, other subgenres include mashups and slash fiction, which features same-sex pairings. These nonheteronormative readings, as Holly Luetkenhaus and Zoe Weinstein have argued, lead to new ways to understand and appreciate Austen's canon.[6]

Despite a few notable exceptions, academic work on Jane Austen and sex has not been nearly as plentiful or diverse. As the only woman writer widely accepted as part of the literary canon of "great" British authors, Austen has long been the focus of work that reflects the dominant interests of those who embrace the study of literature as a profession. During the second half of the twentieth century, as Claudia Johnson eloquently explains, the prevailing view of the author was that of an instructor whose novels promoted "orthodox morality, conservative politics, and strenuous propriety," through the marriage plot.[7] Promoted primarily by a "middle-class professoriate," this view of Austen was aggressively heteronormative, "disciplining and displacing an older (and as these professors claimed) effete and belletristic model of novel criticism."[8]

Within this academic arena, almost no room was made for discussing sex—heteronormative or not—within the novels. One reason for this, as Alice Chandler explains, was the "popular and pervasive stereotype" of Austen as "genteel spinster," or, as Marvin Mudrick describes her, a frigid virgin, for whom "sexual vitality is a rebel, an enemy of [a] system" in which "marriage [is] the means of consolidating privilege and passing it on."[9] Another, Chandler remarks, is Austen's style:

> The coolness and deftness of her surface and the interplay of irony and wit have made her novels seem more purely cerebral than they are and have reinforced the presumptions about her temperament. A merciless satirist of false or excessive feeling, she has wrongly been seen as suspicious of all feeling; and her very desire to subsume sex within marriage has somehow made her seem to be endorsing marriage without sex.[10]

To remedy the situation, Chandler wrote "A Pair of Fine Eyes" (1975), which makes the case that Austen's novels are all about sex. Jan Fergus and Susan Morgan followed suit in the 1980s with "Sex in a Social Context" (1981) and "Why There's No Sex in Jane Austen's Fiction" (1987).[11]

Although each focused primarily on heterosexual relations, their insistence that sexual desire and Austen are not antithetical (or, in Morgan's case, that they are antithetical for a reason), paved the way for two pieces that directly challenged those who preferred their Austen chaste and her protagonists subdued and straight. Eve Sedgwick's "Jane Austen and the Masturbating Girl" (1991) dared Austen's readers to consider the autoerotic elements in *Sense and Sensibility*, while "Sister-Sister," Terry Castle's review of Deirdre Le Faye's edition of Austen's letters (1995), explored the homoeroticism of Austen's bond with her sister, Cassandra.[12] The response to both scholars was swift and sensational. They were pilloried in the popular press and received considerable pushback from some Austen scholars, especially those outside the academy.[13] Castle, though she denied claiming that Austen was a lesbian, defended her interpretation of the sisters' intimacy as not only the "most important emotional relationship" of Austen's life, but one that "had its unconscious homoerotic dimensions."[14] Sedgwick struck back at the "repressive" school of Austen criticism, framing her work as an alternative to its "timidity" and "banality," which misreads Austen as an agent of normalization.[15] This pivotal work in the 1990s opened new possibilities for exploring sexual desire in Austen's novels and subsequent scholars, most notably those involved in Queer (now LGBTQ+) and Gender Studies, have deepened the discussion. Clearly, the environment for these conversations has changed.

To date, however, Jill Heydt-Stevenson's *Unbecoming Conjunctions*, which explores Austen's bawdy humor, remains the only academic book to focus exclusively on sex in Jane Austen's novels.[16]

What accounts for the comparative paucity of academic work in the rich field of Austen and sex? One explanation, we suggest, has to do with the different ways academics and Austen's nonacademic fans talk about Austen and envision themselves in relation to the novels. From the moment Darcy hit the water in 1995, Austen fandom began to multiply exponentially. Many readers and moviegoers talked about Austen's characters not only as if they were real people, but also as objects of desire. To some academics, it seemed that Austen had become synonymous with sex and romance in the popular imagination. For scholars to dwell on the erotic heat in the novels and the film adaptations threatened to destabilize traditional divisions between academics and everyday readers.[17] To write about how Austen's novels generate physical and emotional responses might, for example, involve abandoning an authority buttressed by the assumption that those who study literature as a profession are objective and emotionally detached from their material. It also raised the possibility that scholars might not be better interpreters of Austen than everyday readers, including those who regard themselves as her most ardent fans.

While the issue of sex remains somewhat of a special case, a vital strand in twenty-first-century Austen studies has directly addressed—and begun to bridge—the divide between academic and popular responses. Drawing on recent developments in fan studies, as well as studies in popular culture, adaptation, celebrity, film, and digital media, this work highlights the dynamic interchange between Austen's texts and the broader cultural contexts in which they circulate.[18] Early scholars of fan studies sought to overturn the image of fans as "uncritical, fawning, and reverential" and "redeem them as creative, thoughtful, and productive."[19] While some assumed a detachment from the fan communities they studied, others began to acknowledge that fan and scholarly identities might overlap. As Henry Jenkins notes, "participation is often as important as observation."[20] To write as both an academic, with access to critical tools for analysis, and a fan, with access to the fan community and its own pool of knowledge, has its advantages, even if these two identities don't always easily align.[21] In *Everybody's Jane*, Juliette Wells addresses the uneasiness of the academic with the amateur's display of *feeling* when she asks, "If you are a literary scholar, would you answer or avoid a question about what Jane Austen means to you? You might answer such a question, but only off the record, lest your colleagues hear you speaking in a way that seems unprofessional."[22] Wells strives to dispel such diffidence, urging all of Austen's readers to "let down our guard" and "take the opportunity to come together, amateurs and scholars alike, and share what we love and have learned about this exceptional author."[23]

Austen scholars have responded to Wells's call in diverse and fruitful ways. Their work has broken new ground in exposing academic readers to fan perspectives. Initially, studies of Austen fandom published by academic presses were authored solely by academic writers. More recent work, like Lawrence Raw and Robert G. Dryden's *Global Jane Austen* and Gabrielle Malcolm's *Jane Austen: Fan Phenomena* has included more diverse voices through interviews with nonacademic Austen readers, specifically fan fiction writers.[24] Devoney Looser and Janine Barchas coedited a special issue of *Texas Studies in Literature and Language* asking, "What's Next for Jane Austen?" in which five scholarly articles share space with nineteen pieces penned by nonacademics who, in varied ways, are "major stakeholders connected to the Austen industry."[25] As Looser and Barchas observe, the "democratization of much scholarly information has brought Austen-inspired academics and fans—ranging on a continuum of those who might read Austen purely for pleasure—into closer proximity and cooperation."[26]

Indeed, as nonacademics have signaled by pitching into such publications, they have also become more open to scholarly approaches to Austen. At annual meetings of the Jane Austen Society of North American (JASNA), Austen scholars and fans of all stripes come together to present panels and lectures, lead workshops, perform Austen-inspired entertainments, display their Regency attire, and dance together. JASNA's two journals, *Persuasions* and *Persuasions Online*, publish articles by both academic and nonacademic contributors. While there remains some "anxiety of affiliation" on the part of both kinds of JASNA members, the relationship between the two groups has evolved significantly in the last several decades.[27] Writers outside of the academy have also published their own studies of Austen fandom. For instance, Deborah Yaffe's *Among the Janeites* turns the tables by profiling celebrated Austen scholars Devoney Looser and George Justice, among other personalities in the Janeite world.[28] Other writers, like university librarians Luetkenhaus and Weinstein, claim a dual identity, insisting, "we are both fans and scholars and approach Austen in combination."[29] Communities that once seemed fundamentally divided have recognized significant points of connection. The result has been, if not a merger, perhaps an alliance, in which diverse types of readers and viewers appreciate how their differences enrich their engagement with Austen.

Jane Austen, Sex, and Romance builds on this work by probing what is at stake for each set of Austen enthusiasts when Eros is added to the equation. While other books allude to sex and romance as one area of debate, ours is the first book to place this provocative topic at the center of a discussion among a wide range of readers and viewers. It blurs the boundaries between academic and popular culture by incorporating voices from diverse backgrounds including journalism, screenwriting, digital media, fiction writing, academia, and Austen fan culture.[30] Many of our contributors write about Austen in styles appropriate to their areas of expertise. Readers of this volume will find, for example, an autobiographical essay by a writer of Austenesque fiction following an academic analysis of falling in love in Austenesque novels. A chapter on creating an online virtual world modeled on Austen's may be read alongside discussions about writing for *The Lizzie Bennet Diaries* or the erotics of teasing in *Pride and Prejudice*. Contrasts like these call attention not only to differences among our writers' approaches to Austen, but also to interests and concerns they share. So do other chapters, in which contributors deliberately adopt styles from outside of their fields. Several literary scholars, for instance, depart from the conventions of academic writing by experimenting with personal narrative. Likewise, contributors from outside the academy demonstrate that those who study and teach literature as a profession do not have a monopoly on insightful textual analysis. By enabling this dynamic exchange of personas, perspectives, and styles, this volume strives to enrich all of our different readings of the novels. Together and separately, our contributors make an eloquent case that sex and romance in all things Austen warrant serious attention.

Jane Austen, Sex, and Romance is divided into four sections, each of which focuses on a different realm in which we engage with Eros and Austen. In Part One: The Novels, three very different types of scholars focus on the representation of desire in Austen's own work. In "Austen's Teasing, or What the Wit Wants," Mary Ann O'Farrell, a university professor, explores the erotics of teasing in Austen's novels. "Sex is in the language" of Austen's fiction, O'Farrell demonstrates. Focusing primarily on *Pride and Prejudice*, she argues that teasing is a way to stir up and maintain "the warmth of novel sex and novel love." While O'Farrell interprets the language of courtship and marriage, Jade Higa and Christien Garcia demonstrate how paying attention to queer desire enriches our understanding of the erotic energy in Austen's novels.

In "Performing (Dis)comfort: Queer Possibilities in Jane Austen's *Mansfield Park*," Higa, who teaches high school, explicitly challenges heteronormative readings of Austen's fourth novel. Arguing that to be "queer" is to experience a consistent sense of discomfort, she examines moments when Mary and Fanny seek solace in one another's bodies. These attempts, she demonstrates, though unsuccessful, identify cracks in the novel's apparent inscription of heterosexual norms. Finally, in what may be the most provocative essay in the collection, Garcia, a postdoctoral fellow and psychoanalyst-in-training, reads Austen's novel through the lens of fisting, a practice that disrupts such binaries as interior/exterior and pleasure/pain. "Taking Hands: The Fisting Phantasmic in *Sense and Sensibility*" traces patterns of desire that are not subsumed by "hetero-genital intercourse" and suggests that the novel may be read as prehistory of sexual practices that have been erased.

What desires move people to read and write Austen-inspired fiction? In Part Two: Austen Fan Culture and Austenesque Fiction, three scholars and a fiction writer answer this question. In "Always Wanting More: Desire and Austen Fan Fiction," Marilyn Francus explores the conventions of Austen fan fiction online. Austen fan fiction, Francus contends, not only manifests but also perpetuates the desires of those who read it and write it. Its satisfactions depend on continuity, on creating more "Austen" for fans to consume. Francus identifies fan fiction with a new type of Janeite, one who engages with Austen through creation, adaptation, and commentary, and whose pleasures stem from fulfillment deferred.

In "Unconquerable Attraction: Darcy and Elizabeth's Falling in Love in Austenesque Novels," Maria Clara Pivato Biajoli zeroes in on the desires driving a specific subgenre of Austenseque fiction. Biajoli argues that in the world of *Pride and Prejudice* fan fiction, the protagonists' method of falling in love is so constantly reformed that with few exceptions, it could be categorized in its entirety as "fix fics." The efforts of these fans, who enlarge on such fantasies as love-at-first-sight or the-taming-of-the-hero, strongly indicate what they sought, didn't find, but are still determined to get from *Pride and Prejudice*.

The two case studies that follow speak to the particularity of the desires that drive individual readers and writers of Austen-inspired fiction. Focusing on *Emma*, regarded by many as the least erotic novel in the Austen canon, Stephanie Oppenheim finds herself disappointed to discover that Austen fan fiction does not elaborate on the erotic energy between Frank and Jane. In "What's Hidden in Highbury?" Oppenheim adopts the persona of a "scholar-fan," which enables her to write criticism that doesn't claim complete objectivity. "Passion and Pastiche," by Diana Birchall, complicates the assumption that all readers and writers outside the academy are yearning primarily for sex and romance. Unlike many of her fellow writers of Austenesque fiction, Birchall was not motivated by a "romantic character or passionate scene." Instead, it was her analysis of Austen's creative technique, especially her observation of character, that moved her to write pastiche. Drawn particularly to Austen's villainous and comic characters, Birchall was inspired by none other than the "obnoxious and reviled" Mrs. Elton to write her most celebrated Austenesque oeuvre, the series of stories ultimately published as *The Compleat Mrs. Elton.*

In Part Three: Austen on Stage, on Screen, and Online, three scholars (one of whom is also a dramaturg and director), a screenwriter, and an online game designer discuss the challenges involved in dramatizing the desires that Austen describes. "In Search of Colin Firth's Bum" begins with a question: how does one translate the erotic energy in Austen's novels to screen? For Nora Nachumi, the logical place to start is with the BBC/A&E *Pride and Prejudice.* The 1995 miniseries is all about looking, Nachumi contends. Departing from the letter of the text, it revels in its affinity for the external. Nachumi explores the ingenious use of visual cues and perspectives to generate sexual tension and contends that these methods—which transform viewers into voyeurs—are what has led to a subgenre of novels and films about twenty-first-century women obsessed with Colin Firth's Darcy. Her essay can usefully be read alongside Rachel Brownstein's piece, "Jane Again," which considers screen adaptations of *Emma* and *Sanditon* released 25 years later. Despite their differences, Brownstein asserts, both suggest that the "Jane Austen movie as a knowing romcom, the genre that has developed since 1940, might be finally exhausted."

Elaine McGirr's essay, "Touching Scenes: Austen, Intimacy and Staging *Lovers' Vows,*" shifts the conversation from the screen to the stage. In what may be the least traditional piece by an academic in the collection, McGirr describes her experience as dramaturge and director of a group of university students staging a pastiche of *Mansfield Park* and *Lovers' Vows.* Interweaving memoir with scenes from her play, she reveals how Austen's insights into the desires of the young people in *Mansfield Park* resonate with the complicated relations among the student performers. McGirr, who was pregnant at the time, describes how the intimacy of staging the play blurred the distinction between personal and professional, private and public, and made her feel closer to the Austen family, who mounted their own private theatricals.

The experience of adapting Austen's world to digital media is the subject of the two essays that complete Part Three. In "Jane's Players: Sex and

Romance in the Virtual World of Jane Austen," game designer Judy Tyrer discusses how sex and romance were handled in *Ever, Jane*, the massively multiplayer online role-playing game (MMORPG) that she created. While debauchery certainly took place in the Regency period, Austen's novels never depict it directly. Therefore, the team responsible for *Ever, Jane* required discretion among the game's players. This was difficult, Tyrer explains; many of the game's players brought twenty-first-century attitudes—as well as experience with more sexually explicit MMORPGs—into the mix. Tyrer's piece examines these tensions and the creative solutions employed (including strict penalties and the creation of an online penal colony called Botany Bay).

Adaptation is always an exercise in translation, all the more so when one's project involves transporting characters from Regency England to contemporary California. In "To YouTube from Gretna Green: Updating Lydia Bennet for the Digital Age," Margaret Dunlap explains how she and her colleagues handled Lydia Bennet's elopement with Wickham in *The Lizzie Bennet Diaries*—a modern-day version of *Pride and Prejudice* told vlog-style on YouTube. Did they really want to imply that premarital sex would ruin a young woman's life and bring shame to her family? No, they did not. But how could they create an equivalent obstacle without coming across as hopelessly sex-negative to a modern audience? Writing with an insider's perspective, Dunlap reveals how she and her colleagues resolved their dilemma.

In Part Four: Austen in Conversation and Contexts, three academics and a journalist-writer consider the ways different communities grapple with Austen, romance, and desire. In "Erotic Austen," Devoney Looser considers the history and relevance of Austen-inspired erotica. Looser takes as her subject the most "blatantly sexed-up" responses to Austen, in print, online, and onstage. Today's readers are choosing their Austen in any flavor but vanilla, Looser asserts. In a discussion that draws on a wide and vivid range of examples, Looser explores the cultural meanings of this phenomenon and concludes that "even among those skeptical of Austen-inspired erotica's literary quality or value, the significance of the subgenre ought to be acknowledged." While Looser focuses on explicitly sexual responses to Austen, Laura Engel's essay, "The Shadow Jane," calls our attention to the implicit. Writing from an interdisciplinary perspective, Engel considers Austen alongside her contemporary, silhouette artist Jane Beetham Read, who had a love affair with the portrait-painter John Opie. Although neither woman left autobiographical evidence, Engel demonstrates how the romantic histories of the two Janes can be imagined through the clues embedded in their works of art. Moreover, she argues, if we consider Austen and Read as shadows or silhouettes of one another, we may attain a closer, more complete picture of the working life of women authors and artists in the late eighteenth century.

The final essay in Part Four underscores our belief that different ways of talking about Austen can enrich each other. "In Bed with Mr. Knightley," by scholar Deborah Knuth Klenck and her son, Ted Scheinman, a writer and journalist, links sex to dancing. Austen's novels, they demonstrate, clearly indicate the character traits that "promise a good time in bed." While these qualities include conversational skills and considerateness, the ability to dance well is the most reliable sign that an Austen character is "a good lover." Knuth Klenck and Scheinman compare and contrast Austen's representations of dancing with the behavior of modern-day Janeites at the country dances held annually at Jane Austen symposia. Although they are far more direct than Austen's characters, they too appreciate the erotic implications of a good dance.

Juliette Wells's substantial afterword, "Sex, Romance, and Representation in Uzma Jalaluddin's *Ayesha at Last*" puts the essays in this collection in a global context by reading them alongside Jalaluddin's novel. Wells argues that Jalaluddin "offers an affirming mirror to fellow members of her own faith community by depicting characters who are fully as witty, sexy, and romantic as Austen's." At the same time, she asserts, Jalaluddin's depiction of restraint in courtship is truer to the "spirit of the original novels" than many Austen adaptations produced today. Wells's essay underscores the value of a multiplicity of perspectives, which together illuminate and enrich the different ways we engage with Austen and desire.

Notes

1. *Sanditon,* screenplay by Andrew Davies. Featuring Rose Williams and Theo James, aired 2019 on ITV; Linda Berdoll, *Mr. Darcy Takes a Wife: Pride and Prejudice Continues* (New York: Sourcebooks, Landmark, 2004); Gwyn Cready, *Seducing Mr. Darcy* (New York: Pocket Books, 2008).
2. Jo Baker, *Longbourn* (New York: Vintage, 2013).
3. Devoney Looser, *The Making of Jane Austen* (Baltimore: Johns Hopkins University Press, 2017); Juliette Wells, *Everybody's Jane: Austen in the Popular Imagination* (London: Continuum, 2011).
4. See Rachel Brownstein, *Why Jane Austen?* (New York: Columbia University Press, 2011); Devoney Looser, *The Making of Jane Austen,* 1–12; Deirdre Lynch, *Janeites: Austen's Disciples and Devotees* (Princeton: Princeton University Press, 2000).

5. Sheenagh Pugh, *The Democratic Genre: Fan Fiction in a Literary Context* (Brigend: Seren, 2005), 27.

6. Holly Luetkenhaus and Zoe Weinstein, *Austentatious: The Evolving World of Jane Austen Fans* (Iowa: University of Iowa Press, 2019), 110.

7. Claudia Johnson, "The Divine Miss Jane: Jane Austen, Janeites and the Discipline of Novel Studies," *Janeites: Austen's Disciples and Devotees,* ed. Deirdre Shauna Lynch (Princeton: Princeton University Press, 2000), 28.

8. Deirdre Shauna Lynch, "Introduction," *Janeites,* 16.

9. Alice Chandler, "'A Pair of Fine Eyes': Jane Austen's Treatment of Sex," *Studies in the Novel* 7, no. 1 (special issue: "Jane Austen," Spring 1975): 88–103; Marvin Mudrick, *Jane Austen: Irony as Defense and Discovery* (Berkeley: University of California Press, 1968 [c152]), 180.

10. Chandler, "A Pair of Fine Eyes," 37.

11. Jan Fergus, "Sex and Social Life in Jane Austen's Novels" in *Jane Austen in a Social Context,* ed. David Monaghan (Totowa: Barnes & Noble Books, 1981), 66–85; Susan Morgan, "Why There's No Sex in Jane Austen's Fiction," *Studies in the Novel* 19, no. 3 (Fall 1987): 346–356.

12. Terry Castle, "Sister-Sister," *London Review of Books,* 17 No. 15 (August 3, 1995): 3, https://www-lrb-co-uk.ezproxy.cul.columbia.edu/the-paper/v17/n15/terry-castle/sister-sister.

13. "Letters," *London Review of Books,* https://www-lrb-co-uk.ezproxy.cul.columbia.edu/the-paper/v17/n15/terry-castle/sister-sister; "Scholars not persuaded by 'gay' Austen," *Independent,* July 31, 1995, https://www.independent.co.uk/news/scholars-not-persuaded-by-gay-austen-1594180.html. Monahan quotes Southam (editor, scholar), biographers Claire Tomalin, Elizabeth Jenkins, Helen LeFroy (a descendant of Jane Austen's close friend, Anna LeFroy) and Tom Carpenter (a trustee of the Jane Austen Memorial Trust).

14. Terry Castle, Letter to the Editor, *London Review of Books,* 17, no.16, August 24, 1995. www-lrb-co-ui.ezproxy.cut.columbia.edu/the-paper/v17/n15/terry-castle/sister-sister.

15. Eve Sedgwick, "Jane Austen and the Masturbating Girl" [1991], *Close Reading,* eds. Frank Lentricchia and Andrew DuBois (Chapel Hill: Duke University Press, 2003), 315. DOI: 10.1215/9780822384595.

16. Jill Heydt-Stevenson, *Austen's Unbecoming Conjunctions: Subversive Laughter, Embodied History* (New York: Palgrave Macmillan, 2005).

17. See Johnson, "The Divine Miss Jane," 30. Writing of efforts to create novel studies as a discipline, Johnson writes that "Janeites constitute a reading community whose practices violate a range of protocols later instituted by professional academics . . . dogmas holding, for example, that you cannot talk about characters as if they were real people; that reading novels requires specialist skills and knowledges developed at universities; that hermeneutic mastery . . . is the objective of legitimate novel criticism; that the courtship lot celebrating

marriage and maturity is the determinative event in Austen's fiction; and that the business of reading novels is solitary rather than sociable."

18. See, for example, Brownstein, *Why Jane Austen?*; Gillian Dow and Clare Hanson, *Uses of Austen* (New York: Palgrave Macmillan, 2014); Claudia Johnson, *Jane Austen's Cults and Cultures* (Chicago: University of Chicago Press, 2012); Looser, *The Making of Jane Austen*; Lynch, *Janeites*; Kylie Mirmohamadie, *The Digital Afterlives of Jane Austen* (New York: Palgrave Macmillan, 2014); Linda Troost and Sayre Greenfield, *Jane Austen in Hollywood* (Lexington: University Press of Kentucky, 2001); and Juliette Wells, *Everybody's Jane*.

19. Jonathan Gray, C. Lee Harrington, and Cornel Sandvoss, eds., *Fandom: Identities and Communities in a Mediated World*, 2nd ed. (New York: New York University Press, 2017), 3.

20. Henry Jenkins, *Textual Poachers: Television Fans and Participatory Culture* (London: Routledge, 2013), 4.

21. Jenkins, *Textual Poachers*, 5.

22. Wells, *Everybody's Jane*, 2.

23. Wells, *Everybody's Jane*, 220–21.

24. Lawrence Raw and Robert G. Dryden, eds., *Global Jane Austen: Pleasure, Passion, and Possessiveness in the Jane Austen Community* (New York: Palgrave Macmillan, 2013); Gabrielle Malcolm, ed., *Fan Phenomena: Jane Austen* (Bristol: Intellect Books, 2015).

25. Devoney Looser and Janine Barchas, "Introduction: What's Next for Jane Austen?" *Texas Studies in Literature and Language* 61, no. 4 (2019): 336.

26. Looser and Barchas, "What's Next," 341. See also Annika Bautz, Daniel Cook, and Kerry Sinanan, eds., *Austen After 200* (New York: Palgrave MacMillan, forthcoming).

27. Elaine Bander, "JASNA and the Academy: The Anxiety of Affiliation," *Persuasions* 39 (2017): 148.

28. Deborah Yaffe, *Among the Janeites* (New York: Mariner Books, 2013).

29. Luetkenhaus and Weinstein, *Austentatious*, 2.

30. Several of our contributors are members of JASNA, which speaks to the increasingly diverse nature of that organization.

Part One

The Novels

Chapter One

Austen's Teasing, or What the Wit Wants

Mary Ann O'Farrell

"How can you be so teazing?"(7).[1] Mrs. Bennet's how-can-yous, sprinkled throughout her conversations in Jane Austen's *Pride and Prejudice*, are complaints, rhetorical expressions of her irritation rather than questions for which she expects an answer; with nerves that need quieting, she is accustomed to living an impacific life, habituated to an irritated mode of being. How can a husband be so tiresome as not to intuit her motivations? (He has, of course, but doesn't want to tell her so.) How can he "abuse" his children "in such a way?" (5). How can he talk "so"? (4). The sos and suches that accompany Mrs. Bennet's complaints are simple indications—how can he tease her *this* way—but pointing out what has irritated her cannot relieve her bewilderment about what makes the world an irritant or what makes a partner want to tease, and pointing out that she has been irritated may even incite more teasing, as only she seems not to know. Mrs. Bennet's fitful question is astute, though, in its insight that those who tease are being as much as acting, assuming an identity that functions for them and tells on them at the same time. Wondering how the teaser can be so teasing, this essay suggests, is crucial to understanding Austen's linguistic erotic, which has been so influential for, now, centuries of readers who have learned from her with luck sometimes to recognize (and with something worse sometimes to misrecognize) in teasing's witful frictions a provocation in the direction of sex or love. Taking Mrs. Bennet's question seriously highlights those moments in her writing when Austen lingers on the interaction of the teaser and the teased. And taking Mrs. Bennet's question seriously—considering why the teaser teases—also means coming to know teasing as a behavior and an identity close to Austen-the-wit at her most contemplative about our reasons for being.

A scene toward the end of Joe Wright's 2005 adaptation of Jane Austen's *Pride & Prejudice* upends the traditional view of the Bennets' marriage. Jane Bennet has just been betrothed to Mr. Bingley, and the camera moves from window to window at the Bennets' home, Longbourn, peering in as if to check on how the family is responding to the changes wrought by the betrothal. Stopping at Mr. and Mrs. Bennet's bedroom, it shows us the couple in bed; it is bedtime, but they have not yet extinguished their candles. Brenda Blethyn's Mrs. Bennet is flopped on the bed, talking with her eyes closed; she is a body enjoying what supine feels like, pleased with its proximity to being (almost) *all* body in sleep. Donald Sutherland's Mr. Bennet is propped up beside her, though still reclining; he is pensive (Figure 1.1). Considering the events of the day, they also look forward, prognosticating about their daughter's life with her husband—their income, their prospects, their temperaments. Imagining that the sweet Jane and sweet Bingley will be taken advantage of by all their servants, they giggle together, warmly and companionably. When Mrs. Bennet says something that surprises Mr. Bennet—she doubles down on her negatives in saying she always knew that Jane could not be so beautiful for nothing—he looks at her. Perhaps it's her unexpected perspicacity or perhaps it's her startling pricing of her daughter's appearance that calls his attention; perhaps it's the way her shut eyes and

Figure 1.1. Mr. and Mrs. Bennet, *Pride & Prejudice*, directed by Joe Wright, 2005. DVD. Universal City, CA: Universal Studios, 2007.

her bedtime lumpenness make her seem an apparently impenetrable other to him, but, whatever it is, he looks at her for a bit (actually *at* her), as if fascinated by her, and, as the camera pulls away to peep in another window, he inclines toward her, we think to give her a kiss. The camera's discreet departure tells us that *it* knows, as we *should*, that this is what intimacy looks like.

These, of course, are not the Bennets we think we know from Austen's novel; theirs is the marriage no one wants to have, readers have long thought, the relationship in which you don't want to grow old. The better-than-that marriage of Wright's film is a product, in part, of the film's contemporizing desire to correct Austen's Mrs. Bennet, remaking her as an entity more palatable for our century. But it does something else for me as a viewer: it makes me want to think more about the Bennet relationship, to wonder about it in a way that stretches a little (even to the extent of twisting it a little out of shape) Austen's explanation of the Bennets' marriage as one that has outlasted Mrs. Bennet's "youth and beauty" (236) as well as Mr. Bennet's affection for them; it makes me want to think of Mr. Bennet as getting *something* from the marriage in its dailiness still, to identify that thing, and to visit some places in Austen's novels that will let us think about it. (I will continue to visit some Austen adaptations in doing so, and I will consider some moments in Shakespeare's plays, too, where, I would suggest, Austen finds instigations for her thoughts about teasing's manifestations and motivations.) Mrs. Bennet's husband is, in short, in it for the teasing, and that's what I'm in it for, too. In proposing that teasing is one of Austen's great subjects, this essay will want as well to think about what we want, what we get, and what we make of teasing.

Of Mr. Bennet, Austen writes that "To his wife he was very little otherwise indebted, than as her ignorance and folly had contributed to his amusement. This is not the sort of happiness which a man would in general wish to owe to his wife; but where other powers of entertainment are wanting, the true philosopher will derive benefit from such as are given" (236). Mr. Bennet's teasing is a fallback, a compensation. He is a philosopher not only in the even acceptance of his misery and in the conversion of said misery to amusement but also in his habit of mind. Teasing is the recourse and the work of Bennet-the-philosopher, a rationalizing product of his contemplation and an extension of it. Though it may look, sound, and feel merely like a buzzing, scratching irritant, teasing is about something. A way of thinking, testing, proving, and then doing it all again, *teasing*, though it is by definition never satisfied, is nevertheless nothing if not persistent.

Despite his famous withdrawals to his study, Mr. Bennet makes his continuing engagement with his marriage, his wife, and their children audible in his teasing, and Austen's novel is its logbook. The elaborate pranking of his wife that occurs early in the novel alerts readers right away to how teasing works in the relationship. Withholding from his wife news of his introductory visit to the man of good fortune who has just come to town—a visit that will make that man available to unfortunate daughters in want of a husband—Mr. Bennet leads his wife to disavow what she most wants: "I am sick of Mr. Bingley," she asserts, until Mr. Bennet tells her that his visit to Bingley has made Bingley in fact available to her. Feigning to believe his wife, he tells her, "as I have actually paid the visit, we cannot escape the acquaintance now" (7). "The astonishment of the ladies was just what he wished," Austen writes, "that of Mrs. Bennet perhaps surpassing the rest," and Mr. Bennet enjoys it until he doesn't (7). *The response* is what the teaser mocks but it is also what he wants, producing it for the mocking, while pushing and pursuing it further and again with faux innocence until it bores him or he bores himself.

Mr. Bennet teases frequently: he teases Mrs. Bennet about her continuing attractions, casting her as a serious rival to her daughters for the admiration of young men. He pretends to her that he will tell Mr. Bingley with frankness that he can have his pick of the daughters; Mrs. Bennet believes him enough to protest that he should not. He teases his daughter Kitty about her coughs ["she times them ill" (6)]. Awaiting Mr. Collins, he withholds the identity of their guest, making his family guess who is coming to dinner. He teases Mrs. Bennet with the illusion of his support when she wants Elizabeth to accept Mr. Collins. [Mrs. Bennet "had persuaded herself that her husband regarded the affair as she wished" (112), Austen writes; I wonder who led her to that persuasion.] He teases Mary about her too-visible desire for musical display: "You have delighted us long enough" (110). He teases Elizabeth about being unhappy in love: "Let Wickham be *your* man. He is a pleasant fellow, and would jilt you creditably!" (138, emphasis in the original). He prods us all to wonder how much he means it when he claims that Wickham will be his favorite son-in-law. He frets Elizabeth with his raillery about Jane's pain: "a girl likes to be crossed in love a little now and then" (137). And he 'well-my-dears' Mrs. Bennet about how she might comfort herself were sick Jane in fact to die: "if your daughter should have a dangerous fit of illness, if she should die, it would be a comfort to know that it was all in pursuit of Mr. Bingley, and under your orders" (31).

Mrs. Bennet answers him on this question of Jane's death, taking the jape seriously, though not the danger: "Oh!" she says, "I am not at all afraid of her dying" (31). Getting some version of the point, Mrs. Bennet misses the teasing that subtends it. The mind that Austen calls "less difficult to develop" (5)—Mrs. Bennet's—pushes back with its density against the irritations of Mr. Bennet's mockery, the more powerfully for not entirely knowing that it does so. For Mrs. Bennet, her husband's aggressions in speech have their uses. "I wish you had been there, my dear," she says to him of an encounter with Mr. Darcy, "to have given him one of your set downs" (13). Her not always quite getting Mr. Bennet's jokes does not mean that she does not know the fact and effects of his teasings; she knows that he can set a person down. "The business of her life was to get her daughters married," Austen writes; "its solace was visiting and news" (5). No solace without first a discomfort that wants soothing. The acts of teasing that are consolation to Mr. Bennet have made for Austen's Mrs. Bennet (if not, perhaps, quite for Joe Wright's) a life marked by the irritations they have produced.

Setting the Bennets alongside the fool and his love object in Shakespeare's *As You Like It*—Touchstone and Audrey, of whom the Bennets have long reminded me—may lead to a fuller understanding of the Bennets and of how Austen understands the work of teasing. The couples are alike. Both are dyads of apparently unequal intelligences (there is something unpleasant in how we have always thought of Austen's Mrs. Bennet, of Shakespeare's Audrey), and the dyads each include a teaser and a teased. Like Mr. Bennet, Touchstone is a wit, or at least he would be thought one, and his choice of the oblivious shepherdess, Audrey, as his partner may seem puzzling. Who expects that the wit will want the woman who does not/will not get the joke? He complains of her and to her: "When a man's verses cannot be understood, nor a man's good wit seconded with the forward child, understanding, it strikes a man more dead than a great reckoning in a little room. Truly, I would the gods had made thee poetical."[2] Touchstone is the restless fool, buzzing, moving, joking, constant and even relentless in his pushing and prodding of Audrey—his teasing her—on questions of her virtue, her honesty, her truthfulness, her earnestness, her ugliness, her goats. The actor who may have first played Touchstone was a noted dancer of jigs;[3] his comedy, that is, may have been physical and energetically supplementary to all that verbosity. From the distance of some centuries, we might be Audreys, all, in understanding Touchstone's jokes. (Some editions of the play are laborious in explaining them; some just give up and gesture toward the mists of time.) And as readers, we are distant, too, from that early and buzzing theatricality. Touchstone is in danger of tiring those who encounter it with the eager energy of his foolery (so is Mr. Bennet): "As the ox hath his bow, sir, the horse his curb, and the falcon her bells, so man hath his desires; and as pigeons bill, so wedlock would be nibbling."[4] When I read Touchstone, I find myself wanting to supplement the words myself by performing Groucho Marx eyebrows; I imagine a Touchstone talking too fast and telegraphing his high estimation of his own jokes—funny and insinuating—by rattling them off in fluctuating nasal tones. By contrast, Touchstone's Audrey is written to seem slow, lacking in understanding—her literal-mindedness evoking a solidity as much of presence as of understanding, the kind of massy material-ity that, as a kind of understanding, we might describe as dense.

And Touchstone finds her fascinating; the nineteenth century thought so, at least. Scenes from *As You Like It* were popular subjects for prints and paintings, and John Seymour Lucas's 1879 oil, *Touchstone and Audrey*, slows Touchstone down to find in him a version of the "deep-contemplative" per-sona Touchstone adopts in mocking the more intellectual and melancholic Jaques in the play (Figure 1.2). The scene in Lucas is familiar to those who have been watching Wright's *Pride & Prejudice* onscreen: the self-conscious wit is slowed, pensive, reclining, and evidently fascinated by the intransi-gence and density of his partner, the object of his teasing. Lucas finds some-thing genuine and even quiet in Touchstone, and he represents it as called forth by Audrey. Lucas's image of Touchstone reveals that the contempla-tive has always been hidden within the fool's action and japery and furi-ous laughter, and this revelation makes clear as well that the activity and frenzy that constitute the foolery, teasing, and wit might have a topic and a task. And like the "true philosopher" Mr. Bennet—imagined as hovering, alongside Mrs. Bennet, somewhere in the cultural ether between and above his shifting iterations in Austen's novel and its adaptations—the contempla-tive Touchstone (Shakespeare's or Lucas's) might be imagined as preoccupied with the question that always occupies the fascinated: what is this that fasci-nates me?

The teaser's fascination with teasing, that is, suggests that something is unknowable about the teased object and, doing so, might make it pos-sible to undo the sense of the teasing dyads (the Bennets and the Audrey-Touchstones) as (only) about unequal intelligences ascribed as lifelong attributes or identities. What might better structure our understanding of these dyads would be to think of them, more simply, as comprising wit and the dense object of its irritation and fascination, of its not knowing. Let the teaser's teasing be then, a kind of exploration. But for the unknowing

Figure 1.2. John Seymour Lucas, *Touchstone and Audrey*. Oil. 1879.

wit or the teaser there is, at the same time, a correspondent unknowing in the object, and a goal of teasing is to make an impression on the dense and unknowing object, to make it have to know.

Austen takes up the matter of teasing most explicitly in a scene in her novel *Northanger Abbey*. Her hero, Henry Tilney, and the heroine she is careful to be sure readers know is unexceptional, Catherine Morland, are discussing their brothers, rivals for the affections of the coquette, Isabella Thorpe. Catherine wants to be comforted, soothed out of her worry for her brother, James (who is Isabella's fiancé), in light of Isabella's flirtation with Tilney's brother, Frederick. Catherine is naïve and asserts a surety about the devotion of James and Isabella that her anxiety belies. Tilney knows better and outlines more bluntly the relations articulated by the triangle: Isabella "is in love with James, and flirts with Frederick."[5] But, despite his better knowing, he builds his reassurance on the foundation of Catherine's doubtful certainty, telling her:

"You have no doubt of the mutual attachment of your brother and your friend; depend upon it therefore, that real jealousy never can exist between them; depend upon it that no disagreement between them can be of any duration. Their hearts are open to each other, as neither heart can be to you; they know exactly what is required and what can be borne; and you may be certain, that one will never tease the other beyond what is known to be pleasant."[6]

Tilney's advice—so logical in structure, so earnest in sound, so comforting to a woman desiring comfort—is itself a kind of teasing: more worldly, more practiced in reading people, more certain in his certainty than Catherine is in hers, he tells her to depend upon what he knows to be undependable. His account of teasing is, then, in the smallest terms, a fantasy that will not be fulfilled; Isabella will exceed what can be borne by James. That Tilney knows this makes the larger and more consequential fantasy his own, a spun-out version of a balanced bliss, in which nothing more than can be borne is required and in which teasing is not vexatious but pleasant and always reciprocal: "They know exactly what is required and what can be borne; and you may be certain, that one will never tease the other beyond what is known to be pleasant." Tilney's fantasy is of teasing in its fullest, loveliest, safest warmth. It's teasing as the politest boundary testing, boundary pushing, boundary breaching. It's teasing with permissions, assured consents, reciprocal intimacy. Reading *Northanger Abbey*, it's easy to imagine that something involving teasing might be Tilney's dream. A baby Mr. Bennet might have looked a little like him. Imagining him so suggests that Mr. Bennet may have wanted teasing's frictional warmth even before he wanted teasing's consolations. And as this likeness might remind us, something about Tilney's fantasy of an equivalence in teasing (however charming it is) yet fails as a representation of how teasing works. Tilney's imagination seems to involve a balancing or even a reckoning over the course of a lifetime. It is nearly contractual: each will tease the other just so much and no more; the principle of alternation will be respected.

But the experience of teasing is by instance or incident; even when roles are swapped, each instance is a moment or series of moments featuring a teaser and a teased. Teasing is both more dangerous and less governable than Tilney's imagination will allow it to be. And it is awfully hard to imagine Catherine Morland teasing Tilney back.

Austen's novels are filled with teasing and filled with teasing dyads of the sort I have been asking us to consider. In addition to the Bennets and the future Tilneys, there are, for example, the Palmers in her *Sense and Sensibility*,

Emma and Harriet in *Emma*, Emma and Miss Bates, Elizabeth Bennet and her sister Jane, Elizabeth and Darcy, and Miss Bingley and Mr. Darcy, as well as *Mansfield Park*'s Mary Crawford and anyone with whom she is left alone. In thinking then, as I mean us to, about what teasing wants, let the Palmers represent that thing in its most frightening daily form. "We can all plague and punish one another," says Elizabeth Bennet, discussing teasing (57).

Plaguing and punishing would seem to structure the relationship between Mr. and Mrs. Palmer in *Sense and Sensibility*. The couple seems to be cut to suit the dyad model I have asked us to consider. He is apparently the more intelligent of the two; she is apparently unable to feel the force of his wit. The Palmer husband is in politics and is married to his wife for the expected reasons; her money facilitates his career. His hostility and even sadism are evident. And yet he is also the one who seems to feel punished and plagued. Mrs. Palmer's obliviousness is the weapon she doesn't know she is wielding. And like the other teasers, he keeps trying to make her *know* by making her hear and feel his aggression. Chiming in on a discussion about the tit-for-tat sequence in which invitations to dine are to be issued and returned, he comments on his wife's mother, Mrs. Jennings, as she comments on turn-taking in hospitality. Mrs. Jennings thinks the formality of alternation in issuing invitations is not to be respected (Tilney's fantasy of alternation in teasing might be doomed to similar social disrespect), saying to her friend, "You and I, Sir John, . . . should not stand upon such ceremony." The conversation continues:

"Then you would be very ill-bred," cried Mr. Palmer.

"My love, you contradict every body,"—said his wife with her usual laugh. "Do you know that you are quite rude?"

"I did not know I contradicted any body in calling your mother ill-bred."

Austen tells us that Mr. Palmer's attitude and remarks give his wife "no pain: and when he scolded or abused her, she was highly diverted." While noting that her husband "is always out of humour," Mrs. Palmer nevertheless whispers, "Mr. Palmer is so droll!"[7]

Imelda Staunton, who plays Mrs. Palmer in Ang Lee's 1995 film version of *Sense and Sensibility*, embodies her with a panting breathiness, eager and quick in intakes and exhalations so rapid as to be nearly indistinguishable, the exhalations lost in a sequence of tiny gasps. Her voice is high pitched, like the voices of the Mrs. Bennets in nearly all *Pride and Prejudice* adaptations.

It is the note of being teased. With her panting speech, her breathy mode of being, and her high-pitched voice, this Mrs. Palmer might be being teased or tickled all the time; she is disposed for it, ready-made to give the response that teasing would provoke. And it is her disposition that facilitates the misunderstanding that leads to her mistaking her husband's aggression for the drollery of teasing; ready to be teased, she hears teasing everywhere. In writing the Palmers, Austen highlights for all of us the aggression in teasing (Mr. Palmer's, for example, in claiming that he contradicts no one in calling his wife's mother ill-bred). But she also identifies the preservative work that teasing does; like a hairstyle that retains its tortured structure in the teased bouffant, the relationship pushed to its airy limits by teasing lets "he's so droll" and 'only teasing!' be what help it keep its shape.

It appalls me then, that when I read about the Palmers, I am more identified with Mr. Palmer, despite his awful meanness, than I am with his wife. As a reader, I resist that which resists knowing and that which, in resisting the knowing the reader craves, resists being known. Something frustrates about Mrs. Palmer's resistance, her intransigence, the misunderstanding that seems like a refusal, an obstacle, a density, the kind of block that makes a person seem a blockhead. Teasing takes that which is unknowing for an obstacle and, poking and prodding, tries to make the unknown unknowing have to know.

So often seeming not quite to get it, *Pride and Prejudice*'s Mr. Darcy is more like Mrs. Bennet in this, more like Mrs. Palmer, more like Shakespeare's Audrey than one might have guessed. "Teaze him—laugh at him," Elizabeth tells Miss Bingley. "Intimate as you are, you must know how it is to be done" (57). But Miss Bingley does not need the urging. With "witticisms" (46), she has already teased Darcy about the pleasure a pair of fine eyes can bestow, about the nuptial implications of his appreciation of those eyes (Elizabeth's, of course), and about the lineage portraits of tradesmen his home will have to accommodate when he welcomes to it the family Bennet. And Miss Bingley's wit, Austen tells us, "flowed long" (27). Elizabeth teases him, too, and Austen's attempt to suggest that their marriage will be a happy one rests in large part on her developing a sense that Elizabeth's teasing will continue as "open pleasantry" and a "lively sportive manner of talking" to Darcy; it will be strong enough, Austen promises, to alarm Darcy's sister (387–88).

Seeming not quite to see what about himself is being noted, laughed at, pointed out, prodded, Darcy can be bad at knowing himself, bad at knowing; Darcy is teasable. "Do not you feel a great inclination, Miss Bennet, to seize such an opportunity of dancing a reel?" he asks Elizabeth (52). As the "dancing a reel" attempt suggests, he is himself bad at teasing; by convention, the teased generally are so.

That Darcy ranks among the teased complicates the gender politics that may have seemed implicit in what I have been saying about Austen's use of teasing. It has looked (hasn't it?) as if it is almost always a story about silly wives. But the unexpected similarity of Austen's hero Mr. Darcy to Mrs. Bennet, to Mrs. Palmer, and even to Shakespeare's Audrey suggests that intelligence and marital status and sex may all be misleading (or at least partial) as ways to understand Austen's articulation of the workings of the teaser-teasing dyad. Treating the dyads in a long relation to one another, for example, may be not so much a gloss on what has so often been understood as Austen's great topic—marriage—as it is a means of slowing down (in order to prolong it) the moment of Austenian teasing in order to make it visible in its full consequentiality and meaning.

Teasable in his resistance to knowing himself, Darcy is also the intransigent block that, setting itself against teasing, seems to invite it. Claiming that she does not know how to tease him, that her intimacy with him has not taught her how, Miss Bingley lies in telling Elizabeth that she cannot do it; this is part of her campaign of flattery. It is unlikely that Darcy would like to think himself teasable, at least not without help in learning to do so. Rejecting Elizabeth's direction to tease Darcy, Miss Bingley responds to her, "Teaze calmness of temper and presence of mind! No, no—I feel he may defy us there. And as to laughter, we will not expose ourselves, if you please, by attempting to laugh without a subject. Mr. Darcy may hug himself" (57). Miss Bingley's idiom (he may hug himself, congratulate himself) bears thinking about as it touches on Darcy. The Darcy who hugs himself might do so not warmly and self-protectively but in an act of cold consolation. The money, the status, the masculinity, the power, are contained in an act that draws the upright man of means more fully erect. Darcy is the monolith; the monolith seems not to have to know.

Let Darcy's stance return us for a moment to Austen's predecessor in teasing, the Shakespeare of *As You Like It*. Teased relentlessly by Rosalind while she masquerades in the forest as the boy Ganymede, Orlando (Shakespeare's hero in the play) has a blocky physicality—a wrestler's body, with its attachment to immovability and to the earth. In his body, Orlando literalizes the blockiness with which I have been figuring the problem the teased represents for the one who teases. Teasing implies two kinds of energies, perhaps two kinds of bodies. And I would like, as this essay moves toward its conclusion, to emphasize the desire of the teaser to move the block and to jostle the obstacle, to produce response and thus to animate intransigent matter. The teased person is a representation (one that giggles and laughs, sometimes even without getting the joke or without having to)—a representation of resistant matter made to move despite itself before it settles back, comfortably and yet discomfittingly, into itself and its shape. (There's a Pillsbury doughboy in here somewhere.) The teaser would poke at matter, would pull it apart and aerate it to make it manageable, as those who work with sheep's wool do to the wool's dense fibers, separating them to make them useful. This process is called teasing.

When a man's "good wit" is not understood, Touchstone tells us, he is struck "more dead" than by a "great reckoning in a little room." Whether facing a bar tab, a hotel bill, a death sentence, or an existential tabulation, the teaser sets the airy ephemerality of wit against death (cold pastoral!) in confronting the challenges of matter and is reassured for a moment when teasing pokes matter into animate life. The teaser, then, is deep contemplative. For the teaser, the stakes are life and not death, meaning and not nothingness, the challenges and comforts (both) of massy matter against the airiness of wit and words. Austen's deep-contemplative, Mr. Bennet, as he buzzes around the not-knowing of Mrs. Bennet, does so seeking an answer to his personal despair in the *repetition* of teasing and not in the end (who wants the end?) of fulfillment or satisfaction. It's a promise, a thing to do tomorrow, his reason for living.

Though, in this essay, I am teasing out the nature of the teaser and thinking out, alongside Austen, those moments when I tease, I know that I am as or more often not teaser but teased and need, with Austen, to think about occupying that position, too. I am acquainted (perhaps you are as well) with its pleasure, punishment, and pain. As a littlest sister, I have had to accept being teased as a condition of existence, and sisters, friends, rivals, and partners alike have spotted what is teasable in me. I am not sure what it looks like, but I believe myself closer to seeing it than I used to be. My partner's teasings have come most often (and, in an odd way, are most valuable) when, thinking I shuck off the shackles of some naïveté, I have announced, tremulously and with great effort, what about myself I have just discovered but what everyone else has known about me all along. What's wonderful in that also-scary teasing is knowing for a moment that which one's intransigence resists knowing on its own and of itself. The moment is a promise, nothing more, because afterward, forgetting, I lapse back into Stay Puft puffery or Pillsbury density.

It may be this moment of self-knowledge that Anne Steele wants or perhaps it is this condition of intransigent unknowing that she would escape when she offers herself up for teasing in *Sense and Sensibility*. Anne is not the Steele sister you remember. That one—Lucy Steele—is the girl with bad grammar who rivals and (come to think of it) teases the novel's heroine, Elinor Dashwood, with the prospect of love unfulfilled. Lucy's sister Anne is notable largely for not being noticed, save when she gives away her sister's deepest secrets or talks about smart beaux we readers imagine are imaginary. Chief among these beaux is the Doctor, a man with whom the sisters have shared a coach. Talking of him, she talks of the teasing and plaguing inflicted on her about him by absent others, no more convincing about their teasing than about the doctor's romantic attentions. "Everybody laughs at me so about the Doctor," she says, "and I cannot think why . . . I never think about him from one hour's end to another. . . . My beau, indeed! said I—I cannot think who you mean. The Doctor is no beau of mine" (218). With no "not" in her unconscious, Miss Steele is of course claiming the doctor as a beau, and asking to be teased about him. But despite one half-hearted attempt by the teasing Mrs. Jennings, which makes her briefly happy, no one does much tease Miss Steele about the doctor. No one cares enough. Dense and unknowing, yet buzzing, energetic, and insinuating at the same time, Miss Steele would be at once and ineffectually the teaser and the teased. Asking to be teased, listing at length the occasions on which she would be at home and receptive to it, Miss Steele would practice teasing on herself. She is a "vulgar" (124) young woman, in Austen's language, too free and too flighty, too unself-aware, and, in being so, she is one of those characters Austen might seem to have us mock and disregard; but we are readers, distant, and, even in our mocking (one heavy step beyond the lightness of the tease), we cannot touch her. Like its embodied cousin tickling, teasing is sociable. Sad Miss Steele's desire for it marks a need and a dependence without object. It cannot be performed alone. Unteasable, Miss Steele might be a slack and impoverished Darcy, left to hug herself.

Hugging herself, perhaps, or conjuring a different Darcy, Elizabeth Bennet addresses him in her thoughts, "Teazing, teazing, man!" (339). The teasing Mr. Darcy about whom she exclaims—the teasing, teasing man—teases by irritating presence rather than, as Elizabeth most often does, by active speech. He has been sitting like a block in the Longbourn parlor, "silent, grave, and indifferent" (339), in Elizabeth's view, teasing as the teased do, by their very being; those who respond to such being by feeling teased—Elizabeth—feel so because they want teasing's attentions and its warming erotic, taking the unfathomable other in its sullenness as a provocation, a tease. That Elizabeth has been sitting in the parlor, too, discouraging alongside Darcy's "indifferent," "grave and silent" (381), suggests that for Darcy as well as for Elizabeth—for Austen—sex and love find their impetus in a response to what teases in the other's dense unknowability, what promises in the possibility of making on that density the impression of one's presence.

Knowing herself in this, as Darcy may not, Elizabeth draws up a usefully imbalanced Tilneyan contract for her marriage to Darcy: "My good qualities are under your protection, and you are to exaggerate them as much as possible; and, in return, it belongs to me to find occasions for teazing and quarrelling with you as often as may be . . ." (381). *The Oxford English Dictionary* tells me a thing I didn't know: that to tease is to stoke, "to feed (a furnace fire) with fuel."[8] If, in Austen's novels, the sex is in the language, as it has to be, Elizabeth's contract is Austen's recognition that the warmth of novel sex and novel love is made and kept in the frictions wrought by teasing. And teasing is a kind of tending, a stirring up to take care.

In suggesting, as I have sometimes here, that teasing is a testing of oneself against the lumpenness of materiality, I cannot help thinking about the density of the text that lies between author and reader. One pokes at it from either position, irritates it, takes with it the efforts that keep aloft the lightness of teasing. Once or twice, while working on this essay, I have spent YouTube time on videos of wool teasers, fascinated by their patience as they teased and combed and carded, changing direction again and again as they disentangled and aerated the fibers in their hands. "I have a very light way of using my carders," one says;[9] there is method in teasing and pride in its practice. When I imagine a teasing Austen who beckons a reader through tiny half-mysteries (who stole the Weston turkeys? who got Hannah that good place?) and sentences that swirl before they balance and resolve, I fantasize that she writes to reach a reader who, made itchy by her wooly teasings, takes up the work of teasing them out.

Notes

1.   Jane Austen, *Pride and Prejudice* in *The Novels of Jane Austen*, volume 2, ed. R.W. Chapman, (Oxford U.K.: Oxford University Press, 1932; reprinted 1988), 7. Subsequent page references in the text will be to this edition.
2.   William Shakespeare, *As You Like It*, ed. Juliet Dusinberre (London: The Arden Shakespeare 2000), 3.3.10–14. References are to act, scene, and line.

3. See Dusinberre's discussion of the likelihood of Will Kemp's having played Touchstone in her introduction, especially her consideration of the "dancing Touchstone" that Kemp may have generated (111–13) and of Richard Dutton's reference to Kemp's "trade-mark jigs" in his *Licensing, Censorship, and Authorship in Early Modern England: Buggeswords* (Basingstoke: Palgrave, 2000), 34, quoted in Dusinberre, 46.

4. *As You Like It* (Dusinberre), 3.3.270–72.

5. Jane Austen, *Northanger Abbey* in *The Novels of Jane Austen*, volume 5, ed. R.W. Chapman, (Oxford: Oxford University Press, 1932; reprinted 1988), 151.

6. Austen, *Northanger Abbey*, 152.

7. Jane Austen, *Sense and Sensibility* in *The Novels of Jane Austen*, volume 1, ed. R.W. Chapman (Oxford: Oxford University Press, 1932; reprinted 1988), 111–12.

8. "tease, v.2". *OED Online*. March 2021. Oxford University Press. http://www.oed.com/viewdictionaryentry/Entry/11125 (accessed April 03, 2021).

9. See Hervor and Weyland, "using hand carders with wool," YouTube Video, 3:42, March 3, 2012, https://www.youtube.com/watch?v=SA8oCxLN7sQ.

Chapter Two

Performing (Dis)comfort

Queer Possibilities in Jane Austen's
Mansfield Park

Jade Higa

"A love of the theater is so general, an itch for acting so strong among young people."[1]

When Tom Bertram brings John Yates to Mansfield Park, he sets in motion the moral downfall of the Bertram sisters. The private theatricals that are extensively rehearsed but not performed spark Maria's inevitable affair with Henry Crawford and Julia's elopement with Yates. But the Bertram sisters are not the only ones endangered by acting. The other young people are all involved—even Fanny Price takes pleasure in watching and prompting the amateur actors as they attempt to learn their lines—and they all suffer disappointment, broken hearts, or at least the wrath of Sir Thomas's displeasure.[1] While critics disagree about the extent to which Fanny is involved, most agree that *Lovers' Vows*—the play that, as Elaine McGirr notes, the young people "spectacularly failed to perform"—contributes to the novel's themes of performance and deception.[2] While scholars examine the effect the play has on the Bertram sisters, Edmund, Henry, and Fanny, few recognize the importance of this play as the pivotal beginning of the queer possibilities

---

1   Jane Austen, *Mansfield Park*, ed. R.W. Chapman (London: T. Egerton, 1814; Oxford: Oxford University Press, 1988), 121. Page references to this edition are in parentheses in the text.

between Mary and Fanny. The heteronormative narrative consistently prevents those possibilities from becoming realized. Yet heterosexual endings in romance novels do not have to determine the fate of our queer readings. We can still find queer potential in the narrative's fissures. Through moments of theatricality in *Mansfield Park*, spaces are opened when we shift focus away from the traditional hero/heroine coupling and consider instead the search for queer comfort between Fanny Price and Mary Crawford.

Queerness in the novel shows itself in the oscillating moments of (dis)comfort that Mary and Fanny experience and the way they embody difference through gender performance. I use "queer" in this essay to mean not strictly heterosexual. While "queer" can be a problematic when used as an umbrella term, it can also function as a convenient shorthand for the kind of desire that complicates the heteronormative. It enables us to name fluid desire without resorting to anachronistic terms like "bisexuality" and "pansexuality." Queer connotes an embrace of the nonnormative, the potentially messy, and the beautifully complex—all of which encompass Mary and Fanny's relationship.[3] Previous queer readings of this novel have explored the desire between Mary and Fanny and the incestuous desire between Fanny and Edmund (as a close representation of William). However, they have yet to consider how both of Fanny's relationships can coexist, ultimately reading the novel, and particularly Fanny and Mary, as exclusively heterosexual *or* lesbian.[4] But we do not need to choose one side or the other. Speaking of Mary and Fanny's desire as queer enables us to embrace a reading in which they desire each other *and* a male love object. Their sexuality is fluid and not fixed.

The basic conception of comfort in terms of queerness and bodies is that queer bodies cannot feel comfortable in a heteronormative society because they are constantly reminded of their difference from the heterosexual "norm." Thus, a body that experiences that difference—divergence from the norm—as it walks through life must endure the discomfort of not quite fitting in *and* tends to seek out other bodies of difference so that it might have a better chance at finding comfort. This sense of discomfort—of not belonging, particularly in issues of sexual difference and racial difference—brings the body to the forefront of one's consciousness: "It is," Sara Ahmed notes, "pain or discomfort that return one's attention to the surface of the body *as body*."[5] So it is an embodied difference—one that is emotionally, psychologically, and physically felt. Mary and Fanny attempt to find comfort in each other's queer bodies and, even in their ultimate failure to find that comfort, an analysis of their queer relationship identifies the cracks in a domestic nov-el's perceived heterosexual ideal.

In *Mansfield Park*, there is no truly happy couple—not even Edmund and Fanny. Throughout the novel, Fanny and Edmund's attraction to each other, particularly on Edmund's part, is not given much space. Nor is it convincing at the end of the novel, which contains little to no description of Edmund's devotion to Fanny. Instead, Austen's narrator "intreat[s] every body to believe that exactly at the time when it was quite natural that it should be so, and not a week earlier, Edmund did cease to care about Miss Crawford, and became as anxious to marry Fanny, as Fanny herself could desire" (470). Upon close inspection, this passage reveals the slipperiness of Austen's words—her careful manner of telling us that Fanny and Edmund are not necessarily perfect for each other. First, the narrator's "intreat[ing]" her audience to "believe" that Edmund finally stopped loving Mary sounds more like a plea than a statement of fact. Rather than state that Edmund simply did transfer his affections, she begs her readers to actively participate in the fantasy by choosing to accept that he did. By doing so, the narra-tor implies that readers must suspend any plausible disbelief in Edmund's love for Fanny. So, we struggle to maintain our investment in Edmund and Fanny's relationship; the illusions of love are flimsy and break down once the novel, or performance, ends.

In a queer reading of *Mansfield Park*, attention to theatricality allows us to explore these illusions, as illusions, and to identify the desires that they mani-fest and disguise. Such a reading begins by identifying what Laura Engel calls Austen's "theatrical narrative strategies." In particular, Engel argues that, in much of her work, "Austen relies on a slippage between illusion and real-ity similar to the experience of being in the theater, where in the specific moment of the performance the spectator believes that what he or she is watching exists but then is always reminded that the performance ends."[6] To this end, the narrative of *Mansfield Park* behaves like a play in that the audience is allowed to recognize the performance. In fact, in characters such as the Crawfords, readers are encouraged to see the conscious facades that the siblings take time to develop and implement.[7] A queer discussion of the novel considers how the text embraces the *sexual* "slippage between illusion and reality." In the case of Mary Crawford and Fanny Price, these performances are means of coping with oscillating sexual feeling in a het-eronormative environment. Therefore, within their own theatrical narrative, they struggle with frequent feelings of discomfort as they try to find another queer body with which to exist. The audience is allowed to see just enough of the cracks in Mary and Fanny's heterosexual masks to assure us that we move between the illusion of a happy hetero ending and the reality of several messy queer moments. However, in order to begin uncovering what happens backstage (or, under the women's masks), we must look more closely at those moments where the seam between illusion and reality is most evident: in moments of deeply felt discomfort.

Fanny's discomfort springs from her fear of desire. This discomfort becomes evident when the group demands that she participate in the private theatricals. Her refusal comes from a place of uncertainty and fear. She is not eager to embrace the stage as an actor, nor is she open to consciously considering her desire for Mary; however, she does gain some pleasure from both, and her desire to be entertained clashes with what she believes her views should be: "[f]or [Fanny's] own gratification she could have wished that something might be acted, for she had never seen even half a play, but every thing of higher consequence was against it" (131). In addition, once she is alone, she reads *Lovers' Vows*: "The first use she made of her solitude was to take up the volume which had been left on the table . . . Her curiosity was all awake, and she ran through it with an eagerness which was suspended only by intervals of astonishment" (137). Fanny's instinctual desire is for pleasure. She longs to see a play—to be entertained and to gaze upon bodies in motion. She greedily consumes *Lovers' Vows* when she is alone, and she stops reading only to allow herself to feel shocked over the roles of Agatha and Amelia that are "unfit to be expressed by any woman of modesty" (137). Fanny recognizes that acting *Lovers' Vows* is improper, particularly for the women. But, as Ruth Yeazell suggests, Fanny's modesty is a complex, conscious performance that propels the narration forward and emphasizes the theatrical elements of the novel.[8] Fanny expects Edmund to "have [Julia and Maria] roused as soon as possible by [his] remonstrance" (137) of the play. Rather than speak up, she waits for Edmund to rescue her cousins and herself from their desire for pleasure. Her embodied difference is largely rooted in her extreme fear of self-indulgence.

This fear is manifested in a sense of embodied discomfort. When she continues to refuse to act and Tom begins badgering her in earnest, she feels "shocked to find herself at that moment the only speaker in the room, and to feel that almost every eye was upon her" (145–146). As others take Tom's side, Fanny continues to decline, but has little ability to stop her fragile modesty from bending: "'You must excuse me, indeed you must excuse me,' cried Fanny, growing more and more red from excessive agitation, and looking distressfully at Edmund" (146). In this moment, Fanny turns to Edmund to rescue her from her inability to take a firm stance. When she is under the scrutiny of "every eye" in the room, Fanny feels her difference keenly. She is neither willing to speak condemnation against acting nor is she able to participate in it. Ahmed reminds us that "pain or discomfort . . . return one's attention to the surface of the body *as body*."[9] Fanny's discomfort manifests in a heightened awareness of her body; the root of this discomfort is a fear of exposure—the fear that those around her might know her true mind. The more aware of her body she becomes, the more she must face the instinctual feelings of mingled pleasure and disapproval—a contrast that she is not willing to confront. Thus, the close attention paid to Fanny throws her into a cycle of body awareness and discomfort—she becomes "more and more red from excessive agitation." Her body betrays her desire even as she struggles to mask it. When she is noticed, others become aware of her desires and she must begin to acknowledge them as she becomes more aware of her body. As her body manifests her desires, her discomfort with them and with being looked at becomes evident.

Fanny's fear of pleasure is particularly evident when contrasted with Mary's indulgence in her pleasure. As a regular horseback rider who finds great pleasure in the activity, Fanny becomes "in danger of feeling the loss in her health" (35) when her old grey pony dies and she no longer has the means to exercise. The narrator here explains what Mrs. Norris and Lady Bertram feel—that Fanny didn't really need her own horse—and what Edmund feels—that "Fanny must have a horse" (37). Yet Fanny never discusses her own desire. Rather than attempt to advocate for herself, Fanny waits until Edmund rescues her by procuring a tame mare specifically for Fanny's daily use. Once Edmund acknowledges Fanny's desire and gratifies it, she is then able to admit that "her delight in Edmund's mare was far beyond any former pleasure of the sort" (36). As Nora Nachumi has argued, horseback riding for both Fanny and Mary is a clear metaphor for "more amorous pursuits."[10] Fanny's consistent inability to admit to her own desires for riding is an indication that she is avoidant of her sexual desire, as well. She will allow herself to sink into the comfort and pleasure of Edmund's horse only when he insists that she do so.

When Mary decides that she also wants to learn to ride, Fanny's pleasure is delayed and she is again unable to advocate for herself and her desires. On only her second day of riding lessons, Mary's "enjoyment of riding was such, that she did not know how to leave off" and she is "unwilling to dismount" (66–67). Mary is clearly able to embrace her pleasure, so much so that she becomes lost in it. Fanny, however, yields to her own passivity, instead. Mary takes the mare out with Edmund several days in a row, and Fanny is left at home with the bossy and overbearing Mrs. Norris. The result, for Fanny, is a headache as well as feelings of "neglect" and "discontent" (74). Yet she could have avoided this if she had answered Edmund honestly when he asked her about Mary taking the horse out again. She tells Edmund she would "rather stay at home" (70)—a clear lie. She does not want her own pleasure to impose on another person. She even has "a great anxiety to avoid suspicion" of being even the least bit impatient while waiting for Mary to return (68). Mary has no trouble embracing her own pleasure, even if it inconveniences Fanny. But Fanny can barely acknowledge the fact that riding does give her pleasure. She allows Edmund to believe that while Mary "rides only for pleasure," Fanny rides "for health" (68). Instead of admitting her love of riding, Fanny denies herself pleasure and her passivity results in physical discomfort.

Identifying the discomfort that Fanny feels in situations involving sexual desire enables us to also identify where the heterosexual narrative breaks down. In order to determine where she feels discomfort, however, we must identify where Fanny discovers—or at least stumbles into—comfort. Here is where queer desire surfaces: Fanny finds some comfort in the body of Mary Crawford and Mary, likewise, seeks out comfort in Fanny's body. The potential comfort is never realized because the heteronormative narrative always interrupts their search. Yet it is the moments of searching themselves that are significant in a queer reading of *Mansfield Park* and that challenge the necessity of the heteronormative trajectory.

Fanny's unwillingness to admit her desire to ride until Edmund acknowledges it is an indication that she can find comfort only when she does not approach desire openly. She needs a mask or buffer of some kind to even begin recognizing her own desire. Fanny is able to explore finding comfort in Mary's body only because she (Fanny) embodies Edmund. This becomes evident in Fanny and Mary's rehearsal. Fanny manages to avoid participating in the actual acting, but Mary convinces her to read as Anhalt in order to help Mary, who plays Amelia, memorize her lines. Heteronormative courtship codes are introduced and questioned through both the play itself—Elizabeth Inchbald's *Lovers' Vows*—and through the reference to and eventual appearance of Edmund Bertram. Mary and Fanny's rehearsal scene reveals the interplay of heteronormative relationships and queer desire. This moment in the novel juxtaposes Mary's character with the play's character, Amelia—a bold and masculine pursuer—and it calls attention to the ways in which Fanny both desires Edmund and tries to embody Edmund in her relationship with Mary. This rehearsal scene is the turning point of the novel for Mary and

Fanny. The performance both women put on, the comfort they aim for, the discomfort they experience, and the ultimate interjection of the heterosexual narrative all contribute to the queer possibilities of the text.

German playwright August von Kotzebue was enjoying a great deal of popularity with English audiences in the late eighteenth century. *The Stranger* (1798), Benjamin Thompson's translation of Kotzebue's *Menschenhass und Reue* (1789), starred Sarah Siddons and was a smash hit at Drury Lane under Richard Sheridan's direction. Covent Garden answered with *Lovers' Vows* (1798), Elizabeth Inchbald's translation of Kotzebue's *Das Kind der Liebe* (1791). The play was so popular that Kotzebue "became the most famous and controversial German playwright in England."[11] While audiences clamored to see the play during its 42-night run, writers like Hannah More railed against the immorality of it—mainly the character of Amelia who "obviously well-versed in the art, manipulates and almost forces Anhalt into confessing *his love for her*. [He is] a victim to her amorous enticements and rhetorical skills."[12] But Inchbald was exceedingly conscious of how scandalous the play could be considered if it were translated verbatim into English. Amelia's character in the original is, according to Inchbald's own preface to the play, "indelicately blunt." She writes, "the forward and unequivocal manner in which [Amelia] announces her affection to her love, in the original, would have been revolting to an English audience."[13] Inchbald's solution is to "attach the attention and sympathy of the audience by whimsical insinuations, rather than coarse abruptness."[14]

While Amelia's speeches are still quite forward for a late eighteenth-century English audience, Inchbald claims to have adjusted the character in such a way that she is forward without seeming vulgar. Yet she still takes on the role of pursuer. For example, when she first declares her love, Amelia appears slightly shy but desires to speak her mind—as a masculine lover might. Anhalt, however, plays the coy, feminine beloved:

AMELIA. I will not marry.
ANHALT. You mean to say, you will not fall in love.
AMELIA. On no! [*ashamed*] I am in love.
ANHALT. Are in love! [*starting*] And with the Count?
AMELIA. I wish I was.
ANHALT Why so?
AMELIA. Because *he* would, perhaps, love me again.
ANHALT [*warmly*]. Who is there that would not?
AMELIA. Would you?
ANHALT. I—I—me—I—I am out of the question.

AMELIA. No; you are the very person to whom I have put the question.
ANHALT. What do you mean?
AMELIA. I am glad you don't understand me. I was afraid I had spoken too
plain [*in confusion*].[15]

In this scene, Amelia takes on the masculine role of pursuer. Although their conversation is focused on love, Anhalt has been charged by Amelia's father to discover if she loves her suitor, the Count, but she takes the opportunity of the conversation topic to declare her love for Anhalt. Inchbald writes her as "ashamed" when she says that she is in love, but when Amelia speaks more openly and says "you," to Anhalt, she is neither ashamed nor shy. Meanwhile, Anhalt takes on the stereotypically feminine role of coy flirt. He asks all the questions, forcing Amelia to make statements. Before Amelia's direct "you," he asks "who?" And once she is more open about her feelings, he balks and says unconvincingly, "What do you mean?" Both Amelia and the audience are aware that Anhalt knows exactly what she means. But, as the coy beloved, he shies away from direct language and forces his lover to declare her feelings again and again. As Amelia says she "was afraid [she] had spoken too plain," she openly admits her attempts to take on the stereotypically masculine role of pursuer. Although she knows that her meaning was clear, her confusion is sincere. After all, why should she not take the initiative if Anhalt remains determinedly coy? But as she says that line, she also understands that the exchange did not follow the gendered codes of heterosexual courtship, and in the dialogue following the quoted scene above she recoils back into a submissive feminine subject position. In this initial lovers' scene shared between Amelia and Anhalt, Amelia is an example of a woman performing a masculine subject position in order to satisfy her desire.

Austen encourages readers to associate Amelia's character with Mary's. Mary's feigned worry about acting the part of Amelia highlights Mary's own gender-bending performance. Susan Allen Ford points out that Mary "defines the role of Amelia in terms of that declaration of love . . . [one that is] made by the heroine before she has been assured of the hero's love."[16] In the novel, Mary worries that "such a forward young lady may frighten the men" (144). Yet Mary appears unafraid of practicing that same forwardness when she uses similar techniques in her own pursuit of both Fanny *and* Edmund; she performs a masculine subject position in order to actively search for comfort with both bodies. However, Mary's performance is a great deal more fluid than Amelia's. Mary is able to move seamlessly between seeking comfort

from Fanny's body into seeking comfort from Edmund's. When Mary and
Fanny are alone together in Fanny's East Room and Edmund shows up unexpectedly, Mary moves easily from encouraging Fanny to engage with her to
indulging in a rehearsal with Edmund. Although Fanny is still in the room,
she "becom[es] too nearly nothing to both" Mary and Edmund (170). As
with horse riding, Mary is quick to indulge her own pleasure—even when its
object shifts. By first reading Amelia's character, then reading Mary's, we get
the strong sense of how much more flexible and daring Mary is, particularly
in her scenes with Fanny.

Mary's queerness manifests in her attempt to make sense of the play and
of her attraction to Fanny. As Mary tries to convince Fanny to rehearse with
her, Mary compares Fanny to Edmund and implies that they are so similar that Mary could imagine Fanny to be Edmund. More important, Mary
wants to imagine Fanny as Edmund; she tells Fanny, "You must rehearse it
with me, that I may fancy *you* him, and get on by degrees. You *have* a look of
his sometimes" (168–169). Although Mary desires Edmund, she also desires
Fanny. She conflates their two bodies in an attempt to find a comfortable
space where her body might be safe desiring both. It is tempting to label
this a lesbian desire that cannot be realized unless it is conducted through a
male love object. However, Austen is very clear that the passion Mary feels
for Edmund is sincere.[17] In a moment such as this scene—in which Mary
and Fanny share homoerotic pleasure—the presence of desire for a male
body must be remembered. Rather than arguing that this scene contains
homoerotic tension in the midst of a story about heterosexual courtship, a
much clearer explanation would be to recognize the queerness in the fluidity
of desire. Desire is neither definitive nor static for Mary. She is capable of
searching for comfort in the bodies of both Fanny and Edmund.

This rehearsal scene also provides insight into Fanny's failure to find comfort in addition to her seemingly ceaseless struggles with discomfort and fear
of her own desire. Although Fanny is magnetically drawn to Mary, she is also
in love with Edmund. The narrator writes of the rehearsal, "[Mary] began,
and Fanny joined in with all the modest feeling which the idea of representing Edmund was so strongly calculated to inspire; but with looks and voice
so truly feminine, as to be no very good picture of a man. With such an
Anhalt, however, Miss Crawford had courage enough" (169). At this early
point in the novel, Fanny's love for Edmund is unrequited. One of the ways
she feels she can become closer to Edmund is through "representing" or imitating him. Fanny would likely feel more comfortable in the role of Amelia
because she would be able to act alongside Edmund. Yet this would also

put her in the masculine position of pursuer, which Fanny could never feel comfortable in. In addition, Mary has already taken on the role of Amelia, so that avenue is no longer an option for Fanny. So rather than simply desiring to be *with* Edmund, she reveals in the rehearsal scene with Mary her desire to *become* Edmund.

Fanny experiments with different types of roles in her search for comfort. Her desire to become Edmund as she rehearses the role of Anhalt with Mary enables her to perform a heterosexual love scene. Yet, as we have seen in *Lovers' Vows*, this is by no means a gender normative role in that social codes are manipulated in the dialogue. In addition, Fanny's female body does not allow her to fully become Edmund. The narrator points out that Fanny was "so truly feminine" it was impossible for her to be like any man. Fanny's performative skills are not nearly as good as Mary's. Fanny wants to take Edmund's place, but her performance fails so she falls short of her aspirations. Conversely, Mary is able to make do with Fanny's poor performance. And the narrator suggests that Fanny's femininity—"with such an Anhalt"—contributes to Mary's "courage." Mary is able to fluidly move between masculine and feminine performances *because* of Fanny's femininity. It is the static nature of Fanny's gender performance that enables Mary's fluid gender performance. Theatricality here allows for fluidity—at least for Mary—and that gives Fanny more space to explore her own desires. Despite that space, any potential comfort that could be found for either woman is cut short by the sudden intrusion of the heterosexual narrative trajectory.

When Edmund arrives unexpectedly, the women's rehearsal is quickly broken up and the attention of both Mary and Fanny shifts back to his body. Edmund has come to the East Room to ask Fanny to rehearse the part of Amelia with him. His intentions are similar to Mary's in that he believes Fanny would "help him prepare for the evening" (170). However, unlike Mary, who sought out Fanny purposefully instead of Edmund, he simply did not realize that Mary was at Mansfield Park. While Mary and Fanny's queer desire oscillates between each other and Edmund, his desire remains firmly in the realm of heterosexuality. Thus, the narrative is pushed back into the heteronormative and does not allow Mary and Fanny to find comfort with each other. But the shift from a potentially queer scene into a heteronormative one is a moment of discomfort within the narrative itself. There is something incomplete left in that rehearsal space as the narrative moves on its hetero-merry way. The scene generates an idea of the queer space that cannot be. Mary takes on a masculine role in reading for the pursuer, Amelia, and Fanny reads for the male role, Anhalt, that is actually positioned as the feminine beloved. Even when Edmund interrupts the rehearsal, the sense of possibility that Fanny could read for Amelia lingers. The potential for all three to perform different heterosexual gender roles even while Mary and Fanny experiment with queer pleasure is excitingly real in this brief moment. Yet it ultimately fails to be realized. And the comfort Mary and Fanny try and fail to seek becomes discomfort that only highlights that queerness of their bodies and desires. We can read Mary and Fanny as bodies on stage, acting and reacting to each other's small movements. Edmund's body—at first just a thought specter and then a material reality—serves as both a conduit for the women's desire (male-body-as-prop) and a disappointing reminder of the heteronormative narrative trajectory. The potential for comfort that is introduced when Fanny and Mary begin rehearsing turns to discomfort when Edmund brings that solidity of the heteronormative trajectory into the fluid theater space.

While *Lovers' Vows* certainly invites readers to consider that section of *Mansfield Park* through a theatrical lens, the novel is full of theatrical moments that do not involve the play. Most evident is the use of objects—or props—to signal a body's desire in parts of the narrative not associated with *Lovers' Vows*. In *The Stage Life of Props*, Andrew Sofer explains that an analysis of props requires the critic to imagine bodies on stage; we cannot look at an object alone. We must see that object in the context of the actors'—or, in the case of a theatrical narrative, the characters'—bodies and how those bodies "manipulate" that object "in the course of performance" or throughout the narrative.[18] He writes, "Props' most common function is to act as various kinds of *visual shorthand* . . . [they] easily slide from metonymy to metaphor."[19] In considering the significance of a prop in a theatrical narrative, we must take into account three things: (1) How the character(s) physically interact with and manipulate the prop; (2) What the prop signifies about the character(s) who handle it; and (3) What the prop signifies in general within the context of the plot. For the purposes of my argument, there are two specific props within *Mansfield Park* that further reveal the queer possibilities within the novel: Mary's harp and Fanny's chain. Ultimately, identifying the harp and the chain as props enables us to visualize the bodies of Mary and Fanny as we might visualize the bodies of actors upon a stage. The physical props are signifiers of Mary and Fanny's queer desire and the discomfort that results.

Mary's primary tool of seduction is her harp, and it is introduced abstractly when she mentions to Edmund that she plays and she is having the instrument sent to the parsonage (57). As readers and audience members, we do not actually see or hear the harp until Fanny sees it in Volume Two. In addition, Mary gifts a chain to Fanny and uses that chain as both her own seduction tool and a surrogate seduction tool for her brother, Henry—who is also interested in Fanny. Both of these objects—the chain and the harp—become tools that Mary and Fanny can use to seek comfort in each other's bodies. Yet both objects also force the narrative back into the heteronormative and, for Fanny especially, create discomfort. An examination of these objects and their function identifies further queer possibilities between Mary and Fanny that are never realized.

The harp as a musical instrument is sensual in its own right, and in *Mansfield Park* its titillating nature emphasizes the sexual tension between Mary and Fanny. In discussing their 2006 exhibit at the Metropolitan Museum of Art, curators Harold Koda and Andrew Bolton used the harp as a central figure in an eighteenth-century music lesson display. They note that the harp has the "ability to project a player's coquetry. In the hands of a voluptuary the harp [is] a powerful instrument of seduction."[20] The harp draws attention to a player's light hands and nimble fingers, and playing form requires one to embrace it with one's entire body. Thus, the listener is invited to gaze upon the player's body as she reaches to pluck the harp's strings. In addition, "the harp was a sexual stimulant for players as well as spectators. Necessitating an intrusion between the legs, the harp became an effective autoerotic apparatus."[21] In *Mansfield Park*, Fanny's captive eyes and ears heighten Mary's onanistic pleasure. The harp serves as love object for Mary's own autonomous stimulation; in addition, as Mary manipulates the instrument, she gives Fanny the pleasure of hearing the music while also gazing upon the player. The moment enables them both to seek comfort in each other's bodies.

The harp also brings to mind the heterosexual trajectory of the narrative that forms a barrier between Mary and Fanny. The harp makes both women think of Edmund, since he was the one who had previously most enjoyed Mary's playing. And it is when Mary suggests she play Edmund's favorite that Fanny, who had previously been attempting to leave, agrees to stay. She "fancied him sitting in that room again and again, perhaps in the very spot where she sat now, listening with constant delight to the favorite air, played, as it appeared to her, with superior tone and expression" (207). The harp is a sign that Fanny desires Edmund even as she expresses desire for Mary. Here, just as in the rehearsal scene, Fanny imagines that she *is* Edmund. The harp is used to represent the space between homoerotic and heterosexual desire. As Mary's fingers pluck the strings, as her arms move back and forth, the motion

and the steady rhythm of the music become signifiers of the fluid sexual feeling present in that space. From this point until Mary is officially rejected by
Edmund, the two women enjoy "an intimacy" which Austen's narrator says
is "something new" for Mary and a "kind of fascination" for Fanny (208).
These emotions are evidence of a brief moment when both women are moving toward comfort. Their queer desire finds a place to sink in and rest for a
short time. Although they eventually separate, the "intimacy" they share is
a direct result of their bodies recognizing each other as queer. Neither can
maintain this feeling of comfort, because the narrative does not allow them
to explore it further. In addition, comfort found with another woman and
not a man is not something one seeks when one's purpose is to secure a husband. Thus, the very nature of this instinctual comfort for both Mary and
Fanny transforms into discomfort, because it is not part of the narrative's
ultimately heteronormative trajectories of desire. The push and pull of erotic
desire that the harp represents transforms into an oscillation between the
comfort and discomfort Mary and Fanny feel in each other's presence.

Shortly after this harp scene, Fanny reluctantly asks Mary to lend her
a chain for a ball.[22] They have an argument about the chain. Mary would
like Fanny to choose one to keep, but Fanny believes this is too generous
of a gift to accept. There is a clear desire on Fanny's part to avoid unnecessary and unwanted obligation. But, as is the pattern in their relationship,
Mary gets her way. The chain Fanny chooses is the one Mary wants her to
choose—one that is "more frequently placed before [Fanny's] eyes than the
rest" (248). The women act out a kind of love scene when Fanny accepts
Mary's gift and allows her to place the chain around Fanny's neck. Fanny is
then moved to an uncharacteristically open expression of emotion: "'When
I wear this necklace I shall always think of you,' said she [to Mary], 'and
feel how very kind you were'" (258–59). The sensation of the chain brings
heightened awareness to her body. Fanny feels Mary's kindness in both an
emotional and physical sense, and allows herself to sink into the comfort
of sharing this moment with another queer body. Its intimate contact with
both Mary's body and Fanny's body—Mary had worn it a few times already
before giving it to Fanny[23]—is indicative of the tantalizing sexual nature of
this particular item. It is an object meant to ornament the body and to call
attention to the woman's neck and chest.[24] Like Mary's harp, Fanny's chain
is meant to be both seen and touched. Marcia Pointon argues that, for jewelry, "touch and look are required simultaneously to deliver the pleasure of
the moment."[25] As Mary and Fanny physically interact with the chain, they

are able to experience a shared pleasure; it is a signal of the desire that passes unspoken and unrealized between the two women.

In addition to Mary's welcome feelings toward Fanny, the chain represents Henry's unwelcome feelings toward her; this prop allows Fanny to briefly move toward comfort but ultimately pushes her back into discomfort when the true owner of the chain is revealed. When Mary tells Fanny that she must think of *Henry* and not Mary because the chain was a gift from him, Mary uses an item from her brother to express her own feelings toward Fanny. The chain metonymically represents Henry, who is trying to pursue Fanny. When Mary mentions Henry's attraction to Fanny, the fragile potential comfort of the queer interaction is broken. Once more, the heteronormative makes its way disappointingly but inevitably back into the narrative, and Mary and Fanny find themselves in a space that causes them both discomfort. In the rehearsal scene, Edmund is at first a conduit for the women's desire but ultimately obstructs the queer narrative. Similarly, here Henry is both a conduit for and obstruction of Mary and Fanny's queer desire. Once again, the queer possibilities are evident but cannot manifest into actualities.

Fanny and Mary represent queer bodies and how they consistently experience small levels of discomfort in spaces where heterosexuality is the norm. Mary and Fanny cannot sink into that familiar, comfortable chair that Sara Ahmed describes in *The Cultural Politics of Emotion* because they do not sit long enough in one identity or one sexuality. For them, discomfort does derive from an embodied sexual difference—but it is not a static difference. Their difference cannot be properly named because it is constantly in motion, and that movement takes them to queer intimacies. Fanny constantly pines for Edmund but is inexplicably drawn to Mary. And while Mary spends the majority of the novel trying to force her body to conform to a narrative of heteronormativity by chasing after Edmund, she often finds herself seducing Fanny instead. Mary and Fanny also both attempt to hide their own embodied difference by using Edmund's body as a shield and a conduit for expressing their mutual desire. The result is a potential for queer comfort that ultimately crumbles within the narrative; yet the existence of this attempt encourages potential pathways to queer love and the possibility of finding queer comfort in a heteronormative narrative.

Upon closer examination of Fanny and Mary's relationship, we find the source of that frustration with the novel's conclusion: Fanny Price does not feel comfortable with Edmund Bertram or, really, any type of sexual desire. Although she is able to search for comfort in Mary's body when she (Fanny) is embodying Edmund, Mary both desires Edmund and persistently looks for comfort from Fanny's body. When Fanny and Mary are alone together, they come close to finding that comfort. Mary and Fanny's interest in each other, their search for comfort in each other, is where we find queer possibilities. While absolute comfort is not an option for Mary and Fanny, we can identify the moments in which they are searching for comfort. The moments of (dis)comfort that Mary and Fanny experience with each other necessitate a more critical examination of the heteronormative ending and encourage readers to embrace queer possibilities.

Notes

1. Scholars such as Paula Byrne, Penny Gay, Elaine Jordan, and Joseph Litvak have explained the moral significance of these private theatricals in Austen's novel. Paula Byrne, *Jane Austen and the Theatre* (London: Bloomsbury, 2007). Penny Gay, *Jane Austen and the Theatre* (Cambridge: Cambridge University Press, 2002). Elaine Jordan, "Pulpit, Stage, and Novel: *Mansfield Park* and Mrs. Inchbald's *Lovers' Vows*," *Novel: A Forum on Fiction* 20, no. 2 (1987): 138–148. Livak is cited below.

2. Elaine McGirr, "Documents of Performance: 'What Signifies a Theatre?'" *Nineteenth Century Theatre & Film* 38, no. 2 (Winter 2011): 75.

3. This essay is not the first to explore a homoerotic reading of Jane Austen's writing. Critics such as Terry Castle and Eve Sedgwick, among others, have identified homoerotic threads in Austen's work. In her extremely controversial book review, "Sister-Sister," Castle suggests that the letters exchanged between Austen and her sister, Cassandra, contain an "underlying eros." See Terry Castle, "Sister-Sister," Review of *Jane Austen's Letters*, edited by Deirde Le Faye. *London Review of Books* 17, no. 5 (1995): 6. In "Jane Austen and the Masturbating Girl," Sedgwick argues that Marianne Dashwood's descriptions of her own body in *Sense and Sensibility* might lead us to consider her having a "masturbatory identity." See Eve Sedgwick, "Jane Austen and the Masturbating Girl," *Critical Inquiry* 17, no. 4 (1991): 837.

4. Aintzane Legarreta Mentxaka looks specifically at the complex relationship between Fanny and Mary Crawford. Mentxaka argues the novel contains a lesbian subplot that can never be fully realized because Fanny could never pursue Mary in the romantic way that Edmund does. Neither could Mary pursue Fanny. The narrator, Mentxaka notes, calls attention to the homoerotic subplot by emphasizing the supposedly naturalness of assumed heterosexuality, but lesbian relations between Mary and Fanny must be a temporary flirtation. The lesbian subplot "in conjunction with the heterosexual romance . . . serves to illustrate the main theme of the novel, a debate on nature versus education." See Aintzane Legarreta Mentxaka, "'Where She Could Not Follow':

The Lesbian Subplot in Jane Austen's Mansfield Park," *English Language and Literature Studies* 3, no. 1 (2013): 3.

5. Sara Ahmed, *The Cultural Politics of Emotion*, 2nd ed (Edinburgh: Edinburgh University Press, 2014), 148.

6. Laura Engel, *Austen, Actresses, and Accessories: Much Ado About Muffs* (New York: Palgrave MacMillan, 2015), Kindle, Introduction.

7. Henry is more than ready for the private theatricals; when the scheme is being discussed, he declares, "I feel as if I could be any thing or every thing, as if I could rant and storm, or sign, or cut capers in any tragedy or comedy in the English language" (123). And Fanny believes, "Mr. Crawford was considerably the best actor of all" (165). Mary takes to acting well, but we see her artifice immediately when the narrator introduces her as a woman with an agenda: "Matrimony was her object, provided she could marry well . . . While she treated it as a joke, therefore, she did not forget to think of it seriously" (42). Her ability to scheme and perform is implied when she sets out to secure a husband.

8. Ruth Bernard Yeazell, "Fanny Price's Modest Loathings," in *Fictions of Modesty: Women and Courtship in the English Novel* (Chicago: University of Chicago Press, 1991), 143–168. Yeazell puts pressure on the tropes of modesty and morality in Austen's novels; she argues that "Mansfield Park does not always distinguish a modest consciousness from a conscious sense of loathing toward the body" (163) and explores the ways in which Fanny Price's "modesty" is often read as "a given" (145).

9. Sara Ahmed, *The Cultural Politics of Emotion*, 148.

10. Nachumi, Nora. "Horses and Hunks: Translating Sexuality in Austen to Film (Part II)." Paper presented at East-Central/American Society for Eighteenth-Century Studies Conference, Cape May, NJ, October 2004.

11. Carlotta Farese, "The Strange Case of Herr von K: Further Reflections on the Reception of Kotzebue's Theatre in Britain," in *The Romantic Stage: A Many-Side Mirror*, eds. Lilla Maria Crisafulli and Fabio Liberto (Amsterdam: Rodopi, 2014), 77.

12. Christoph Bode, "Unfit for an English Stage? Inchbald's *Lovers' Vows* and Kotzebue's *Das Kind der Liebe*," *European Romantic Review* 16, no. 3 (2005): 300.

13. Elizabeth Inchbald, *Lovers' Vows*, 1798, reprint in *Mansfield Park*, ed. R.W. Chapman (London: T. Egerton, 1814; Oxford: Oxford University Press, 1988), 478.

14. Inchbald, *Lovers*, 478.

15. Inchbald, *Lovers*, 505.

16. Susan Allen Ford, "'It Is about Lover's Vows': Kotzebue, Inchbald, and the Players of Mansfield Park," *Persuasions On-line* 27, no. 1 (2006), url: http://www.jasna.org/persuasions/on-line/vol27no1/ford.htm?

17. In fact, she loves Edmund despite herself: her ambitious nature dictates that she should be more interested in Tom (who will inherit Mansfield) or that she should move on emotionally to another family with a more suitable first-born son. It is her ambition that eventually makes Edmund see her as a poor match for himself.

18. Andrew Sofer, *The Stage Life of Props* (Ann Arbor: University of Michigan Press, 2003), 11.

19. Sofer, *Stage Life,* 20–21.

20. Harold Koda and Andrew Bolton, *Dangerous Liaisons: Fashion and Furniture in the Eighteenth Century* (New York: Met Publications, 2006), 46.

21. Koda and Bolton, *Dangerous Liaisons*, 46.

22. The cross Fanny wants this chain for is from her real brother, William, who is often compared to Edmund. For a reading of incestuous possibilities within Fanny and William's relationship, see George Haggerty, "Fanny Price: Is she solemn?—Is she queer?—Is she prudish?" *The Eighteenth Century* 53, no. 2 (2012): 175–188.

23. This is an assumption I'm making that I believe the text implies. Mary tells Fanny "You see what a collection I have . . . more by half than I ever use or think of. *I do not offer them as new*" (258, my emphasis). As I read it, there is an implication here that Mary has worn all of the necklaces and chains she shows Fanny.

24. Marcia Pointon refers to the bosom as "a display case" for jewelry. Marcia Pointon, "Valuing the Visual and Visualizing the Valuable: Jewellery and Its Ambiguities," *Cultural Values* 3, no. 1 (1999): 15.

25. Marcia Pointon, "Women and Their Jewels," in *Women and Material Culture, 1660—1830,* eds. Jennie Batchelor and Cora Kaplan (New York: Palgrave Macmillan, 2007), 23.

Chapter Three

Taking Hands

The Fisting Phantasmic in *Sense and Sensibility*

Christien Garcia

1.

Jane Austen's hands present a paradox. On the one hand, hands in her novels do the symbolic work of neat and tidy matrimonial pairing—the metaphorical taking of hands in marriage. On the other hand, as this chapter aims to show, hands make a mess of the fantasy that the erotic trajectory of her novels is one of straightforward coupling. This two-handedness is mirrored in the ongoing reception of Austen's work and the author's enduring popularity. On the one hand, Austen's name in the popular imagination remains a near synonym for genteel social organization. And on the other hand, the enduring canonization of her work depends on a veritable cottage industry of disrupting the image of the polite and sexless "dear Aunt Jane."[1]

One handy flash point in the history of this schism came in 1990 via Eve Kosofsky Sedgwick. The American critic whose scholarship on sexuality in literature helped form the foundations of queer theory, sparked an uproar with a conference submission titled "Jane Austen and the Masturbating Girl." Even in an era before social media, the title quickly made the rounds as evidence of the degeneracy of academic discourse in the humanities.[2] Sedgwick later noted that the paper had yet to be written, let alone published, before the jeremiads began, and thus, that there must have been something self-evidently scornful about the mere association of Austen and masturbation. But what? Masturbation is no longer the execrated act of self-defilement that it once was. Whether today or in the late twentieth century, it is more likely

seen as a healthy part of sexual development and self-care. Given this reha-
bilitation, a more likely account of the furor, Sedgwick postulates, is that the
developmental infantility associated with the masturbating girl challenged
something we hold dear about the seriousness of Austen's novels, and more
specifically, the unspoken role "mature" sex, which is to say procreative het-
ero-genitality, plays in defining "the literary."[3]

In the publication that would eventually come out of this talk, Sedgwick
explores the onanistic subjectivity represented by *Sense and Sensibility*'s sister
protagonists, one restless, impertinent, and often listless, and the other the
watchful disciplinarian. This coupled subjectivity, Sedgwick argues, speaks
to the nascent techniques of medicalization and surveillance enacted during Austen's time to regulate sexual behaviors into binary forms of sexual
identity—gay/straight, closeted/out, and disordered/healthy. Paradoxically,
because masturbation serves as the "proto-form" of modern sexual subjectivity, there remains little evidence of its role as forebear to the dominant
sexual politics of today.[4] It is hard to imagine masturbation as a serious sexual identity. And thus, the erotic charge of the novel is easily overlooked
in favor of confirmation of our contemporary lens of alloerotic partnership.
In Sedgwick's words, "the dropping out of the autoerotic term is also part
of what falsely naturalizes the heterosexist imposition of these books, dis-
tinguishing both the rich, conflictual erotic complication of a homoerotic
matrix not yet crystallized in terms of 'sexual identity,' and the violence of
heterosexual definition finally carved out of these plots."[5] In order to reani-
mate this (auto)erotic term, Sedgwick's approach to criticism is to ground
the rich and conflictual field of associations between bodies, signs, moods,
gestures, sensations, patterns, and sounds that subtend the narrative out-
comes of the courtship drama.

Thus, as well as using the novel to unpack the Western genealogy of sexuality, Sedgwick challenged the kinds of criticism that are deemed valid in
the academy. "Austen criticism," she writes, "is notable not just for its timidity and banality but for its unresting exaction of the spectacle of the Girl
Being Taught a Lesson."[6] As if to counter the "would-be-damning epithet
'mental masturbation',"[7] many Austen critics focus on Elinor's, and especially, Marianne's moral education, culminating in the conjugal "fruition"
of her marriage to Colonel Brandon, those critics themselves taking on the
role of disciplinarian. While contemporary scholars are less likely to describe
Marianne's character in terms of moral and sexual atonement, there remains
in the literature a strong indication that the enduring value of these works
rests in their ability to help us navigate "different but analogous" social

conventions.[8] Sedgwick wants to upend these critical impulses and center the undisciplined pleasures of Austen's language, freeing reader, author, and character alike to play with each other and, of course, themselves more freely. Sedgwick's objective is to "make available . . . an alternative, passionate sexual ecology—one fully available to Austen for her exciting, productive, and deliberate use,"[9] which is precisely my goal here.

In particular, this chapter uses Sedgwick's article as inspiration to make available another sexual phantasmatic in *Sense and Sensibility*, and an altogether different taking of hands than is usually associated with Austen, the sexual practice of fisting. In line with the objectives of this collection, my goal is to center a different kind of reader before *Sense and Sensibility* as a way to help illuminate Austen as a different kind of writer than what is typically asserted. Although this work no doubt constitutes an example of what Vincent Quinn calls "loose reading,"[10] nothing is closer to the letter of the novel than to say that *Sense and Sensibility* is about the ritualized mingling of pleasure and pain that arises from the deferment of heterosexual, genital couplings, and the deliberate stretching of bodies to their physical limit.

2.

Gayle Rubin defines fisting as "a sexual technique in which the hand and arm, rather than a penis or dildo, are used to penetrate a bodily orifice. Fisting usually refers to anal penetration, although the terms are also used for the insertion of a hand into a vagina."[11] Fisting is often assumed to be inherently brutal and dangerous. Its practitioners, however, emphasize its deliberate, meditative, and nuanced characteristics. Because fisting "involves seducing one of the jumpiest and tightest muscles in the body,"[12] it typically involves numerous cycles of slow, gradual stretching. David Halperin likens it to "anal yoga"[13] as it requires the kind of intensity that only tranquility can offer. And as Dinesh Wadiwel describes,

> The practice is by nature gentle and . . . requires care and skill on the part of its practitioners . . . fisting also involves an elaborate web of communication strategies, as well as the often-painstaking process of 'coaxing' the body into a position of comfort where this practice may become possible . . . a connection and synergy between body organs.[14]

Fisting thus both intensifies and inverts the dynamics of penetrative intimacy, centering "intensity and duration of feeling, not climax."[15] The elasticity of the anus and rectum literally shapes the rhythm of the penetration along with the top's alloy of sensitivity and force.

For these reasons, the power exchange involved in fisting is not as clear cut as in other kink practices. Despite the overlap between fisters and sadomasochists, the former is generally less hierarchal, less decorous, less "noisy"[16] than its deviant sibling. If fisting does constitute something like a minority identity, it is a loose and layered one. It both intersects and remains distinct from other kink practices. As a queer subculture, it has its own rituals, codes, organizations, paraphernalia, social events, and even a podcast. The representation of fisting, however, is widely censored. Australia[17] and the United Kingdom[18] ban fisting in porn production and the popular adult entertainment site OnlyFans prohibits fisting on its platform.[19] It is hardly a darling of gay culture either.[20] *The Joy of Gay Sex,* considered by many a hallmark of post-Stonewall, pre-AIDS American gay-male sexual liberation, condemns fisting.[21] Rubin makes the incisive point that fisting with gloves might have been a powerful weapon in the arsenal of safer sex practices during the rise of AIDS but was instead excluded from health policy conversations. During this period, fisting was isolated from the wider gay community and fisting venues shuttered.[22] Despite all this, today fisting is widely practiced and arguably a growing aspect of queer and kink cultures.

Fisting and masturbation might appear to share very little in common. But beside the role hands play in both, where they come together is as bookends of the developmental paradigm of sexuality. Masturbation is seen as merely a trial run for the development of mature sexuality, while fisting is seen as an add-on that could come only after sexual modernity. Because ostensibly no record of fisting exists before the late twentieth century,[23] scholars have attested (somewhat circumstantially) that it may be the only sex act invented in the last century.[24] Thus, whether at an individual or historical level, both practices are outliers understood through the achievement of penile-vaginal sex. The question seems naturally to arise, how can we read fisting, or masturbation for that matter, in *Sense and Sensibility* when the novel doesn't even portray sex "itself"? By this logic, however, reproductive sex will constantly reproduce itself as the frame through which "other" forms of sex must be comprehended. This obscures the fact that in *Sense and Sensibility*, erotic connection has far more to do with fraught forms of stretching the reception of others than it does with conjugal cathexis. Which is why many of the most libidinally charged moments in Austen's writing take place between those who don't end up together.

What fisting and masturbation share, then, is a capacity to de-familiarize the symbolic structures that disguise the less disciplined erotic textures and rhythms of literature. As Sedgwick argues in a different context, "what is so productive about the fisting image as a sexual phantasmatic is that it can offer a switchpoint not only between homo- and heteroeroticism, but also between allo- and autoeroticism . . . and between the polarities that a phallic economy defines as passive and active."[25] Fisting flickers rhythm, forms, textures, and sensations in ways that abnegate the symbolism, truths, and meanings of reproductive sex. Much like the practice of fisting, the society of *Sense and Sensibility* dramatizes the coaxing of bodies, using the hand specifically to couple intensity and composure, force and passivity. Blurring the boundaries of social and physical sensation, Austen performs pleasure at its limits, using hand and body as a site for the interplay of realism and fantasy, plot and imagery, and between character, author, and reader. In these ways, Austen's "fisting-as-écriture"[26] imagines sex at the limits of what bodies can or should do, rather than as the realization of what "we" assume happens when the lights go out at the end of the story.

3.

Fisting scenes are not so commonplace in Jane Austen's novels that readers get jaded with their chiaroscuro of force and tenderness.[27]

> She started up, and pronouncing his name in a tone of affection, held out her hand to him. He approached, and addressing himself rather to Elinor than Marianne, as if wishing to avoid her eye, and determined not to observe her attitude, inquired in a hurried manner after Mrs. Dashwood, and asked how long they had been in town. Elinor was robbed of all presence of mind by such an address, and was unable to say a word. But the feelings of her sister were instantly expressed. Her face was crimsoned over, and she exclaimed, in a voice of the greatest emotion, "Good God! Willoughby, what is the meaning of this? Have you not received my letters? Will you not shake hands with me?"

> He could not then avoid it, but her touch seemed painful to him, and he held her hand only for a moment. During all this time he was evidently struggling for composure. Elinor watched his countenance and saw its expression becoming more tranquil. After a moment's pause, he spoke with calmness.[28]

This encounter is Austen's way of bringing to a head the question of Marianne and Willoughby's possible engagement. She does this with Marianne's hand. It lingers outstretched for so long that, by the time Marianne implores Willoughby to take it, it seems to have been absorbed into the narrative. The hand brings with it a layered sequence of ceremony, pressure, shock, pain, release, and tranquility.

The scene could easily be read as a spectacle of Marianne's public humiliation. Willoughby pretends to hardly know the woman he has been actively courting for the past several months. But there is also a brazenness, even sadistic quality, in the way Marianne actively disrupts the polite composure of those around her by putting her hand where it does not belong. After all, "her joys, could have no moderation . . . she was every thing but prudent" (7). Indeed, this interaction of force and receptivity is the foundation of Marianne and Willoughby's intimacy. On the occasion of their second encounter, we are told,

> Their taste was strikingly alike. The same books, the same passages were idolized by each—or if any difference appeared, any objection arose, it lasted no longer than till the force of her arguments and the brightness of her eyes could be displayed. He acquiesced in all her decisions, caught all her enthusiasm; and long before his visit concluded, they conversed with the familiarity of a long-established acquaintance. (56)

In this light, the party scene is both a culmination of their intimacy and its rupture. Marianne uses the party to make a public spectacle of Willoughby's previously private acquiescence. In a letter soon after this meeting Willoughby confesses his "desire of a release" (209) from his attachment to Marianne. As much as this initiates abhorrence to the man for misleading Marianne, it also underscores the way in which Austen understands desire itself through sensations of slowly built tension and sudden release. What better way to explore this than with hands, which signify the ability of humans to grasp and intricately manipulate their surrounding environments?

Earlier in the narrative, when Marianne observes a ring on Edward's hand and presumes it to be evidence of his attachment to her sister, Austen directs readers to the "conspicuous" work of hands in her novel (113). In this case, the hand proves to be misdirection. The ring is adorned with Lucy's hair and not Elinor's as Marianne assumes. Yet, by the end of the novel Marianne's assumption proves to be correct. Hands, in other words, subtly gesture to the unreliability of signs as they pertain to the conjugal imperative of the novel. In another instance, a hand similarly signals the affective limits of language.

When Colonel Brandon enlists himself to retrieve the ailing Marianne's mother, he takes leave of Elinor by "only pressing her hand with a look of solemnity, and a few words spoken too low to reach her ear" (352–23). Brandon's gesture is not simply a complement to the expressivity of voice and explanation, but also an insistence on that "which may not want, need, or be capable of louder articulation."[29] Regardless of what Brandon says, nothing is lost from the intimacy of the scene in Elinor's not hearing it.

This polysemic economy of touch is all the more intricate between the Dashwood women. Hands do far more than merely console, as might first appear. More often they tip sensation over the edge. This is the case when Marianne is "overcome" by "her mother's silently pressing her hand" (95). When Mrs. Dashwood, escorted by Colonel Brandon, arrives to see the convalescent Marianne, and is greeted by Elinor, there is a frenzy of breathless touch between the party: "shedding tears of joy, though still unable to speak, [Mrs. Dashwood] embraced Elinor again and again, turning from her at intervals to press Colonel Brandon's hand, with a look which spoke at once her gratitude, and her conviction of his sharing with herself in the bliss of the moment" (378). Here the hand works as a conduit for the intensity that courses through them. The pleasure that arises with news of Marianne after Mrs. Dashwood's suspenseful journey is conveyed with a hand that both confirms and dissolves the physical boundaries of bodies.

Perhaps nowhere is this boundary play more evident than during the scene between Elinor and Willoughby just before Mrs. Dashwood's arrival. Elinor portrays an almost unexplainable openness to the man she previously seemed hardly willing to countenance. At first Elinor is the picture of self-possession. Impervious to him, "her hand was already on the lock" (359). Slowly, however, she is coaxed, wavering in intervals between "acquiescence" (359), and "hardening her heart anew" (364) until finally she is persuaded to have empathy for the man. The erotics of the scene are crafted through this push and pull. It is done with a medley of "command" and "supplication" (359). The scene ends with a reversal of the party scene: "He held out his hand. She could not refuse to give him her's," whereby "he pressed it with affection" (375). With this mirroring, Elinor stands in for Marianne who never gets her romantic reunion. At the very least, Elinor's ability to forgive Willoughby stretches the limits of what we know of her character. The scene envelops Elinor into a pattern of corporeal interlocution first initiated by Marianne—a climatic, almost shocking imposition, the assuaging of jumpy reflexes, a kind of giving in or letting go that is active, and finally, a wave of calm that succeeds this acquiescence.

What these fisting scenes reveal is that the taking and releasing of actual hands in *Sense and Sensibility* is one important way the novel foregrounds erotic exchanges that run alongside the current of matrimonial coupling. What is more, the taking and releasing of hands frame desire in Austen's language as the oscillation between bodies that couple and bodies that merely fold intricately into one another without ever merging. By tracing patterns of gripping and letting go, the very entity that can "I do" is repeatedly displaced by webs of desire, pleasure, and bodies, thus weaving the inarticulacy of erotic sensation into the more explicit narrative of conjugal unity. As the novel builds towards its closure and the latter becomes more pronounced, we see this folding in the way Marianne seems to bend herself to Elinor's more reserved image (reversing the openness Elinor exhibited in her scene with Willoughby). Near the end of the novel Marianne presses Elinor's hand (393), as if to siphon some of her character as she promises to live by Elinor's "example" (392) and to be more "regulated" in her desire (393). After this atonement, Elinor recounts the details of Willoughby's apology, which Austen glosses in favor of this image: Marianne "caught every syllable with panting eagerness; her hand, unknowingly to herself, closely pressed her sister's, and tears covered her cheeks" (394). Marianne's grip invokes the threat of her being completely washed away by emotion, but it is also what keeps her "unknowingly" to her new determination of self. This unknowingness assures that Marianne's moral transformation is far from unambiguous.

It is telling that this is arguably the last truly gripping exchange in the novel. Even when Edward arrives at Barton Cottage to ask Elinor to marry him, it is Mrs. Dashwood who takes his hand, leaving Elinor to only "wish" she had done the same (204). As for Marianne, the manner in which she gives her hand to Brandon as soon as he walks into the sick room after bringing her mother to her—"receiving the pale hand which she immediately held out to him" (244)—rests in sharp contrast to the vigor with which she reaches out to Willoughby. Accepting Brandon, her pallid hand is like a lifeless prop. In a novel that understands the very nature of desire through the delay and escalation of the force of hands, the fact that Brandon's is taken immediately robs the exchange of Marianne's sexual agency.[30] There is none of the gradations or contradictions of either of the sister's scenes with Willoughby. By the time the reader is told, at the end of the novel, that Marianne has decided "voluntarily to give her hand to another!" (429) taking hands has lost the sensual dexterity of actual hands and is reduced instead to its pat metaphorical usage.[31]

4.

Part and parcel of the queer, critical reading tradition cultivated by Sedgwick is the practice of telling stories about stories, thus reintegrating the phantasmatic and critical. Just as criticism can be thought of as a form of intellectual self-eroticism, so too can we think about it as a form of fisting, stretching a text in ways that reveal new forms of pleasure and connection that were there all along. By expanding contemporary Austen criticism beyond "this is what Austen can teach us about today" ways of thinking, we center reading as itself a polymorphously perverse practice, which is to say, not requiring healthy reproduction or reproducibility.

Thus, this chapter's one-upping of the onanistic with the fisting imaginary is not simply about putting a queer "spin" on a literary classic, it is rather about illustrating the restrictive effects naturalized ideas about sex have on how we think about literature broadly. The fact that we tend to assume that Austen's erotic social tableaus work in the service of hetero-genital intercourse, and not, say, fisting or masturbation, says more about how the enduring fantasy of healthy, mature, and reproductive sex works as a silent arbiter of serious literature than it does about the imagined sexual proclivities of Austen's characters. Countering this, fisting can offer a whole host of potentially transformative metaphors for desire that owe very little to the politics of individual sovereignty, genital coupling, reproductive futurity, health, or even seriousness.

And finally, reading *Sense and Sensibility* as a fisting drama helps us think more critically and creatively about the history of fisting itself. Fisting may not have existed as a recorded practice of sexual identity until the twentieth century; but its unique orientations between bodies and patterns of sensation certainly did. Although not explicitly vaginal or anal, the insertive hand and receptive body as erotic device is far from merely latent or secret in the British literary cannon. This fisting phantasm suggests that the prehistory of fisting may be much larger and richer than previously thought possible.

Notes

1. The "dear Aunt Jane" persona was famously promulgated by her nephew's 1869 *Memoir*. J. E. Austen-Leigh, *A Memoir of Jane Austen* (London: Richard Bently, 1870).

2. Perhaps most notably, Roger Kimball cited the title as proof of the "ideologically motivated assaults on the intellectual and moral substance of our

culture." Roger Kimball, *Tenured Radicals: How Politics Has Corrupted Our Higher Education* (Chicago: Ivan R. Dee, 1998), 11–12. And in the *New York Times,* it was listed, along with such triggering titles as "Brotherly Love: Nabokov's Homosexual Double," and "A Womb of His Own: Male Renaissance Poets in the Female Body," as the Q.E.D. of "political correctness" gone awry. Bernstein, Richard, "The Rising Hegemony of the Politically Correct: America's Fashionable Orthodoxy," *New York Times,* October 28, 1990, sec. 4.

3. Eve Kosofsky Sedgwick, "Jane Austen and the Masturbating Girl," *Critical Inquiry* 17, no. 4 (1991), 825.
4. Sedgwick, "Masturbating Girl," 826.
5. Sedgwick, "Masturbating Girl," 826.
6. Sedgwick, "Masturbating Girl," 833.
7. Sedgwick, "Masturbating Girl," 820.
8. Tom Keymer, *Jane Austen: Writing, Society, Politics* (Oxford: Oxford University Press, 2020), 28.
9. Sedgwick, "Masturbating Girl," 834.
10. Vincent Quinn, "Loose Reading? Sedgwick, Austen and Critical Practice," *Textual Practice* 14, no. 2 (2000): 305–26.
11. Gayle S. Rubin, "The Catacombs: A Temple of the Butthole," in *Deviations: A Gayle Rubin Reader* (Durham NC: Duke, 2012), 402n6.
12. Rubin, *Deviations,* 230.
13. David Halperin, *Saint Foucault: Towards A Gay Hagiography* (Oxford: Oxford University Press, 1995), 91.
14. Dinesh Wadiwel, "Sex and the Lubricative Ethic," in *The Ashgate Research Companion to Queer Theory,* ed. Noreen Giffney and Michael O'Rourke (Aldershot: Ashgate, 2009), 495–496.
15. Halperin, *Saint Foucault,* 101.
16. Rubin, *Deviations,* 232.
17. Zahra Stardust, "'Fisting Is Not Permitted': Criminal Intimacies, Queer Sexualities and Feminist Porn in the Australian Legal Context," *Porn Studies* 1, no. 3 (July 3, 2014): 242–59.
18. Christopher Hooton, "A Long List of Sex Acts Just Got Banned in UK Porn," *The Independent,* December 12, 2014, https://www.independent.co.uk/news/uk/long-list-sex-acts-just-got-banned-uk-porn-9897174.html.
19. E. J. Dickson, "Sex Workers Built OnlyFans. Now They Say They're Getting Kicked Off," *Rolling Stone* (blog), May 18, 2020, https://www.rollingstone.com/culture/culture-features/onlyfans-sex-workers-porn-creators-999881/.
20. See David Bergman, *The Violet Hour: The Violet Quill and the Making of Gay Culture* (New York: Columbia University Press, 2004), 161.

21. Charles Silverstein and Edmund White, *The Joy of Gay Sex: An Intimate Guide for Gay Men to the Pleasures of a Gay Lifestyle* (New York: Simon and Schuster, 1977), 82.

22. Rubin, *Deviations,* 237–38.

23. Bergman, *Violet Hour,* 206–7.

24. "It may have been practiced earlier," Rubin elaborates, "but it really became popular in the late 1960s and early 1970s, and then spawned its own unique subcultural elaboration and institutionalization." Rubin, *Deviations,* 308.

25. Eve Kosofsky Sedgwick, *Tendencies* (Durham: Routledge, 1994), 101. Like Sedgwick, others have argued that "fisting subverts the phallic economy." See Jonathan A. Allan, *Reading from Behind: A Cultural Analysis of the Anus* (Regina: University of Regina Press, 2016), 138.

26. Eve Kosofsky Sedgwick, *Touching Feeling: Affect, Pedagogy, Performativity* (Durham: Duke UP, 2003).47–48.

27. This sentence is a riff on one from Sedgwick's article, "Masturbating Girl," 822.

28. Jane Austen, *Sense and Sensibility,* ed. Edward Copeland, *The Cambridge Edition of the Works of Jane Austen* (Cambridge UK: Cambridge UP, 2006), 201. Additional citations in text.

29. Anne-Lise François, *Open Secrets: The Literature of Uncounted Experience* (Stanford, CA: Stanford University Press, 2008), 16.

30. This hand shake is similar to the sisterly way in which she meets Edward earlier in the story—"She met him with a hand that would be taken, and a voice that expressed the affection of a sister" (275).

31. This distinction recalls D. A. Miller's reading of *Sense and Sensibility* and his argument about the ways the novel releases meanings that escape the narrative closure of the novel's final paragraphs. In this vein, we might say, the novel itself releases Marianne, and to an extent Elinor, from its grip, precisely because of the tidy pairing off that takes place in their names. D. A. Miller, *Narrative and its Discontents: Problems of Closure in the Traditional Novel* (Princeton: Princeton University Press, 1981).

Part Two

Austen Fan Culture and Austenesque Fiction

Chapter Four

Always Wanting More

Desire and Austen Fan Fiction

Marilyn Francus

Austen fan fiction is an endless tease: a manifestation of the desire for more Austen originals, which can never be fulfilled, by writing Austen-inspired literature to compensate for that lack. By continuing to create "Austen," the Austen fan fiction archive is open-ended and ever expanding, like any fan fiction archive;[1] it is "A World Without End for Fans of Jane Austen" as Pamela O'Connell titled her *New York Times* article on austen.com and the Republic of Pemberley.[2] In this essay I argue that Austen fan fiction and its conventions articulate a specific set of desires as they attempt to fulfill them, but the fulfillment of those desires remains perpetually out of reach.

First, a few comments about the context in which Austen fan fiction flourishes. Popular culture, commercialism, postmodernism, and technology facilitated the rise of Austen fan fiction, which has been in full swing since 1995.[3] The modern Austen invasion began with the critical and commercial success of Austen's works on film and television between 1995 and 1999, as Austen's works permeated modern culture.[4] Austen fans celebrate: the 200th anniversaries of publications of her six major novels in the 2010s sustained, if not amplified, Austen culture. Austen is cross-marketed: her novels are sold with covers featuring actors from the film and television versions—and images of Austen (or what people think of as Austen), her characters, the actors playing her characters, and quotes from her works appear on posters, watches, mugs, towels, T-shirts, bags, calendars, and buttons. Austen fans behave like fans in other fandoms do, and they sustain these markets: on June 17, 2021, a search of "Jane Austen" on the cafepress.com search engine yielded 2,003 results. A search for "Jane Austen" on Etsy yielded 16,304 items that day.

Austen attracts fans all the time—and one of the ways that fans express themselves is by writing Austen fan fiction, which fits into and builds upon Austen culture. The literary devices that characterize modern and postmodern literature—pastiche, transposition, altered points of view, and metafiction—readily generate fan fiction.[5] The Austen-inflected novels that have been published within the past 20+ years—like Helen Fielding's *Bridget Jones's Diary* (1996), Stephanie Barron's Jane Austen mystery series (1996–present), Amanda Grange's *Darcy's Diary* (2005), Laurie Viera Rigler's *Confessions of a Jane Austen Addict* (2007), Seth Grahame-Smith's *Pride and Prejudice and Zombies* (2009), and the Austen Project Book Series, featuring Joanna Trollope's *Sense & Sensibility*, Val McDermid's *Northanger Abbey*, Alexander McCall Smith's *Emma,* and Curtis Sittenfeld's *Eligible* (2014–2016)—use these devices to engage with Austen, and in terms of technique, they are Austen fan fictions.[6]

Fan fiction, however, is usually defined by the amateur status of the writer, and the lack of profit. The Internet makes the dissemination of fan fiction far easier than the early days of *Star Trek* fan fiction mailings in the 1960s and '70s—and technology entices writers of fan fiction with a large, easily accessible audience.[7] Occasionally online Austen fan fiction writers win large publishing contracts—as in the case of Pamela Aidan, whose online *Fitzwilliam Darcy, Gentleman* series elicited a $150,000 advance from Simon and Schuster, who published her three novels under their Touchstone imprint.[8] Increasingly, Austen fan fiction writers are removing their work after they receive feedback in order to self-publish on Amazon or Kindle, but the majority of Austen fan fiction writers still keep their stories online for free, finished and unfinished, building an ever-growing archive of Austen fiction.[9]

While Austen culture, commercialism, postmodernism, and technology have facilitated the rise of Austen fan fiction, the psychology of desire is the primary engine for this phenomenon—and the conventions of Austen fan fiction online reveal the desires of Austen's current fandom *and* the mechanisms that sustain those desires. Sheenagh Pugh cites a fan fiction writer who "once remarked . . . that people wrote fanfic because they wanted either 'more of' their source material or 'more from' it."[10] The verb choice "want" is important here, as signaling desire, but I would argue that there is more at work in Austen fan fiction than "more of" and "more from" the source material, although those desires are certainly in play. The fan fiction writer also wants to be recognized and validated by the fan community: to be acknowledged by others who share the same desire and know the fan culture, which helps the writer fulfill their desire. But for the desire to perform—for an audience, a community—a fan fiction writer would have no reason to post their work online.

There is also the desire of the Austen fan fiction reader (who may or may not be a fan fiction writer as well) who seeks out Austen fan fiction on the Internet—who wants more Austen and who reads fan fiction "Austen" to get it. As Luetkenhaus and Weinstein write:

> By changing details, small or large, we get to spend more time with characters and places we love, experiencing the joy we had that first time we picked up Austen and falling in love with them all over again. *This* is the allure of JAFF [Jane Austen fan fiction], *this* is why Austen spinoffs, adaptations, and reimaginings will continue to sell: because we all want to feel that way again. The first flush of feeling Darcy's eyes on Elizabeth during a ball. The desperation of Marianne running through a storm, heartbroken over Willoughby. The vindication of knowing Fanny was right to not trust Henry Crawford. Fanfiction offers us new ways to experience that rush, to get our Austen fix. And it is exciting because we think we know what is going to happen in the end, but we don't know *how* we are going to get there.[11]

We all want to feel that way again. Note the communal "we," the inclusive "all," that important "want" signaling driving desire, and that incessant "again." Fan fiction is repetitive and addictive—and Luetkenhaus and Weinstein characterize it with the language of the rush and the fix that cannot be fully satisfied[12]—but they also describe it with the rhetoric of devotion, joy, and love, the language of desire. The fan fiction reader may lurk online reading silently or provide feedback to authors; either way, the fan fiction reader desires satisfaction from the fan fiction text, from the community, and if providing feedback, from the attention of the writer. The Austen fan fiction reader keeps reading, seeking satisfaction for their desire. Lastly, there's the desire of fan community itself, the "we" that hosts websites and in some cases sets up parameters to regulate the content to fulfill their desires to maintain the reputation and fandom of Austen and "Austen."[13]

My comments on the conventions of Austen fan fiction online are based on the stories and comments available on FanFiction.net (FFN), the Derbyshire Writers Guild (DWG), and Archive of Our Own (AO3), the largest Austen fan fiction websites, which post thousands of stories.[14] In this

essay, I will identify and analyze five conventions of online Austen fan fiction. There may be more conventions, but I believe that these five are suf-
ficient for my argument that Austen fan fiction is a source of and a response
to fan desire.

First, it is a convention of online Austen fan fiction that Austen's works
are universal—universal in the sense that her work can be transposed to any
time or place, fitted into or mashed up with any genre. Arguably this holds
true for all fan fiction, although I suspect that *Star Wars*, *The Avengers*, and
the *Harry Potter* series are not transposed to the Regency as often as *Pride and
Prejudice* is shifted to the present or to outer space. On FanFiction.net for
instance, one can find *Pride and Prejudice* stories under the genre categories
of fantasy, crime, suspense, horror, humor, parody, sci-fi, and mystery.[15]

This convention—the universality of Austen—reflects the desire to *be*
Austen, and in being Austen, to use her plots, characters, and attitudes. Fan
fiction authors regularly acknowledge Austen in their opening disclaimers to
their fan fictions; they proclaim their devotion as they cite her as their inspiration and pay homage, as a brief sampling of comments shows:

> Love, love, love *Pride and Prejudice*, it's one of my favourite novels in existence!
> I hope I do Jane Austen justice. Disclaimer: I do not own the fabulous works
> of Jane Austen, nor do I own the characters, I am making no profit out of this
> either. This is merely for my own amusement!—"Not Handsome Enough to
> Tempt Me" by imafeckingstarr[16]

> The canon characters do not belong to me. They are the creation of the lovely
> Miss Austen, to whom we all owe a great debt.—"One Great Love" by I found
> my Mr. Darcy

> Okay. If I owned *Pride and Prejudice*, do you really think I would be here on
> Fanfiction? No. I would totally be sitting in some awesome mansion and work-
> ing away on my next masterpiece. And I'm not, so therefore I don't own *Pride
> and Prejudice*.— "Simply Tolerable" by nikkitusa[17]

> I did not write *Pride and Prejudice* and/or *And Then There Were None*. I'm not
> Jane Austen or Agatha Christie either. (But if any of you knows how I could
> become Christie and Austen at the same time, PM me. I'm more than will-
> ing to sell both of my kidneys. And my soul.)—"There Were The Proud, The
> Prejudiced, And Then There Were None" by narcissagrey[18]

> Welcome! I hope that you enjoy Friendship Afire. After completing my first
> P&P Fanfiction (An Unwanted Engagement), I am hooked. I love Austen's

characters and it's great playing with them. I can't wait to hear what you think of this new story so hit Review and let me know. Thanks!—"Friendship Afire" by LilLamb24[19]

As some of these comments suggest, fan fiction authors wish that they were Austen.[20] But they do not rewrite or re-envision Austen's works because they expect to attain her craft—Austen fan fiction writers know that they are not Jane Austen. Rather, the desire to be Jane Austen reflects on the affection for—and projections upon—Austen's authorial persona as much as it reflects the devotion to her works. Austen (like Shakespeare) is famously present but absent in her works; there are multiple Austens, depending upon the way people read her comedy, irony, satire, politics, tone, and biography. So being Austen is a fantasy filled with possibility. It is a fantasy of performance. This distinguishes the desire of the Austen fan fiction writer from the fans who write *Lord of the Rings* fan fiction, *Star Wars* fan fiction, Marvel fan fiction, and possibly even *Harry Potter* fan fiction. Those fan fiction writers are undoubtedly devoted, but they may not want to be—or identify with or love—J.R.R. Tolkien, George Lucas, Stan Lee, or J.K. Rowling the way that Austen fan fiction writers love Austen and want to *be* Austen.

The ability to tinker with Austen's plots and characters (to play with Austen's toys, as LilLamb24 suggests) is a considerable compensation, for it is a way to be "Austen," and follow in the steps of the master. Playing with Austen's characters and plots does not have automatic or recognizable closure; the game can always be reset and played again. So it is possible to write an infinite number of Austen fan fictions, which means that pleasure, and the desire for more pleasure, can be produced indefinitely. As noted previously, the strategies of postmodernism—adaptation, transposition, mashup, and so on—readily generate more text. For instance, modern fan fictions of *Pride and Prejudice* feature Elizabeth and Darcy in a wide variety of professions: as doctors, lawyers, detectives, reporters, teachers, political campaigners, businesspeople, space explorers, camp counselors, artists, and ice skaters.[21] There are fantasy fan fictions with zombies and werewolves, and crossovers with *Harry Potter, The Hobbit, Anne of Green Gables, Batman,* and other works.[22] Some fictions shift the class status of the characters, making Elizabeth affluent or Darcy poor; some switch their genders; others envision Elizabeth being forced to marry Darcy for a variety of reasons. All work through issues of relationships and character, which suggests that both the writer and reader of Austen fan fiction do not necessarily want more plot, but they want more "Austen" character and society for more venues for analysis.

There are prequels and sequels that provide more plot, and many Austen fan fictions extend Austen's narrative: by providing scenes that are alluded to, but not depicted in Austen's novels; by rewriting scenes from the point of view of minor characters; and by changing and adding scenes outright.[23] All of these mechanisms are used by filmmakers when they adapt Austen's novels to the screen, and it is not unusual for scenes from film adaptations (like Darcy in the pond, or Elizabeth and Darcy getting caught in the rain in the folly) to appear in fan fiction.[24] As a result, fan fiction participates in establishing and stabilizing an Austen popular culture canon, much as the winking references to Colin Firth's wet shirt in popular culture reinforce each other.[25] Other fan fictions present modern Austen fans reading her works, and then living (consciously or not) Austen narratives, much like Shannon Hale's *Austenland* (2007; film version, 2013), Alexandra Potter's *Me and Mr. Darcy* (2007), and the television series, *Lost in Austen* (2008).[26] Here too, the writer of Austen fan fiction responds to the reader's desire and their own for more Austen, by creating more platforms for the discussion of (and engagement with) Austen and "Austen." The amount of "more" is potentially infinite, and the desire insatiable, because the fan fictions are "Austen" but not Austen.[27] The fan fictions then are always asymptotic; at best they get close to Austen, but they can never be Austen. So fan fiction "Austen" is always supplementing Austen.[28]

Second, it is a convention that the *knowledge* of Austen's works is universal within the online fan fiction community, as it is assumed that everyone knows the plots, characters, and language of Austen's six major novels. According to Sheenagh Pugh, the knowledge of the source text—which is the canon of the fandom—is expected within any given fandom.[29] There is a corollary here: that the people who do not know Austen yet really should, which is not necessarily the case for other fandoms. Many fans recognize that people outside their fandoms perceive them to be precious and obsessed— and Austen fans are seen that way too—but Austen fans also know that Austen is seen as canonical beyond her fandom. Austen's combination of popularity and canonicity is comparatively unusual, as the major fan fiction sites host thousands of Austen stories. As Mike Goode notes, "Austen fanfiction also constitutes a special case of this common media behavior. For one thing, there is the sheer size of the archive relative to the age of its canonical sources. Aside from Arthur Conan Doyle's Sherlock Holmes stories and the monster–scientist dyad from Mary Shelley's *Frankenstein*, no other classic literary text, characters, or oeuvre can boast an archive of fanfiction even remotely as robust as Austen's novels. Charlotte Brontë's *Jane Eyre* (1847)?

Fewer than 500 tagged entries on AO3 and FanFiction.net combined. The entirety of Charles Dickens's corpus? Fewer than a thousand."[30] Not surprisingly, it is a convention of online Austen fan fiction that knowledge of Austen and her literature is established, public, available, and open—rather than a boutique, specialist-only culture.

This convention—the universal knowledge of Austen's works—reflects a desire for the modern world to be Austen's world, where Austen's codes and values are known, respected, and followed, so that Austen serves as a reliable guide. Perhaps that is why there are so many versions in which *Pride and Prejudice* is transposed to the present. The escapism of this desire—in its resistance to (and resentment of) modern society—is manifested by the effort to avoid or circumvent modernity and overwrite it with Austen. Part of the success of *Bridget Jones's Diary* can be attributed to Helen Fielding playing with Austen *and* engaging in metafiction about her literary play, and her readers recognizing and enjoying the game. Arguably, fan fiction as a genre tends towards escapism, for it not only seeks a respite from reality but even from the conventions of literary fiction itself, as fan fictions increasingly incorporate texts, mood boards, and other media. It also seems significant that the fandoms that generate the most fan fiction are based on science fiction and fantasy: *Star Trek*, *Star Wars*, Marvel and DC superheroes, *Lord of the Rings*, and *Harry Potter*. Austen's novels are anomalous in this regard, but that's part of the point here: as noted by Goode, canonical literature generally does not generate a lot of fan fiction, for it does not seem to transcend its historical moment as Austen does. Of course, modern society does not conform to the Austen social code (Bridget Jones was not a virgin), just as modern Austen fan fictions can only approximate Austen's originals. One would think that the inability to turn back time and conform to Regency codes would lead to thwarted desire and frustration, but instead it leads to creativity and enhanced desire, as the plethora of modern Austen fan fictions with versions of Austen's values makes evident. Here too, the desire for the modern world to be Austenian cannot be realized fully, so the desire remains, which generates more fan fictions in an effort to satisfy it.

Third, Austen fan fiction emphasizes the romantic elements of her work—and romance is a genre that is committed to the production and satisfaction of desire. While other elements of Austen's works (such as class, family dynamics, country society, and so on) may be emphasized in online fan fiction, those elements do not displace romance as the primary focus. If, as Pugh suggests, fan fiction "happens in the gaps between canon, the unexplored or insufficiently explored territory," then there is no space more waiting to be explored than Austenian romance.[31] Courtship culture is central in Austen's novels, and anticipation, anxiety, and desire, which respond to and generate gaps, are everywhere. The reader sees Austen's young female characters social-izing—attending balls, dinners, visits, a picnic—as they determine (or have determined for them) their destiny on the marriage market. The emotions and desires of Austen's female protagonist are delineated clearly, even if she is not always self-aware. But everyone else has gaps waiting to be filled. Where are the men, and what are they doing? What are they thinking and feeling? What of other women's romances, not just the protagonist? What of homo-sexual romance, and the queer resonances in Austen?[32] There are inscrutable looks, gazes, and behaviors, and confusing conversations: what are these peo-ple thinking? Do others notice? How does it affect their relationships? People are separated from their beloveds for weeks, months, and sometimes years. What are they doing? How do they respond to separation? How do people overcome misunderstanding and the obstacles in their way? Austen famously avoids proposal scenes—except the comically awful ones, like Collins's in *Pride and Prejudice*. Another gap to be filled. What happens after couples unite? Do they live happily ever after? Does romance survive marriage? How do Austen's couples navigate sex? Do Austen's couples have children, and what are they like as parents? What are their children's romances like? The possibilities for romance in Austen fan fiction are endless.

Accordingly, the desire to be an Austen protagonist is evident in the third convention of Austen fan fiction. In her survey of Austen fan fiction readers, Marina Cano provides evidence that they identify with Austen's characters ("I wanted to be Elizabeth" and "I was Elizabeth")[33] and that Austen fan fic-tion readers derive considerable pleasure from reading romantic narratives:

> What my female respondents enjoyed about romantic fan fiction was watching the Austen couples come together again and again. Changes of circumstance notwithstanding, they were clear that stories should be truthful to the original romance. Irene claimed to read fan fiction to 'see the couples come together over and over again in myriad ways', and ColleenL 'loved reading Darcy and Lizzy falling in love over and over again' at a different time or place. Wanda also claimed to 'love Lizzy and Darcy and love the different scenarios' to such an extent that she read *Pride and Prejudice* fan fiction only. My readers welcomed, and even sought, the insistent repetition of Darcy and Elizabeth's love story. The characters might meet in a different context or historical period, as ColleenL and Wanda suggest, but the romantic resolution must remain intact.[34]

It is not surprising that the Elizabeth-Darcy pairing of *Pride and Prejudice* is the most frequently revisited and rewritten fan fiction narrative in the Austen canon.[35] In re-envisioning the Elizabeth-Darcy relationship, many fan fictions present their courtship from Darcy's point of view, which is how Pamela Aidan, who received the publishing contract from Simon and Schuster, started writing fan fiction.[36] There's a desire to know Darcy's thoughts—or any attractive, inscrutable man's thoughts—or better yet, to *determine* such a man's thoughts. There's a cognate fantasy about Elizabeth too: the desire of being the pretty (but not beautiful) woman who wins the heart of the desirable man—the desire to be the woman who is loved for her wit, her character, and her intellect. Austen's courtship narratives fulfill desires for romance, but the online fan fiction suggests that that fulfillment is fleeting—readers cannot truly *be* Elizabeth or Darcy—so fan fiction authors and readers re-enact the narrative over and over again, generating and satisfying desire in an endless cycle.

Romance is perceived as a stereotypically female, conventional genre, but it has also been read as a genre that enables women to subvert convention, which can be useful for fan fiction's creative, revisionist impulses.[37] Ann Haker, the founder of austen.com, remarked that there is a desire for sexually explicit Austen in the fandom: "The implicit nature of Austen's writing collides with our modern sensibilities and desires for the explicit . . . As Jane Austen failed to write of these things, we feel compelled to do so in her place."[38] Yet Austen fan fiction is predominantly heterosexual in its sexually explicit fan fiction, unlike some other fandoms. Slash fiction developed early in the *Star Trek* fandom with multiple stories featuring Kirk and Spock as lovers. Pugh writes that *Star Trek* fan fiction writers in the late 1960s and 1970s—the majority of whom were women—found it difficult to write convincing fiction about the show's few female characters because there was so little material to work with.[39] That meant either inventing female characters in the *Star Trek* universe (and run the risk of being accused of writing Mary Sues, that is, idealized versions of themselves), or to "concentrate on the more developed male characters and the emotional relationships between them."[40] Hence Kirk/Spock (K/S) slash fiction was born. The largest fandoms, in which the source material is dominated by male characters, abound with slash fiction: comic book fan fictions (with pairings such as Tony Stark/Steve Rogers, Bucky/Steve Rogers, Tony Stark/Peter Parker), *Lord of the Rings* fan fictions (Sam/Frodo and Gimli/Legolas) and *Harry Potter* fan fiction (Harry Potter/Draco Malfoy, Harry Potter/Severus Snape, and Sirius Black/Remus Lupin).[41]

But Austen's novels are not dominated by male characters. Austen's feminocentric narratives are placed in worlds where the demographics tend towards gender equality. Austen's works refer to nonheterosexual behavior, like Mary Crawford's sly comment about rears and vices in the Navy in *Mansfield Park*, and the cross-dressing of Chamberlayne in *Pride and Prejudice*.[42] While Pugh suggests that Austen's language and voice complicate the writing of slash fiction, I doubt that is the issue.[43] Since the impetus for slash fiction is the investigation of emotional relationships, the question is, are there homosexual and homosocial relationships in Austen, as there are in male-dominant narratives? The answer is "yes," and the few *Pride and Prejudice* slash fictions focus on Elizabeth Bennet/Charlotte Lucas, Kitty Bennet/Georgiana Darcy, Darcy/Bingley, and Darcy/Wickham.[44] If one remains reasonably faithful to the novel, three of these pairs undergo separations of varying lengths and significance, and one pair (Kitty/Georgiana) is never together, which complicates matters. But there are prequel possibilities for Elizabeth/Charlotte, Darcy/Bingley, and Darcy/Wickham; the sequel possibilities are open for Kitty/Georgiana, and there are potential options for Darcy/Bingley as well. (Sequels for Elizabeth/Charlotte seem less likely, and highly unlikely for Darcy/Wickham). As Luetkenhaus and Weinstein note, Austen adaptations are not absolutely heterosexual: Curtis Sittenfeld's novel *Eligible* considers lesbianism (via Mary Bennet) and transgender sexuality (through a character partly based on George Wickham), and *Lost in Austen* envisions Caroline Bingley as a lesbian.[45] For now, given the fandom's strong investment in Elizabeth and Darcy, it is less likely that any slash pairing, particularly any pairing with Elizabeth or Darcy with another partner, will be pursued extensively. The fandom receives too much pleasure from Elizabeth and Darcy to look elsewhere for long.[46]

The fourth convention of fan fiction is repetition, and the expectation of repetition, in Austen fan fiction. As Jenkins writes—and Cano's survey respondents confirmed—"Rereading is central to the fan's aesthetic pleasure. Much of fan culture facilitates repeated encounters with favored texts."[47] Or as Luetkenhaus and Weinstein put it, "we all want to feel that way *again*."[48] But it is not only repetition that is involved here. Coppa argues that fan fiction functions like theatre: people see the same play with different actors, and each performance is different, and each interpretation of the play is different.[49] The script of a play functions as a blueprint for the performance— which can vary from night to night, even with the same cast—much as a source text functions as a blueprint for a fan fiction. So repetition allows the fan fiction reader to derive pleasure by recognizing and analyzing the ways that the fan fiction author fills in the gaps in Austen's narrative or changes Austen's narrative, as well as enjoying a well-written narrative. Those analytical and aesthetic pleasures satisfy readers' desires as well as the Austen fan fiction writer's performative desires. And it is even better when the fan fiction provides interpretive insight into Austen.

The desire associated with repetition is the desire to live *in* Austen's world—which is related to, but different from, the desire for the modern world to *be* Austenian. Both desires are escapist, but to live in Austen's world does not look to transform the present. Both moves—the universalism and the repetition of Austen—reflect the desire for Austen's narratives to be accessible to the modern reader, and both reflect the desire for Austen to be a reliable guide to life. But repetition also expresses a desire for certainty—to know what will happen, and to know how people will behave—and perhaps most importantly, a desire for things to work out according to plan. People often report that they find reading Austen to be comforting and therapeutic[50] and it is significant that Austen was given to soldiers and civilians to read during wartime.[51] The fan fictions augment this therapeutic response by repeating Austen's narratives, for the desire for comfort and security is ongoing. There is faulty nostalgia in escaping into Austen's world, however; the Regency was a difficult place for women, people of color, the disabled, and the poor, and the lack of sanitation and medicine would be daunting to a twenty-first-century sensibility. But desire is not necessarily rational or pragmatic. Living in Austen's world exists as a fantasy which cannot be realized—it can only generate repetitions of reading Austen and Regency-period Austen fan fiction.

Finally, there are conventions of community. Austen's works and their derivatives form a code that binds, elevates, and regulates those who know it, those who are learning it, and those who want to discuss and analyze Austen, her fictions, her fan fictions, and her fans.[52] The ability of Austen's works to generate community has a long history: from Austen's friends and family asking her for more information about her characters (which is how we know that Kitty Bennet will marry a clergyman, and Mary Bennet will marry a clerk in her Uncle Philips's office), to the Austen community of British soldiers in Rudyard Kipling's 1926 story "The Janeites," to the establishment of Austen societies in the UK in 1940, the US in 1979, and Australia in 1989.[53]

For media theorist Henry Jenkins, it is community that distinguishes the fan from the cultural consumer: the fan participates in a community with others who enjoy the same text/event/cultural phenomenon. Fan fiction as a genre is community-oriented, whether or not Austen is the subject, because fans rely on community to valorize their identity as fans. The desire to be recognized and valued as an Austen fan is an enormously powerful motivator to seek out and participate in Austen culture. Online communities support the fan fiction author: whether by providing an editor (a beta reader) before posting work online, or running discussion boards that analyze the fan fictions as they are posted, encouraging authors to write, or all of the above.[54] Online communities support the fan fiction reader—not only by providing text, but also providing venues for the reader to comment on text, and engage with fan fiction authors and other readers. These communities of readers and writers function as a brain trust, an instance of what Jenkins calls "collective intelligence." On some websites, such as the Derbyshire Writers Guild, there is a separate discussion board, where people post queries and get answers: about Regency culture, Austen's life, current Austen culture (on and offline), and general advice (which ranges from personal to professional issues).[55] The online community can become a platform for participation in offline community as well, providing information about Austen conferences, festivals, and performances. As fan fictions are being posted on other platforms, and links to fan fictions are posted on Tumblr, LiveJournal, Facebook, and other media outlets, the community becomes larger and more networked—and there are more venues to participate in, and more venues for personal validation as an Austen fan, and for validation of the Austen fandom itself. These conventions of Austen fan fiction online community align with what media theorist Henry Jenkins calls "convergence culture"—the phenomenon of fans generating content across different media platforms, working collaboratively, manifesting collective intelligence—which, for Jenkins, defines the current media revolution.[56]

In light of these conventions, the notion that Austen fan fiction perpetuates the desires of Austen fans does not seem amiss. Austen fan fiction recognizes the psychology of the Austen fan—the desire to identify with Austen, her characters, and her works, the desire for more Austen, and the desire for validation and community—and perpetuates the conditions of desire and the fandom by creating more "Austen" for the fan to consume. Arguably, the modern cultural landscape features a new type of "Janeite": not a keeper of the flame who protects and secures an ideal Austen, but one who engages with Austen through creation, adaptation, and commentary. Accordingly, I would suggest that Austen fan fiction is about process, not product. It's not about closure—as Busse and Hellekson would say, it is about the work in progress.[57] In so far as Austen fan fiction is about desire, those desires are continuous, not finite.

Of course, there is the possibility of a surfeit of "Austen"—of a moment of personal and/or cultural saturation of Austen, when the desire for Austen diminishes or even evaporates. The market of cultural interest, particularly in popular culture, has its ups and downs after all. But Austen's resilience seems comparable to that of Shakespeare, and like Shakespeare, Austen seems to be in the process of becoming inextricably woven into the fabric of Western culture. If that is the process that we are witnessing—that Austen is moving beyond traditional canonization to a new form of cultural permanence and permeability—then there will always be new instantiations of Austen. Any strong version of Austen will reinvigorate a potentially waning Austen culture. Then the Austen fan fiction community will respond, and provide more.

Notes

1. Abigail Derecho, "Archontic Literature: A Definition, a History, and Several Theories of Fan Fiction," *Fan Fiction and Fan Communities in the Age of the Internet,* eds. Karen Hellekson and Kristina Busse (Jefferson, NC: McFarland & Co., 2006), 64.
2. Pamela Licalzi O'Connell, "A World Without End for Fans of Jane Austen." *The New York Times,* January 13, 2000.
3. Austen fan fiction existed long before 1995, but it was not extensive. As Francesca Coppa, observes, "it's only when stories get *embodied* [i.e., in film] that they seem to generate truly massive waves of fiction." "Writing Bodies in Space: Media Fan Fiction as Theatrical Performance," *Fan Fiction and Fan Communities in the Age of the Internet,* eds. Karen Hellekson and Kristina Busse (Jefferson, NC: McFarland & Co., 2006), 229. Austen's nieces wrote works based on *The Watsons* and *Sanditon*: Catherine Hubback's *The Younger Sister* (1850), and Anna Le Froy's continuation of *Sanditon,* which was probably written in the late 1840s and published in 1983; see Deirdre Le Faye, "*Sanditon*: Jane Austen's Manuscript and Her Niece's Continuation," *Review of English Studies,* n.s., 38, No. 149 (Feb. 1987): 56–61. Sybil Brinton's novel *Old Friends and New Fancies* (1913), which combines characters from Austen's novels, is often considered the first Austen fan fiction; see Claire Harman, *Jane's Fame: How Jane Austen Conquered the World* (New York: Henry Holt and Company, 2009), 216; and Holly Luetkenhaus and Zoe Weinstein, *Austentatious: The Evolving World of Jane Austen Fans* (Iowa City: University of Iowa Press, 2019), 13–14. Sarah Glosson suggests Eliza Leslie's "The Beaux" (1842) and Andrew Lang's "From Catherine Morland to Miss Eleanor Tilney" (1890) as instances of early Austen fan fiction; *Performing Jane: A Cultural*

History of Jane Austen Fandom (Baton Rouge: Louisiana State University Press, 2020), 44–51.

4. The initial Austen wave was powerful because of the number and quality of works produced in a short period of time: *Pride and Prejudice* directed by Simon Langton (1995*); Sense and Sensibility* directed by Ang Lee (1995); *Clueless,* directed by Amy Heckerling (1995); *Persuasion* directed by Roger Michell (1995); *Emma* directed by Douglas McGrath (1996; starring Gwyneth Paltrow); *Emma* directed by Diarmuid Lawrence (1996; starring Kate Beckinsale); and *Mansfield Park* directed by Patricia Rozema (1999). According to a June 2021 Internet Movie Database search of "Jane Austen," fifty Austen films, television series, and web series were produced between 2000 and 2020. While most of these works are based on Austen's fiction, the results also include versions of Austen's life, like *Miss Austen Regrets* (2007) and *Becoming Jane* (2007); narratives that combine Austen characters, such as *The Jane Games* (2014–2015) and *Austentatious* (2015); films about Austen readers, like *The Jane Austen Book Club* (2007); and films about Austen fans, like *Lost in Austen* (2008) and *Austenland* (2013). The quality of these works is not as consistent as the initial 1995–1999 wave, but many achieved critical acclaim and/or cultural impact, such as the 2005 *Pride and Prejudice* and *The Lizzie Bennet Diaries* (2012–2013). Both the number and range of these works are significant, however, for they represent the depth of the Austen cultural field and the degree to which Austen has permeated contemporary culture.

5. For the purposes of this essay, I am defining "fan fiction" as a literary text that engages with at least one other text, adding to an ever-expanding archive of literature and culture. Fan fiction may engage with a text in many ways: by transposing a text to another place, time, or culture; by envisioning a text from another character's point of view; by filling in the missing scenes of a text; by adding scenes to a text; by changing an element in a text and following through the implications (like changing the gender, class, or race of a character or characters); by combining texts in a mashup; by combining genres; as a prequel or sequel; etc. The possibilities are endless. The term "fan" in "fan fiction" tends to signal devotion, or at least admiration, for the text that the fan fiction author is engaging with. But that does not mean deference; the fan fiction author has knowledge, intent, and agency, and is engaged in an act of literary play, which may involve resistance, too. (The literature often cited in discussions of fan fiction—like Jean Rhys' *The Wide Sargasso Sea*—resists Brontë's *Jane Eyre* mightily). Accordingly, the intertextuality of fan fiction is creative—not necessarily derivative or appropriating—and as Derecho suggests, additive.

6. Helen Fielding, *Bridget Jones's Diary* (1996; New York: Penguin, 2001); Stephanie Barron, "Jane Austen Mysteries." Francine Matthews. Accessed June

15, 2021, https://francinemathews.com/stephanie-barron-books/jane-austen-mysteries/; Amanda Grange, *Darcy's Diary* (London: Robert Hale, 2005); Laurie Viera Rigler, *Confessions of a Jane Austen Addict* (New York: Dutton, 2007); Jane Austen and Seth Grahame-Smith, *Pride and Prejudice and Zombies* (Philadelphia: Quirk Books, 2009); Joanna Trollope, *Sense & Sensibility* (New York: HarperCollins, 2013); Alexander McCall Smith, *Emma* (New York: Pantheon Books, 2014); Val McDermid, *Northanger Abbey* (London: Borough Press, 2014); and Curtis Sittenfeld, *Eligible* (New York: Random House, 2016).

7.   For a short history of modern fan fiction from its origins in 1960s through the early 2000s, see Francesca Coppa, "A Brief History of Media Fandom," *Fan Fiction and Fan Communities in the Age of the Internet,* eds. Karen Hellekson and Kristina Busse (Jefferson, NC: McFarland & Co., 2006), 41–59. For the dissemination of fan fiction by mail and fan conventions, and the impact of the Internet on fan fiction, see Sheenagh Pugh, *The Democratic Genre: Fan Fiction in a Literary Context* (2005; Rpt. Bridgend: Seren Books, 2015), 117–19.

8.   See Luetkenhaus and Weinstein on fan fiction as a nonprofit gift economy, the changing publishing practices of fan fiction writers, and Aidan in *Austentatious,* 48, 51–52. For information on Aidan, see John Jurgensen, "Rewriting the Rules of Fiction," *The Wall Street Journal,* Saturday/Sunday September 16–17, 2006, Pursuits Section, P1, P4 and Deborah Yaffe, *Among the Janeites: A Journey through the World of Jane Austen Fandom* (Boston: Mariner Books/Houghton Mifflin Harcourt, 2013), 89–90.

9.   For examples of authors removing their work to publish on Amazon and other venues, see "Christmas at Netherfield" by GeorgianLover (FanFiction. net, updated June 15, 2017, https://www.fanfiction.net/s/12186338/1/ Christmas-at-Netherfield); "Duty and Honor (NOW: COURAGE RISES)" by Melanie Rachel (FanFiction.net, published June 18, 2016, https://www. fanfiction.net/s/12005910/1/Duty-and-Honor-NOW-COURAGE-RISES); and "Mr Darcy Came to Dinner" by Jack Caldwell (jvcla25) (FanFiction. net, published September 23, 2011, https://www.fanfiction.net/s/6960104/1/ Mr-Darcy-Came-to-Dinner).

10.   Pugh, *Democratic Genre,* 19. See also Henry Jenkins, who argues that "the fans' response typically involves not simply fascination or adoration but also frustration and antagonism, and it is the combination of the two responses which motivates their active engagement with the media." *Textual Poachers: Television Fans & Participatory Culture* (New York: Routledge, 1992), 23. While fascination and adoration are manifestations of desire, arguably the alleviation of frustration and antagonism can be construed as a desire, too, and motivations for fan creativity.

11.   Luetkenhaus and Weinstein, *Austentatious,* 54.

12. Marina Cano discovered a similar rhetoric of fan fiction addiction in her survey of 300 Austen fan fiction readers; she writes that "reading Austen fan fiction is beyond voluntary control for many of my respondents." *Jane Austen and Performance* (Chaim, Switzerland: Palgrave Macmillan, 2017), 178.

13. See Pugh's comments about the Republic of Pemberley (which no longer accepts new fan fiction), which was prescriptive about the Austen fiction posted on the site (*Democratic Genre,* 37–40). See also the guidelines of Derbyshire Writers Guild website (www.dwiggie.com). Sites like FanFiction. net (www.fanfiction.net) and Archive of Our Own (www.archiveofourown. org), which serve multiple fandoms, are more concerned about writers' work being stolen or misattributed than maintaining the reputation of a particular fandom.

14. On June 17, 2021, Archive of Our Own (AO3) listed 3,124 stories for *Pride and Prejudice* & Related Fandoms; 304 for *Persuasion*; 260 for *Emma*; 234 for *Sense and Sensibility* (All Media Types); 210 for *Mansfield Park* (All Media Types); and 115 for *Northanger Abbey,* for a total of 4,247 complete and incomplete stories. On the same day, FanFiction.net (FFN) listed ~5,200 for *Pride and Prejudice*; 380 for *Emma*; 243 for *Sense and Sensibility*; 203 for *Persuasion*; 88 for *Mansfield Park*; and 64 for *Northanger Abbey,* for a total of 6,178 complete and incomplete stories. The Derbyshire Writers Guild (DWG) website has an Epilogue Abbey for Regency period Austen stories, and listed 1,596 stories, and a Fantasia Gallery for non-Regency Austen stories, of which there were 1,313 stories, for a total of 2,909 complete and incomplete stories. The Republic of Pemberley's Bit of Ivory website does not provide totals of the stories available there (https://pemberley.com/?page_id=5270). There are smaller websites, such as Austen Interlude (http://austeninterlude. com), and fan fiction sites that require log ins, like the Meryton Literary Society's "A Happy Assembly" (www.meryton.com). And there are the sites set up by individuals, such as Rika Hopewell's "An Unexpected Song" (http://darcymania.com/aus/, last updated January 15, 2015) and Sandy W's "Netherfield's Library" (https://netherfieldslibrary.blogspot.com). The Jane Austen Fan Fiction Index (JAFF) provides a general overview of Austen fan fiction on the Internet (http://www.jaffindex.com/).

15. On AO3, the categories for Austen fiction include Humor, Angst, Fluff, Alternate Universe: Modern Setting, and Alternate Universe: Canon Divergence.

16. Imafeckingstarr, "Not Handsome Enough to Tempt Me," FanFiction. net published May 6, 2014, https://www.fanfiction.net/s/10328541/1/ Not-Handsome-Enough-to-Tempt-Me.

17. Nikkitusa, "Simply Tolerable," FanFiction.net, updated December 14, 2010, https://www.fanfiction.net/s/5600422/1/Simply-Tolerable.

18. Narcissagrey, "There Were The Proud, The Prejudiced, And Then There Were None," Fanfiction.net, updated March 16, 2016, https://www.fanfiction.net/s/11840951/1/ There-Were-The-Proud-The-Prejudiced-And-Then-There-Were-None.

19. LilLamb24, "Friendship Afire," Fanfiction.net, updated May 24, 2017, https://www.fanfiction.net/s/8633134/1/Friendship-Afire.

20. Emma Thompson engaged in this form of Austen play—the desire to be Jane Austen—in her Golden Globe acceptance speech for the best screenplay for *Sense and Sensibility* in 1996. After acknowledging the "genius of Jane Austen," Thompson then performed as Austen attending the Golden Globes. See "Emma Thompson—Golden Globes 1996 (Best Speech ever!)" on YouTube, posted May 5, 2012 (https://www.youtube.com/watch?v=AHUgsDIOoNQ).

21. For an example of a fan fiction with Elizabeth and Darcy as doctors, see Phia-Karenzia's "Solemnly, freely, and upon my honor," Archive of Our Own, updated July 18, 2021, https://archiveofourown.org/works/28470276/chapters/69763212; Beth M's "Coast to Coast" for Elizabeth as a lawyer and Darcy as the head of a communications tech company (Derbyshire Writers Guild, published January 23, 2004, https://www.dwiggie.com/derby/old_2004/bethm1.htm); Kate F's "Pride at Sea" for Elizabeth as a lawyer and Darcy as a private investigator (Derbyshire Writers Guild, published December 26, 2001, https://www.dwiggie.com/derby/old_2001/katef1e.htm); Judy Lynne's "Honestly" for Elizabeth as a writer and Darcy as a magazine editor (Derbyshire Writers Guild, published June 10, 2003, https://www.dwiggie.com/derby/old_2003/judyly18.htm); Em's "Ten Weeks at Meryton" for Elizabeth as a student teacher and Darcy as a head teacher (Derbyshire Writers Guild, published August 1, 2002, https://www.dwiggie.com/derby/old_2002/em1.htm); Rosie J's "Gardiner for America" for Elizabeth and Darcy as political campaigners (Derbyshire Writers Guild, published July 4, 2014, https://www.dwiggie.com/derby/rosiej2.htm); Cheryl K's "Pemberley, Inc." for Elizabeth and Darcy in property development and business management (Derbyshire Writers Guild, published July 28, 1998, https://www.dwiggie.com/derby/olda/cherylk2.htm); Kathy's "A Space Between," for Elizabeth and Darcy and space exploration (Derbyshire Writers Guild, published March 5, 2010, https://www.dwiggie.com/derby/kathy14.htm); Tamara's "Smart Kids!" for Elizabeth and Darcy as camp counselors (Derbyshire Writers Guild, published September 26, 2003, https://www.dwiggie.com/derby/old_2003/tamz12.htm); Victoria Lynn's "The Development" for Elizabeth as a sculptor, and Darcy as a photographer (Derbyshire Writers Guild, published February 12, 2005, https://www.dwiggie.com/derby/old_2006/viclyn6.htm); and Annie's "Kiss and Cry" for Elizabeth and Darcy as ice skaters (Derbyshire Writers Guild, published April 14, 1998, https://www.dwiggie.com/derby/olda/annie9.htm).

22. For mashups and crossovers with *Pride and Prejudice,* see Skjcartwork's "Pride and Polyjuice Potion" (*Harry Potter*) Archive of Our Own, published February 12, 2021, https://archiveofourown.org/works/29352786/chapters/72100368; malazuzu22's "Proud and Prouder" (*The Hobbit*) Archive of Our Own, published December 23, 2016, https://archiveofourown.org/works/8042263/chapters/18419410; disjointed_scribblings' "Lizzie of Green Gables" (*Anne of Green Gables/Lizzie Bennet Diaries*) Archive of Our Own, published April 3, 2017, https://archiveofourown.org/works/10530348; Paula J's "The Dark Knight" (*Batman*) Derbyshire Writers Guild, published June 2, 1999, https://www.dwiggie.com/derby/olde/paulaj3.htm; Felicia's "The P-Files I & II" (*The X Files*) Derbyshire Writers Guild, published August 12, 1998, https://www.dwiggie.com/derby/oldb/felic1.htm; and Karen A.'s "Pride and Prejudice Meets Shrek." Derbyshire Writers Guild, published April 2, 2009, https://www.dwiggie.com/derby/old_2009/karena2.htm. For Darcy as a werewolf, see Autumn D's "Nature of the Beast," Derbyshire Writers Guild, published July 13, 2013, https://www.dwiggie.com/derby/autumnd.htm. The fan fictions of *Pride and Prejudice and Zombies* provide multiple examples of Austen's work mixed with zombies.

23. For examples, see KatherineRose2000's version of Darcy asking Mr. Bennet's permission to marry Elizabeth in "So Great A Man." Archive of Our Own, published October 25, 2020, https://archiveofourown.org/works/27138892; for a revision of a scene, see Lupin111's "A Small Matter," in which Lady Catherine notes over dinner at Rosings that Darcy gave Wickham money (Archive of Our Own, published April 13, 2021, https://archiveofourown.org/works/30648644); for a perspective of a minor character, see Hill's perspective on the Bennet daughters in sheepsleet's "On Writing Letters," Archive of Our Own, published October 2, 2015, https://archiveofourown.org/works/4917919.

24. For examples, see Abby C's "A Departure from Cannon," Derbyshire Writers Guild, published September 22, 2002, https://www.dwiggie.com/derby/old_2002/abbyc2.htm, in which Darcy complains about the pond scene from the 1995 film version of *Pride and Prejudice,* or Recoveringjaddict5's "Admire and love you," a re-envisioning of the proposal in the rain scene from the 2005 film version of *Pride and Prejudice* (Archive of Our Own, published January 19, 2021, https://archiveofourown.org/users/Recoveringjaddict5/pseuds/Recoveringjaddict5). See Glosson, *Performing Jane,* on fan fictions based on film adaptations, 155–59.

25. Luetkenhaus and Weinstein, *Austentatious,* 10.

26. See, for example, Amanda2's "Wish Upon A Darcy," Derbyshire Writers Guild, published April 16, 2002, https://www.dwiggie.com/derby/old_2002/amanda2.htm and blue_sweater_spike's "Pride and Prejudice . . . and Buffy?" Archive of Our Own, last updated May 16, 2020, https://archiveofourown.

org/works/17176898/chapters/40386953#workskin. See also, Shannon Hale, *Austenland* (New York: Bloomsbury, 2007); *Austenland,* dir. Jerusha Hess, Screenplay by Jerusha Hess and Shannon Hale (2013), Alexandra Potter's *Me and Mr. Darcy* (London: Hodder and Stoughton, 2007), *Lost in Austen,* dir. Dan Zeff (2008).

27. See Glosson: "Fans create [these] effigies to stand in for something lost, such as a past affective experience related to their beloved text. However, it is a substitute that can never produce an exact fit and is destined to disappoint. Therefore, one must continuously audition new stand-ins in the hopes of finding a better match" (*Performing Jane,* 14; cf. 147–48).

28. See Coppa on fan fiction as supplement, "Writing Bodies," 238.

29. Pugh, *Democratic Genre,* 26, 40.

30. Goode, "Letters from Austenland," *Romantic Capabilities: Blake, Scott, Austen, and the New Messages of Old Media* (Oxford Scholarship Online. 2020). DOI: 10.1093/oso/9780198862369.001.0001.

31. Pugh, *Democratic Genre,* 92. Pugh argues that early media fan fiction was driven by a desire for character and emotional development, which is related to my argument about Austen and romance. Pugh claims that "the biggest canonical gap in [*Star Trek*] was any kind of character or relationship development at all.. . . you could have watched the episodes of the *Star Trek* TV series completely out of order and made very little difference to the experience" (92–93). For Pugh, the lack of emotional development in the *Star Trek* characters enabled fan fiction writers to fill multiple gaps, and fan fiction proliferated.

32. Austen has attracted gay and lesbian attention for years; see Claudia L. Johnson's seminal essay, "The Divine Miss Jane: Jane Austen, Janeites, and the Discipline of Novel Studies," which looks to "genealogize the perceived queerness of many of her readers" in *Janeites: Austen's Disciples and Devotees,* ed. Deirdre Lynch (Princeton: Princeton University Press, 2000), 28. For the queerness of Austen and queer readings of Austen, see Luetkenhaus and Weinstein, *Austentatious,* 102–113.

33. Cano, *Jane Austen and Performance,* 161.

34. Cano, *Jane Austen and Performance,* 170.

35. See note 10. On July 1, 2021, a search for Elizabeth and Darcy among the 5,200 *Pride and Prejudice* stories on FFN yielded 2,200 results, or 42.3%. On the same day, AO3's *Pride and Prejudice* & Related Fandoms listed 3,146 fan fictions, and an Elizabeth/Darcy search generated 1,101 stories, or 35% of the total.

36. See Pamela Aidan's comments about the BBC series motivating her to write fan fiction about Darcy: "There was a story to be told. Why was he like this, and why did he change?" So Aidan wrote her first fan fiction, "Be Not Alarmed, Madam," about Darcy's thoughts after his first proposal to Elizabeth (Yaffe, *Among the Janeites,*77; 78–82, 88–91). There are many novels written

from Darcy's point of view: see, for example, Janet Aylmer, *Darcy's Story* (1996; New York: Harper, 2006), Marjorie Fasman, *The Diary of Henry Fitzwilliam Darcy* (Los Angeles: New Leaf Press, 1998), Amanda Grange, *Darcy's Diary* (London: Robert Hale, 2005) and Mary Street, *The Confession of Fitzwilliam Darcy* (London: Robert Hale, 1999). See also Juliette Wells, on Austen motivating readers to write, *Everybody's Jane: Austen in the Popular Imagination* (London: Continuum, 2011), 94–96.

37. See Derecho's comments in "Archontic Literature" on the romance as subverting patriarchal culture, based on Janice Radway's argument in *Reading the Romance* (72); also see Luetkenhaus and Weinstein, *Austentatious*, 56–57.

38. Cited in O'Connell, "World Without End." See also Jun Xu's linguistic analysis of 37 *Pride and Prejudice* sequel fan fictions, which demonstrates that Austen uses terms like "passion," "desire," "longing," "pleasure," and "anger" with significantly lower frequency than the Austen fan fiction writers; See Xu, "Austen's fans and fans' Austen," *Journal of Literary Semantics*, vol. 40 #1 (2011): 91. Xu writes, "the fans' words and phrases in depicting romance are not consistent with those of Austen's. Rather, they belong to the linguistic register of modern romance. . . . The comparison between the ways in which *pleasure* is used illustrates a major cultural difference: *pleasure* in love is all about sexuality to the fans but not to Austen. *P&P*'s fanfic can be identified as contemporary romance fiction from this perspective" (92; original italics).

39. See Pugh's comments about women, *Star Trek,* and the origins of fan fiction, *Democratic Genre,* 19–20; Coppa's comments on women and the history of fan fiction, "Brief History" 45–47; Jenkins, *Textual Poachers,* on the dominance of women in the science fiction fan community, 48. See also Derecho's comments about fan fiction as a subversive, subordinate, resistant practice, pursued by women, "Archontic Literature" 68–72.

40. Pugh, *Democratic Genre,* 93.

41. Based on an analysis of AO3 on July 1, 2021, slash fiction constitutes 2.3% of Austen fan fiction, which is significantly less than other fandoms. On July 1, 2021, Archive of Our Own's *Pride and Prejudice* & Related Fandoms listed 3,146 fan fictions: 14 for Darcy/Wickham (.45%), 16 for Elizabeth/Charlotte (.51%), 21 for Darcy/Bingley (.67%) and 21 for Kitty/Georgiana (.67%), for a total of 2.3% for the category. *Avengers (Marvel) All Media Types* listed 189,809 fan fictions in its film category. Of those, 26,754 were Tony Stark/Steve Rogers (14.1%), 18,343 were Bucky/Steve Rogers (9.7%) and 11,439 were Tony Stark/Peter Parker (6.0%)—for a total of 29.8% of the category. The *Harry Potter* listing (which was the same for film and book) listed 307,644 fan fictions; 48,552 for Harry/Draco (15.8%), 24,305 for Sirius Black/Remus Lupin (7.9%) and 12,850 for Harry/Severus Snape (4.2%), for a total of 27.9% for the category. *The Lord of the Rings—All Media Types* in

the film category listed 28, 310 fan fictions; 1,649 for Sam/Frodo (5.8%) and 1,479 for Gimli/Legolas (5.2%), or a total of 11%.

42. Jane Austen, *Mansfield Park,* ed. John Wiltshire (Cambridge: Cambridge University Press, 2013), 71; and *Pride and Prejudice,* ed. Pat Rogers (Cambridge: Cambridge University Press, 2013), 245.

43. Pugh, *Democratic Genre,* 104. Also see Wells, *Everybody's Jane* 199, n. 30, for additional sources on the absence of slash from Austen fan fiction. Glosson notes that the adult content ban on Tumblr in December 2018, which led to a 30% drop in traffic to that platform, did not seem to affect the Austen blogs there (*Performing Jane,* 120).

44. For an example of Elizabeth/Charlotte fan fiction, see Lefaym's "In Preparation," Archive of Our Own, published May 3, 2010, https://archiveofourown.org/works/84278; for Kitty Bennet/Georgiana Darcy, see kmairif's "Prudence and Peril," Archive of Our Own, published June 20, 2019, https://archiveofourown.org/works/14721173/chapters/45883345#workskin; for Darcy/Wickham, see MildredMost, "In vain have I struggled," Archive of Our Own, published February 14, 2017, https://archiveofourown.org/works/9609047; for Darcy/Bingley, see FrizzyDreams' "DearestBingley," Archive of Our Own, published July 13, 2019, https://archiveofourown.org/works/19353952.

45. For Luetkenhaus and Weinstein, the *Lost in Austen* adaptation is more successful than *Eligible* because it is more nuanced and aware of its sexual politics (*Austentatious,* 104–108). See Wells on Ann Herendeen's *Pride/Prejudice: A Novel of Mr. Darcy, Elizabeth Bennet, and their Forbidden Lovers* (185).

46. See Luetkenhaus and Weinstein: "What is the point, however, in fans *wanting* two characters to be together when they know the end of the story is going to thwart their hopes? . . . Charlotte Geater explains: 'We never expect our [LGBTQ+] ships to become canon. That's the first thing you need to know . . . we never expect our favourite relationships—the potentially romantic relationships we see between characters in the stories the world tells us—to be sanctioned by anyone but us.' Fans ship characters in queer relationships not because the queerness is going to happen, but because the loop never closes: there is always unsurety in romance and in sex and in identity, and to use queer subtext to ship characters or to cast characters or to imagine characters is to use that open loop" (*Austentatious,* 103; original italics).

47. *Textual Poachers,* 69. See the analysis of familiarity and novelty in fan fiction works on AO3 by Jing et al. In their abstract they write, "Contrary to the balance theory, we find that the lowest-novelty are the most popular and that popularity declines monotonically with novelty. A few exceptions can be found: extremely popular works that are among the highest novelty within the fandom. Taken together, our findings not only challenge the traditional theory of the hedonic value of novelty, they invert it: people prefer the least novel

things, are repelled by the middle ground, and have an occasional enthusiasm for extreme outliers. It suggests that cultural evolution must work against inertia—the appetite people have to continually reconsume the familiar, and may resemble a punctuated equilibrium rather than a smooth evolution." In fan fiction, familiarity would usually mean similarity to the source text. Elise Jing, Simon DeDeo and Yong-Yeol Ahn. "Sameness Attracts, Novelty Disturbs, but Outliers Flourish in Fanfiction Online." Preprint. April 17, 2019. https://arxiv.org/pdf/1904.07741v1.pdf.

48. Luetkenhaus and Weinstein, *Austentatious,* 54, emphasis added.
49. Coppa, "Writing Bodies in Space," 236–237.
50. See Cano, *Jane Austen and Performance,* 162–63, 165.
51. Harman, *Jane's Fame,* 144–149. See also Claudia L. Johnson, *Jane Austen's Cults and Cultures* (Chicago: University of Chicago Press, 2012), 127–30, 151–52.
52. For many media scholars, what defines fandom is emotional engagement, creativity, and participating in community; see Henry Jenkins, *Convergence Culture: Where New and Old Media Collide.* New York: NYU Press, 2006, Jenkins, *Textual Poachers,* and Pugh, *Democratic Genre.* The scholarship on Austen's fans and the culture that they generate continues to grow apace. See Cano, *Jane Austen and Performance*; Glosson, *Performing Jane*; Harman, *Jane's Fame*; Devoney Looser, *The Making of Jane Austen* (Baltimore: Johns Hopkins University Press, 2017); Luetkenhaus and Weinstein, *Austentatious*; Lynch, *Janeites*; Wells, *Everybody's Jane*; Yaffe, *Among the Janeites*; and Xu, "Austen's fans and fans' Austen."
53. For Austen telling her family about her characters, see James Edward Austen Leigh. *A Memoir of Jane Austen* (Oxford: Oxford UP, 2002) 119. For the origins of the Jane Austen Society of North America, the Jane Austen Society of the United Kingdom, and the Jane Austen Society of Australia, see the pages "Our Beginnings" (http://jasna.org/about/), "History of the Society" (https://janeaustensociety.org.uk/about-us/history-of-the-society/), and https://jasa.com.au/ respectively.
54. For examples of fan fiction authors requesting feedback on their work, see "Through My Fine Eyes" by hopelessromanticlove (FanFiction.net, published September 7, 2011, https://www.fanfiction.net/s/7361005/1/Through-My-Fine-Eyes); "The Road to Recovery" by LadyElizabethDarcy (FanFiction.net, published October 28, 2014, https://www.fanfiction.net/s/10787029/The-Road-to-Recovery); and "Eavesdropping" by Lynne George (FanFiction.net, published March 23, 2015, https://www.fanfiction.net/s/11134070/1/Eavesdropping). For an example of a fan fiction author thanking a beta reader, see "your eyes whispered, "have we met?" by Herskirtsarentthatshort (Archive of Our Own, published May 27, 2016, https://archiveofourown.org/works/6982417); for an example for a fan fiction author seeking a beta reader,

see "The Benevolence of Scandal" by thecorkrose (Archive of Our Own, updated February 6, 2021, https://archiveofourown.org/works/26573299/chapters/64785061). See also Bronwen Thomas's analysis of the online community for "Ae Fond Kiss," an unfinished modern *Pride and Prejudice* fan fiction set in Scotland, the ways readers responded to chapter postings and to the author when she became ill, "What Is Fanfiction and Why are People Saying Such Nice Things about It?" *Storyworlds: A Journal of Narrative Studies,* vol. 3 (2011), 16–20.

55. The Republic of Pemberley has a Knowledge Base with information about Regency practices: https://pemberley.com/?page_id=12315.

56. See Jenkins, *Convergence Culture.* Increasingly, fans not only shape fandom, but they also shape the culture that they consume—as media producers acknowledge the power of fans by surveying fan opinion at fan events like Comic-Con, tracking fan websites, influencers, and so on.

57. Kristina Busse and Karen Hellekson, "Introduction: Work in Progress," *Fan Fiction and Fan Communities in the Age of the Internet,* eds. Karen Hellekson and Kristina Busse (Jefferson, NC: McFarland & Company, 2006), 7.

Chapter Five

Unconquerable Attraction

Darcy and Elizabeth's Falling in Love in Austenesque Novels

Maria Clara Pivato Biajoli

When Jane Bennet asks her sister how she has fallen in love with Mr. Darcy, Elizabeth answers: "It has been coming on so gradually, that I hardly know when it began."[1] Throughout the process that reframed *Pride and Prejudice* as the most romantic novel ever written, "gradually" became an odious adverb, at least when describing the feelings of ODC—"our dear couple," in fan fiction terms. It was, however, a strong foundation for happiness in Jane Austen's view. The description of Elizabeth's despondency in seeing Darcy leave the inn in Lambton had already introduced the notion:

> If gratitude and esteem are good foundations of affection, Elizabeth's change of sentiment will be neither improbable nor faulty. But if otherwise—if regard springing from such sources is unreasonable or unnatural, in comparison of what is so often described as arising on a first interview with its object, and even before two words have been exchanged, nothing can be said in her defence, except that she had given somewhat of a trial to the latter method in her partiality for Wickham, and that its ill success might, perhaps, authorise her to seek the other less interesting mode of attachment.[2]

Here, a regard springing from "gratitude and esteem" is opposed to one arising "on a first interview"; hence, the gradual development of amorous feelings is the opposite of the celebrated lightning strike of love at first sight. Because we've discovered Mr. Wickham's true character alongside Elizabeth and are now learning that Darcy "was exactly the man who, in disposition and talents, would most suit her,"[3] we share her lesson about the errors of first impressions. Additionally, as readers, we are encouraged to question our desire for protagonists always to fall madly in love from the beginning.

Darcy also needs to learn many things, and he needs time. Austen could not be more resolute with this plan, having her hero, on his first appearance, call her heroine tolerable, and many months later admit about his feelings: "I cannot fix on the hour, or the spot, or the look, or the words, which laid the foundation. It is too long ago. I was in the middle before I knew that I *had* begun."[4] This "deliberate rejection on Austen's part of the love-at-first-sight formula," affirms Emily Auerbach, is a novelty in the fiction of Austen's time, but it is not unique in her work.[5] Take, for example, the narrator's description of Henry Tilney's feelings for Catherine Morland in *Northanger Abbey*: "for, though Henry was now sincerely attached to her, though he felt and delighted in all the excellencies of her character and truly loved her society, I must confess that his affection originated in nothing better than gratitude, or, in other words, that a persuasion of her partiality for him had been the only cause of giving her a serious thought."[6] Again, Austen chooses an unusual path towards a happy ending. Tilney does not give Catherine a serious thought before realizing she likes him. His love is the consequence of gratitude, thus, we can infer, it is of a gradual rise. Even for Marianne Dashwood in *Sense and Sensibility*, so immediately enchanted by Willoughby and his gallant rescue of her, the narrator tells us that "[h]is society became *gradually* her most exquisite enjoyment."[7] That dreadful adverb shows up once more. How different from the scene in the 1995 movie where we see Colonel Brandon (Alan Rickman) arriving late to a dinner party only to be bewitched by the image of Marianne (Kate Winslet) playing the pianoforte.

In short, love takes its sweet time in Austen's novels. The unions of Emma and Mr. Knightley, Anne and Captain Wentworth, and Fanny and Edmund Bertram take years of waiting on the part of at least one of the lovers. Bertram also rubs salt into the wound by falling in love with another woman first and making our heroine watch them together. No wonder many Austen fans today dislike him and wish that Fanny had accepted Mr. Crawford—at least with him, she was not a plan B. Moreover, the refusal of the love at first sight *topos* in *Pride and Prejudice* is an essential part of the refusal of first impressions, and, most importantly, of not allowing them, either positive or negative, to guide our actions. This message, however, has lost its importance in the contemporary reception of the novel. As I stated earlier, *Pride and Prejudice* went through a long process of re-signification that reframed the novel foremost into a love story. Its enduring appeal is, no doubt, an effect of this process, conducted in part by adaptations for the big and small screen, and in part by the use of Austen as the reference for more modern subgenres of romantic fiction in different media (from Georgette Heyer's Regency novels, to *Bridget Jones* movies, and to the *Bridgerton* TV series). This appeal is also the basis for the phenomenon of "Jane Austen Fan Fiction" (JAFF), which, judging from the disparity between the number of stories derived from *Pride and Prejudice* and all the other novels combined, could be justly called "*Pride and Prejudice* Fan Fiction" or even "Mr. Darcy Fan Fiction."

In the fan fiction genre, there is a subcategory called "fix-it," where fans alter a specific part, or parts, of the original material that made them unhappy. The death of a beloved character. A couple separated or paired with the "wrong" person. Lack of punishment for the villains or antagonists.[8] Even something *fans* consider out of character is open for fixing. In the *Pride and Prejudice* fan fiction world, it is the protagonists' method of falling in love that is constantly reformed, so much so that, with few exceptions, its whole group in JAFF stories, from sequels, variations, modern retellings, alternative universes, and so on, could all be categorized as "fix fics."

In the next pages, I will examine this specific trait of the JAFF phenomenon, focusing on examples from "Austenesque novels." They must be distinguished from fan fiction written and posted solely in online communities, since, as the term indicates, these novels are fan fiction stories published as books or, more frequently, as e-books. Although many of their authors have started as fan-readers and fan-authors of online fics, these novels have become a phenomenon of their own, with characteristics closer to traditional novel writing than fan fiction writing. For example, one of the main aspects of a fanfic community is the participation of readers, particularly when fan-authors post their stories in installments. Readers will comment, criticize, and give suggestions and encouragement, in a process that calls to mind the serialized publication of the nineteenth century. It is not the case when a book is published, even if it's self-published, as a complete story, notwithstanding the practice of posting reviews on Amazon or Goodreads, for example. Also, one of the core features of fan fiction is its free access. Many authors of Austenesque novels, however, have earned enough money to make a career out of it, and many more earn at least a little bit by making their stories available for low prices or through a subscription system like Kindle Unlimited. Since the community of Austen fans has started, by itself, to recognize these differences, the term "Austenesque novels" has been adopted to mark the existence of these two different types of fan fiction. Finally, the choice of restricting the analysis to Austenesque novels is a practical one: it is much easier to catalog, keep track of, and return to published novels and their authors than to online stories that run the risk of disappearing from the archives of fan pages.

Now, why fan fiction in the first place? To better understand Austen's popularity, it is essential to turn to her readers, to the audience for the adaptations, and her fans, since the current Austenmania phenomenon is a combination of media, paper, screen, and cloud. The usual method for this kind of readers' reception study would be to gather their opinions through interviews and questionnaires, or nonacademic reviews (fans' blogs, for example). Fan fiction, however, offers a new source of information. Fan-authors rewrite Austen's work according to their views, ideas, and feelings about the original story, highlighting and developing aspects they like, and changing or excluding aspects they do not (such as in the "fix-it" genre). In this sense, their stories are testimonies of their perceptions and preferences, which is related, on one level, to their personal experiences—such as with the birth of the "Mary Sue" fanfic subgenre, promoted by the need of a *Star Trek* female fan to see women in higher ranks in that universe. However, on a second level, fan fiction reading and writing is also connected to a collective experience, in this case, the Austen fandom and its community. Therefore, close reading a single fan fiction story will tell us more about a fan-author than about Austen; but close reading a large corpus of stories, alongside TV and movie adaptations, might elicit patterns that can help us answer the question "What does Austen mean today in popular culture?" Because the JAFF phenomenon is mostly centered on replaying Elizabeth and Darcy's courtship and happy ending, I believe one possible answer is that, when reading the original, that relationship is what stands out for most fans. That is why their fiction will usually rely on common romantic tropes, such as love at first sight, or the taming of the dangerous hero, both analyzed in the following sections—because JAFF authors and readers are, to some extent, motivated by a desire to relive the experience of the first reading in different ways, an experience closely connected to *Pride and Prejudice*'s love story.

The Rise of the Hero

The importance allotted to Mr. Darcy in Austen's current popularity is undeniable. Many critics have already traced the rise of this character to the 1995 BBC adaptation of *Pride and Prejudice* and Andrew Davies' additions of scenes of Darcy bathing, fencing, riding, writing, playing billiards, and diving in a lake. Davies explains that he confined himself to "writing the scenes that [Austen] didn't write, really . . . [But] I thought that could help a lot, especially since I was writing such a pro-Darcy adaptation in 'Pride and Prejudice'. If they saw him suffering or just doing something very physical, the audience would treat him more like a real person, and not just have Elizabeth's view, where she sees him only when he's in a bad mood all dressed up in evening dress."[9] Davies built a new Darcy, one whose feelings for Elizabeth grow in front of us so we can like him better and forget his pride and his offenses. In this sense, the 1995 *Pride and Prejudice* speaks to the fact that adaptations of Austen, as Cheryl Nixon puts it, "add scenes to add desirability to her male protagonists."[10] Indeed, as Lisa Hopkins states, this specific adaptation blatantly fetishizes Darcy and offers him up to the female gaze.[11]

As a result, Darcy has gained a larger presence in fans' understanding of *Pride and Prejudice*, sometimes larger than Elizabeth's. Darcy's comparative lack of space in the original, therefore, is seen as one of the problems fans want to fix. Since the publication of Janet Aylmer's *Darcy's Story* soon after the airing of the BBC adaptation, many fan-authors have brought us Darcy's point of view. For instance, a very popular Austenesque work, Pamela Aidan's trilogy *Fitzwilliam Darcy, Gentleman*, dedicates a whole volume to letting us know where Darcy goes and what he does between the Netherfield ball and his reencounter with Elizabeth in Kent—but, most importantly, how he is constantly tormented by his feelings for her. Although an exception, there is also the case of Lily Granson's *Mr. Darcy's Sorrow and Redemption*, where Elizabeth, we are told, died during childbirth, leaving Darcy desolate. Many years later, he's open to repairing his broken heart with another woman. In a way, Elizabeth has become secondary to our longing for Darcy, which, as Ashley Tauchert puts it, "remains a sticking-point in our aesthetic and cultural understanding of Austen," despite "having plentiful of critical tools with which to demystify this illusory object of an outmoded romantic desire."[12]

Finding a Darcy of one's own is a fantasy easily identified in the novel *Austenland*, by Shannon Hale, adapted to film in 2013. Jane Hayes, the protagonist, is incapable of overcoming an obsession with Mr. Darcy, a constant obstacle to her real life, as her aunt tells her: "'I've seen the movie. I know who Colin Firth is, my dear. And I think I know what you've put your life on hold to wait for.'" Jane responds: "'Listen, I don't actually believe I can somehow end up married to Mr. Darcy. I just . . . nothing in real life feels as right as . . . oh, never mind, I don't want you believing your great-niece is living in a fantasyland.'"[13] Jane tries to explain that real life does not measure up to what she sees on the TV series (not in the novel) while refusing to admit that she is indeed living in a fantasyland. Her wish is to find someone like Mr. Darcy, "[s]omeone who made me feel all the time like I felt *when I watched those movies*."[14] As a sort of family intervention, her aunt sends Jane to spend a period in a "resort" in England that reproduces the lifestyle of the aristocracy in the Regency era. There, Jane gets involved with two men, one a seducer *à la* Wickham, the other, a Mr. Nobley, distant and moody *à la* Darcy. She ends up disillusioned with that (fake) nineteenth-century world and returns to the United States with a new perception: "She believed now in earnest that fantasy is not practice for what is real—fantasy is the opiate of women."[15] Her realization makes for a good ending except for the fact that Mr. Nobley follows her across the ocean. Their union contradicts the final message of liberation from her Darcy-obsession. After all, Jane's happy ending is with Nobley/Darcy, and not with the Wickham-like character.[16] Jane may assert that "Mr. Nobley . . . helped her say no to Mr. Darcy,"[17] but, in truth, that isn't the case; instead, she merely says "yes" to someone who finally measures up to his image in real life. Granted, she doesn't end up with the real Mr. Darcy; that privilege is reserved for Amanda Price in *Lost in Austen* (2008). However, Jane's happy ending is the next best thing because she achieves what she wanted from the beginning: to find someone who makes her feel what she feels watching *Pride and Prejudice* on TV.

How and why did Mr. Darcy become such an object of desire? Linda Troost and Sayre Greenfield have shown us how, in the nineteenth century, *Pride and Prejudice* was lauded not because of its hero but, shockingly, because of Mr. Collins and many other comic characters.[18] Today, however, and despite ongoing debates about whether Darcy, Wentworth, Knightley, or (since the 2007 film) Henry Tilney is the best Austen hero, Darcy usually wins first place. Contemporary women may long for his handsome and tall person, nostalgic chivalry, and Pemberley; yet, the true fantasy that encloses this character is the dream, in Janet Todd's words, of "the worthy lowly girl catching or taming a deliciously arrogant master," which she sees as "a utopian exultation at the feminine erotic power that can bring the monster to heel with minimal effort."[19] Hence, instead of pride and prejudice, we have Beauty and the Beast.

Darcy begins the story as rude and arrogant: "he was discovered to be proud; to be above his company, and above being pleased."[20] Against his principles and resolve, he falls in love with Elizabeth, and, strongly supported by a belief in his superiority, he proposes and expects an acceptance. She refuses. Her response to his offenses works as a mirror to show him his faults, which, with time, promotes a change in Darcy—a change that must continue after the closing of the novel. He learns to recognize his mistakes, acts to fix them, and when he proposes a second time, he is accepted because now, in his own words, he is worthy of Elizabeth. According to Emily Auerbach, "Darcy's ability to overcome his snobbish sense of superiority in order to accept Elizabeth as his equal and to measure her relatives by worth rather than birth marks perhaps the greatest personal evolution any Austen hero undergoes."[21] He is inserted in a tradition of men tamed by heroines, from Mr. B and Rochester to pop-culture Christian Grey, and acts as the bridge between these characters; he is seen as the perfect combination of a romantic and mysterious hero, and a faithful knight down on his knees in front of the woman who refused to be conquered by his view of the world. Darcy is, therefore, the ideal example of a man who changes for love.

In *Pride and Prejudice* fan fiction, the "taming of the hero" fantasy appears constantly, based on the premise that Darcy is the first to fall in love *and* unwillingly: as in the original, Elizabeth's success is usually "unconsciously done."[22] Darcy is defeated by her qualities, to which he initially is blind due to circumstances and his shortcomings, which sometimes are expanded to make Elizabeth—and, vicariously, her female readers—more powerful. It's a most satisfying fantasy for a woman, probably surpassing even the fantasy of love at first sight. Caitlin William's *The Coming of Age of Elizabeth Bennet* is a complex and intriguing example of these two particular fantasies that are not mutually exclusive. It brings a Darcy with more pride and self-importance, and a very young Elizabeth, into a forced marriage scenario, in which a scandal gives them no other choice but to marry against their will. Darcy takes a long time to overcome his resentment and inability to deal with their situation, while Elizabeth responds with a reserve of her own due to many misunderstandings. In a way, this Darcy is transformed into the powerful and distrustful hero archetype that the original character has helped to create. However, he learns with time to recognize his flaws and embrace his love for Elizabeth. In the excerpt below, we see the moment when he is finally prostrated by her without her knowledge and desire to have him so:

> Then he opened the parlour door and fell in love. Though he had never experienced it before, he knew it straight away. It was the surest emotion he had ever felt. He had burned for her before, been desperately attracted to her since the day he had returned to Pemberley. He constantly wanted to be near her and she

had certainly ignited that basest, most beastly part of him, his needs and his passions. This was an entirely new emotion, however. It made him shake; such was
the force with which it took hold of him. He didn't just adore the sight of her,
he realised, he adored everything about her, who she was, what she had become.
Elizabeth was sat with a small child on her lap, a fork full of cake poised in mid-
air, laughing at the boy's cries for more. When Darcy entered, she turned her
head his way, but her smile, which usually faltered or disappeared upon seeing
him, remained, and its breadth and warmth, the joy in it, sent him spiralling.[23]

Darcy, after many years of marriage with Elizabeth—most of it spent travel-
ing alone to escape it—recognizes first his physical desire for her; later he
is struck by the lightning of love while Elizabeth is entertaining a friend,
completely unaware of what's happening. It's her victory, which she obtained
without any effort, that illustrates the desire of the modern woman to be
loved and cherished just as she is. Even though it is not Elizabeth's love that
causes the transformation in Darcy's view and feelings, it's clear that her presence in his life is responsible for it. Caitlyn William's novel does not oblit-
erate Elizabeth, as many Austenesque variations end up doing by focusing
so much on Darcy; on the contrary, she remains the main character and is
forced to grow and learn many things by herself from a tender age. Apart
from that, the scene in the parlor is also an example of a variation on the
love at first sight plot. They have met before, being married for seven years;
however, that moment is almost as if Darcy really sees Elizabeth for the first
time. Love hits him on the chest—there is nothing gentle or gradual about
the experience—but only once he is open to it. It is an interesting twist since
love at first sight in Darcy's case is usually also against his will, but not here.
In this novel, he has to go through a lengthy process of change to merit the
wife he already had but didn't value.

    In *Obligation and Redemption* (2016), by Georgia McCall, there is another
interesting case of a "Darcy made worse." The scenario is the same, a forced
marriage, but in this case, Darcy is so altered by his frustration and jealousy regarding Elizabeth that he is more like the dangerous and dark hero
of many Harlequin novels. He even forces Elizabeth to have sex with him.
Since marital rape is not something many fans are prepared to accept about
Darcy, there are several vehemently negative reviews of this novel, indicating
that there is indeed a limit to what fan fiction will embrace. Undoubtedly,
the more dangerous the hero in the fantasy of the man who changes for love,
the sweeter is his surrender to the heroine in the end; however, there is a line
that must not be crossed, and that usually lies in the fact that the hero can
be dangerous, even violent, with anyone, but not with the heroine. So much

so that, in many variations of the forced marriage scenario, Darcy is usually respectful of Elizabeth's reticence towards consummating their union; or, when he does act on his "husband's rights," he is caring and concerned with her enjoyment as well. It is also an indication of how important questions raised by the feminist movement impact current readers' views, even if its subsequent waves, according to Janet Todd, "make no dent in the mass phenomenon of the modern cultural idea of romantic 'true love,' the utopian desire of female readers for a special kind of romance and a special kind of hero."[24] Specifically, modern women have long learned to despise domestic violence, which in turn has made the heroes of popular romantic fiction less and less prone to abuse; on the other hand, however, these same women still cherish fantasies associated with Byronic, heterosexual, powerful Alpha males, and, more dangerously, with curing them through love.

The Heart Wants What It Wants

The "taming of the dark hero" fantasy is indeed a powerful one, and it has found a large space in *Pride and Prejudice* variations. However, the main tendency in Austenesque novels veers in the opposite direction. Instead of making Darcy worse, most cases of *Pride and Prejudice* fanfic will correct or excuse him. For example, in *Sense of Worth*, by Deborah Kauer, Elizabeth realizes that "his aloofness was a sign of shyness and reserve that he experienced when in the company of people he did not know or were only minimally acquaintances. Since he was not as aloof as she first suspected, it also made her accept the fact that he was not as proud as he first appeared; at least not proud in the sense that he felt himself above everyone around him."[25] This description portrays a much better man than Darcy's admission: "I was spoilt by my parents, who . . . allowed, encouraged, almost taught me to be selfish and overbearing; to care for none beyond my own family circle; to think meanly of all the rest of the world; to *wish* at least to think meanly of their sense and worth compared with my own."[26] In essentials, as Elizabeth asserts to Wickham, Darcy is good. The fact that he can be a good landlord, a loving brother, as well as an arrogant and proud man makes him more interesting. Instead, recreating him as a perfect man just weakens a complex character into a superficial one.

Eliminating Darcy's flaws has interesting effects. An improved Darcy is not motivated to change by Elizabeth's refusal because he doesn't need to; he is already worthy of her. Elizabeth's power, then, is diminished when Darcy appears the perfect man from page one, particularly if we compare it to the taming of the hero fantasy. If the refusal of the first proposal is included in the plot, we feel sorry for Darcy and evaluate Elizabeth somewhat negatively because instead of standing up for her principals by rejecting an as-yet unimproved Darcy, she has rejected a suitable suitor, a marriage that could solve all her family's problems, *and* a truly good man. Moreover, the balance is all wrong. The happy ending of Austen's novel is one of equilibrium. The protagonists both need to change before they can meet again and be reconciled. But when Darcy is faultless, only Elizabeth must learn to understand him correctly, creating a teacher-pupil relationship. Finally, if there is no inner growth needed, then the plot must be sustained from the outside. Austenesque novels rely heavily on the usual social obstacles to an unequal union—family opposition due to inferiority of status, lack of fortune and connections—and on all kinds of miscommunications and misunderstandings, or, on occasion, overt manipulation by the villains to keep them apart until the very last minute. In fact, some stories resemble a lot Austen's "Plan of a Novel, according to Hints from Various Quarters," and not in a satirical way: "the scene will be for ever shifting from one Set of People to another—but all the Good will be unexceptionable in every respect—and there will be no foibles or weaknesses but with the Wicked, who will be completely depraved & infamous, hardly a resemblance of Humanity left in them."[27] Without entering the problematic and generic question of literary quality, then, we can still evaluate fan fiction concerning Austen's work by showing how most cases end up resorting to narrative solutions that, as Deirdre Lynch points out, "Austen loved to burlesque."[28] They pay homage to Austen by using elements she didn't appreciate in the fiction of her time.

Since this "Darcy 2.0" does not need taming, the most common fantasy associated with him is love at first sight. It can range from that lightning strike we already saw, to a slower shift from denial to admission, beginning usually with physical attraction and curiosity. Far from thinking her merely "tolerable," this Darcy must be affected by Elizabeth from the beginning. In Valerie Lennox's *Compromised by Mr. Darcy*, the Meryton dance passage is retold from Darcy's point of view. We already know that he doesn't want to dance because he is concerned with locating Mr. Denny, and in this scene he is grasping for any excuse to convince Bingley to leave him alone without revealing his intent:

> [Darcy] was rather preoccupied, but he did remember that Bingley had shown special preference to a girl, dancing with her twice, and Darcy decided not to

offend his friend by allowing that Bingley's favorite was "the only handsome girl in the room." He settled upon another excuse, that he was not interested in dancing with ugly women. He pronounced them all below his standard. It was another stupid excuse, but he did not care. Bingley would likely believe it of him. Darcy had been teased, after all, during their time together at school, for being too particular about various things, something that may have been true when he was a boy, used to being catered to in his own household, but had been quite eradicated from him during his schooling. He was no more fastidious now than other men he knew, and he certainly didn't mind dancing with women, whatever their appearance. He supposed there was nothing worse than a frightfully dull conversationalist, but that couldn't be discerned by looking at a woman, could it? Bingley did indeed latch onto this and cried out that Darcy was just the same as ever, and that he would not be like him. And then he pointed out the sister of his favorite. Darcy turned to look at the woman, intending to do it cursorily, and to reject her out of hand. Instead, he quite felt as if his breath was knocked out of him.[29]

We learn that Darcy wants to *appear* fastidious, and fully intends to use his—mostly undeserved—fame of being difficult to please to be rid of his friend. He plans to slight Elizabeth, but is not prepared for how she will destabilize him:

> It was the kind of beauty that might make Darcy decide he didn't care as much about conversation after all, and he gulped at that, because he didn't consider himself a shallow man, turned by a pretty face or the curve of a knowing smile, like the one Bingley's favorite's sister was giving him now. "Miss Elizabeth Bennet," said Bingley in a whisper. "You cannot tell me she is not lovely." "She is . . ." Mr. Darcy choked, still gazing at her like a man adrift at sea. "Tolerable, but not handsome enough to tempt me."[30]

Calling her tolerable, therefore, is a falsehood, a disguise of his true feelings. His rudeness is explained as a ruse, necessary to his urgent mission to discover from Denny what really happened to his sister at Ramsgate, and one that he finds difficult to maintain. His character is dissociated from Elizabeth's accusation of his "arrogance," "conceit," and "selfish disdain of the feelings of others."[31] In addition, the reader finds it pleasing to have it confirmed once again that he never stood a chance against Elizabeth's power.

Some variations choose to alter the way Darcy and Elizabeth first meet and, using "fix-it" logic, avoid that first insult altogether. In Arthel Cake's *Pemberley in Peril*, Darcy is introduced to Elizabeth as his potential bride for an arranged marriage orchestrated by both their fathers:

"Mr. Darcy, may I present Mrs. Bennet and my daughters Elizabeth, Mary, Catherine, and Lydia?" Darcy bowed. He had a brief impression of a plump, pretty woman of middle age with suppressed excitement in her glance, three young ladies of varying ages, and a fourth standing a little apart. She was indeed small and fair, her hair coiffed more simply than he might have expected, the color of burnished ebony. When she straightened and her eyes rose to his, his breath stopped. Remarkable eyes, loveliest eyes. The words spun through his mind. They were the color of wood violets, flecked with blue with a thin black ring around the iris. He had met ladies with violet eyes before, if rarely. But these were the pure color and Darcy thought, as he struggled to respond in a rational manner, that a man could fall into those eyes and drown.[32]

Instead of offending Elizabeth, Darcy civilly speaks to her during dinner, but her first impact on him is, again, very potent. She muddles his brain and his rational thoughts even before saying a single word, by just being there. His reaction, therefore, is not anchored in reason but in the heart, restoring sentimental tropes of the eighteenth century that Austen ingeniously mocked. For her part, Elizabeth is at least curious about Darcy, as in many fan fiction stories in which Darcy's response is stronger or more immediate than hers. Although falling in love at the same time is a common romantic device in JAFF, making the hero work for the heroine's hand might be more exciting. In any case, it is always clear that Elizabeth is Darcy's destiny.

The concept of soulmates is a trope similarly popular in Austenesque novels. The plot of *Haunting Mr. Darcy* is a significant example. After an accident that leaves Elizabeth in a coma, her soul is detached from her body and reappears in Darcy's house in London. Obviously, he is the only one who can see her. Their connection is so strong that Elizabeth—in her ghost form—can't be more than a few feet away from Darcy, being "pulled" to follow him everywhere. Since this whole situation occurs before she develops any feelings for him, it is clear that her soul knows their bond before she does. In a plan to wake Elizabeth up from her coma, Darcy travels to Longbourn to bring her spirit back to her body. After several failed attempts, Darcy discovers that the only thing that can stir Elizabeth is a kiss:

As he pressed his lips to hers, slowly the feeling that grew in prominence against all the other exquisite sensations was that of extreme rightness. *It was as if he was destined to this end.* Though the kiss was brief, it was no less powerful to the gentleman, who found himself quite breathless as he lifted his head. He looked down at the lady and was astonished, paralyzed suddenly in shock, as he felt her stir beneath the hand still resting tenderly on her cheek. "William!" Elizabeth's voice drew his attention to her ghostly self. She had turned herself during the kiss, and her hand was resting unbelievingly upon her lips. "I feel something. I . . . Something is happening." Wide-eyed, Darcy watched as her vision wavered before him. . . . Again, the cheek resting in his hand stirred, and he was seized with a hope that drove him to bend over her lips again. . . . This time he poured forth all the love he felt in his heart and allowed it to manifest skin to skin as *he connected his very soul to hers.*[33]

This passage reinforces concepts that have become permanent among Austen fans, such as the fact that Darcy and Elizabeth are meant to be together. That is not to say that there aren't any fan fiction stories where Darcy and Elizabeth's HEA—"happily ever after"—doesn't happen. However, in my observation, these daring choices are rare and generally restricted to the universe of online fan fiction. The migration to the published universe of Austenesque novels, despite even the self-publishing system of Amazon, seems to work as a filter, and not everything available online is well-received everywhere.

An Unconquerable Attraction

In addition to one or more of the aforementioned fantasies, Austenesque novels are built on one nonnegotiable foundation: a powerful physical attraction between the protagonists. John Mullan has noted how even "some recent academic criticism, discover[ed] more sex implicit in Austen than narrative logic allows," while also consenting that Austen occasionally required her readers to recognize that "humans are driven by sexual appetites."[34]

Richard Jenkins, for example, points out that "[o]ne reason for [Darcy's] popularity is that he is the hero in whom sexual desire is most overt and overpowering. For what is he doing when he makes his first proposal to Elizabeth but telling her that he is so desperate to get her into bed that he will marry her even though it will be a degradation to him?"[35] Claudia Johnson and Clara Tuite, in turn, take issue with Charlotte Brontë's complaint that passions were unknown to Austen. In doing so they point out how Elizabeth and Darcy "argue, they taunt, they insult each other, they expose each other's faults, pain, and weakness, and often while alone. . . . One would have to be willfully unimaginative—or insensate—not to recognize such exchanges as passionate, even vehement."[36] I will let other pens dwell on the matter of how large a part sex played in the original novel; I'll say, however, that for the Austen fandom, Jenkins' view is canon, i.e., it's a fixed interpretation among fans. We have already seen, for instance, how Caitlin William's Darcy first burns for Elizabeth but falls for her later.

This attraction is not one-sided; Elizabeth experiences the same. If a fan fiction story follows the ban on women knowing too much about sex in the Regency period, then Elizabeth feels but can't understand her desire. In modern variations, however, there is no problem. Take the example of Curtis Sittenfeld's *Eligible*. After a short race that translates Darcy and Elizabeth's verbal sparrings, we read:

> Her limbs [Elizabeth's] burned, her heart pounded; she was exhausted, possibly nauseated, but also giddy. As they faced each other, there was between them such a profusion of vitality that it was hard to know what to do with it; they kept making eye contact, looking away, and making eye contact again. At last—surely he was thinking something similar and she was simply the one giving voice to the sentiment—she said, "Want to go to your place and have hate sex?"[37]

Their engagement in "hate sex" is a perfect illustration of a couple who yields to a mutual desire, despite their opinion of each other, supplanting the heart in the process of recognizing their soul mates.

As I stated earlier, the 1995 miniseries championed this interpretation by offering new glimpses of a more human Darcy—a man, therefore, of flesh and blood. It started a tradition of exploring Darcy's feelings, and not only of the heart. In the 2005 film adaptation, after Darcy helps Elizabeth into the carriage, we see the famous "flexing hand" moment, their ungloved hands having just touched skin to skin. Later, in the heat of their argument after his first proposal, both get a touch too close, stealing a glance at each other's lips—a silent code for considering, or wanting, a kiss. That scene informs the film adaptation of *Pride and Prejudice and Zombies* (2016), in which the argument, replete with many sexual hints, is depicted as an actual fight, where buttons fly off, breasts are almost exposed, and Darcy ends up on top of Elizabeth.

Since fan fiction is a transmedia genre by nature, the relationship between sex and romance depicted by all these adaptations is absorbed and incorporated by Austen's fandom. Even if the sentimental language of the heart takes precedence over reason in Austenesque novels, it is undoubtedly accompanied by the notion that, apart from your heart, your body also knows best. For example, although Elizabeth always recognizes Wickham's beauty and charm, and engages in flirtatious dialogue, she is, at most, only mildly attracted to him in fan fiction. She rarely has sex with him in modern retellings—and when she does, it is a lukewarm experience in comparison to what she eventually experiences with Darcy. By contrast, the unconquerable attraction between Elizabeth and Darcy must arise as the first step of their falling in love, and as theirs is the quintessential true love, so is their love-making the best both ever had. This sexualizing of *Pride and Prejudice* is not only approved of but expected by many fan fiction readers and writers. The "fix-it" efforts of these fans, which add and enlarge the fantasies of love at first sight or the taming of the hero, along with the addition of lots of sexual content, are a strong indication not only of what they sought but didn't see enough of in the original, but also of what they are determined to get from *Pride and Prejudice*.

Notes

1. Jane Austen, *Pride and Prejudice* (Cambridge: Cambridge University Press, 2006), 414.
2. Austen, *Pride and Prejudice*, 308.
3. Austen, *Pride and Prejudice*, 344.
4. Austen, *Pride and Prejudice*, 421.
5. Emily Auerbach, *Searching for Jane Austen* (Madison: The University of Wisconsin Press, 2004), 154.
6. Jane Austen, *Northanger Abbey* (Cambridge: Cambridge University Press, 2006), 252–53.
7. Jane Austen, *Sense and Sensibility* (Cambridge: Cambridge University Press, 2006), 58, my emphasis.
8. Just as Austen refuses love at first sight, she also resists exemplary punishments for her "villains." Fan fiction is ripe with new endings for Wickham, who usually dies or is transported. Lydia is more of a debate. Those who think she was a victim send her on a path of reformation. Those who disagree prefer sending her away, such as to a strict school for rebellious young ladies, to give ODC a respite.
9. Andrew Davies interviewed in Deborah Cartmell, and Imelda Whelehan, "A practical understanding of literature on screen: two conversations with Andrew Davies," in *The Cambridge Companion to Literature on Screen* (Cambridge: Cambridge University Press, 2007), 244.
10. Cheryl L. Nixon, "Balancing the Courtship Hero. Masculine Emotional Display in Film Adaptations of Austen's Novels," in *Jane Austen in Hollywood*, ed. Linda Troost, and Sayre Greenfield (Lexington: The University Press of Kentucky, 2001), 27.

11. Lisa Hopkins, "Mr. Darcy's Body. Privileging the Female Gaze," in *Jane Austen in Hollywood*, ed. Linda Troost, and Sayre Greenfield (Lexington: The University Press of Kentucky, 2001), 122.
12. Ashley Tauchert, *Romancing Jane Austen. Narrative, Realism, and the Possibility of a Happy Ending* (New York: Palgrave Macmillan, 2005), 23–24.
13. Shannon Hale, *Austenland* (New York: Bloomsbury, 2008), 6. Kindle.
14. Hale, *Austenland*, 189, my emphasis. Jane Hayes' love of Austen because of adaptations is very real. See, for instance, Juliette Wells's interviews with visitors at Jane Austen's House Museum. *Everybody's Jane: Austen in the Popular Imagination* (New York: Continuum, 2011).
15. Hale, *Austenland*, 180.
16. Jane Hayes can also be compared to Catherine Morland and her penchant for reading life through fiction. The fact that Mr. Tilney followed Catherine home to propose is another similarity, evident in the casting for Mr. Nobley's role in 2013: J.J. Feild, who played Tilney in the 2007 adaptation of *Northanger Abbey*.
17. Hale, *Austenland*, 180.
18. Sayre Greenfield and Linda Troost, "Before It Was All About Mr. Darcy: Nineteenth-Century Views of Austen's Characters," *Persuasions On-Line* vol. 38, no. 1 (Winter 2017). https://jasna.org/publications-2/persuasions-online/vol38no1/troost-greenfield/.
19. Janet Todd, "The Romantic Hero," in *The Cambridge Companion to Pride and Prejudice*, ed. Janet Todd (Cambridge: Cambridge University Press, 2013), 153.
20. Austen, *Pride and Prejudice*, 10.
21. Emily Auerbach, *Searching for Jane Austen*, 160.
22. Austen, *Pride and Prejudice*, 212.
23. Caitlin Williams, *The Coming of Age of Elizabeth Bennet* (Amazon Digital Services LLC, 2016), Kindle.
24. Todd, "The Romantic Hero," 157.
25. Deborah Ann Kauer, *Sense of Worth. A Pride and Prejudice Variation* (Deborah Ann Kauer, 2016), Kindle.
26. Austen, *Pride and Prejudice*, 409–10.
27. Jane Austen, "Plan of a Novel, according to Hints from Various Quarters" in *Later Manuscripts* (Cambridge: Cambridge University Press, 2006), 228.
28. Deidre Lynch, "Sequels," in *Jane Austen in Context*, ed. Janet Todd (Cambridge: Cambridge University Press, 2007), 164.
29. Valerie Lennox, *Compromised by Mr. Darcy: A Pride and Prejudice Variation* (Punk Rawk Books, 2020), 15–16, Kindle.
30. Lennox, *Compromised by Mr. Darcy*, 16.
31. Austen, *Pride and Prejudice*, 215.

32. Arthel Cake, *Pemberley in Peril. A Pride and Prejudice Vagary* (CreateSpace Independent Publishing Platform, 2017), 56, Kindle.
33. KaraLynee Mackrory, *Haunting Mr. Darcy* (Oysterville: Meryton Press, 2014), Kindle, my emphasis.
34. John Mullan, *What Matters in Jane Austen? Twenty Crucial Puzzles Solved* (New York: Bloomsbury Press, 2012), 163, 178.
35. Richard Jenkins, *A Fine Brush on Ivory. An Appreciation of Jane Austen* (Oxford: Oxford University Press, 2007), 86.
36. Claudia L. Johnson and Clara Tuite, *30 Great Myths about Jane Austen* (Hoboken: John Wiley and Sons, 2020), 9.
37. Curtis Sittenfeld, *Eligible: A Modern Retelling of Pride and Prejudice* (New York: Random House Publishing Group, 2016), 236, Kindle.

Chapter Six

What's Hidden in Highbury?

Stephanie Oppenheim

As a reader of Jane Austen with academic credentials, I used to be leery of sequels, retellings, mashups, and other spin-offs produced by nonacademic fans of Austen's novels. Yet the recent explosion of Austen-inspired writing, as well as new critical approaches focusing on Austen's popular reception, finally tempted me to give fan fiction a chance.[1] Reading the fiction I had previously scorned, I underwent a conversion experience. I discovered that fiction written by and for Austen fans can function as critical commentary, not unlike an academic article. Like scholars, fan fiction authors call attention to aspects of the work that have been overlooked, offering new possibilities for interpretation. And if Austen fans resemble Austen scholars, perhaps I might embrace the fact that scholars resemble fans. We are in it not *only* for intellectual satisfaction, but to satisfy more private, less professional, desires.

With this premise, I embarked on a course of reading Austenesque novels based on *Emma* to see what insights they might provide not only into Austen's novel but into my own fannish tendencies as a reader.[2] I chose *Emma* because it is my favorite Austen novel and because I have always found it oddly titillating. In my reading, the secret engagement of Jane Fairfax and Frank Churchill generates palpable heat. I wondered what writers of *Emma*-inspired fiction could bring to my understanding of the novel by tapping into the erotic energy that we literary critics often disregard. What might their more subjective responses to literature tell us about our reading practices? And how might they illuminate Austen's craft, which heightens erotic tension even as she keeps it hidden? In other words, I wanted to have it both ways: to enjoy the dramatization of Frank and Jane's backstory that I expected to find in the fiction, and to paper over my salacious interest in their sex life with academic questions.

This attempt to balance analysis with enthusiasm, combining aspects of academic and fan identities, places me in a hybrid position described by scholars of fan studies. As Cornel Sandvoss argues, "Fan studies has . . . eroded the boundaries between audiences and scholars, between fan and academic more than any other field."[3] The identity of those who attempt to cross the boundary has been given various names. John Wyver, for instance, uses the term "aca-fan" to denote an academic who embraces the fan's deep identification with her object of study.[4] Matthew Hills distinguishes between the "scholar-fan" and the "fan-scholar" depending on the subject's primary affiliation. He argues that what divides fans and scholars is not so much what they do as how they position themselves; "the different guiding discourses and ideals of subjectivity . . . which are linked to cultural systems of value and community."[5] I am by Hills's taxonomy a scholar-fan, whose bread is buttered by an academic institution. Hills describes the challenges inherent in this position: "The scholar-fan must still conform to the regulative ideal of the rational academic subject, being careful not to present too much of their enthusiasm while tailoring their accounts of fan interest and investment to the norms of 'confessional' (but not overly confessional) academic writing."[6] Hills cautions those who would forge their fan and academic identities to "remain sensitive to those institutional contexts which disqualify certain ways of speaking and certain ways of presenting the self."[7] Indeed, I have been warned against writing in the first person if I want my work to count towards academic promotion. Yet I am doing so here, blending aspects of personal narrative with an academic essay, because I feel it best expresses my hybrid position as a scholar-fan. The sensitivity I feel about this mode of writing is compounded by the mode of reading it describes. I am reading for pleasure as well as for insight, and for erotic pleasure at that.

To validate my choice of reading *material*, I turn to Austen for precedent. After all, the first Austen fan fiction was produced—and therefore encouraged—by Austen herself. In James Edward Austen-Leigh's *A Memoir of Jane Austen,* the author, Austen's nephew, recalls how his aunt "would, if asked, tell us many little particulars about the subsequent career of some of her people."[8] In providing the first sequels to her own novels, Austen invited just the kind of fantasy or speculation that fan fiction writers trade in. According to Austen-Leigh, his aunt's revelations about *Emma* were that "Mr Woodhouse survived his daughter's marriage, and kept her and Mr. Knightley from settling at Donwell, about two years; and that the letters placed by Frank Churchill before Jane Fairfax, which she swept away unread, contained the word 'pardon.'"[9] What especially interests me about the "little particular" regarding Frank and Jane is that, unlike the other details Austen-Leigh mentions, it is *not* about the "subsequent career" of the characters. It concerns what's *really* going on in the world of the novel: the subtext, the secrets, the concealed story of Frank and Jane. It suggests that there is indeed something hidden in Highbury; something that we might uncover if we only probed deeply enough. This seems to authorize the work of Austen variations, which retell the stories with material added, viewpoints shifted, background illuminated, secrets revealed. I have to admit that since first reading Austen-Leigh's memoir, I have always experienced the scene mentioned as really containing Frank's plea for "pardon"; and that this has increased my pleasure in it, and informed my understanding of Frank's character, and of the relationship between Frank and Jane. With her tantalizing glimpse of Frank's private message, Austen has invited readers (and writers) to embellish the narrative with their own imaginings.

Whether or not writers of fan fiction have adopted the label of fan-scholar, the interpretive work they perform has been suggested by those who study fandom. Sheenagh Pugh, for instance, provides a relevant introduction to what motivates and inspires writers of fan fiction in *The Democratic Genre: Fan Fiction in a Literary Context*. Her extensive survey of the field uncovers two primary motivations among writers: "they wanted either 'more of' their source material or 'more from' it."[10] The first group is so enthralled by the "canon"—the material of the original work—that they can't get enough of it. Members of the second group, by contrast, "see possibilities in it which were never explored as they might have been."[11] Such possibilities are frequently offered by "missing scenes" in the canon; those "incidents, conversations, interactions" that may be alluded to or implied, but are not spelled out on the page.[12] Clearly, the initial meeting and engagement of Frank and Jane in *Emma* constitutes an extended missing scene (or series of scenes). As Pugh elaborates: "Fanfic happens in the gaps between canon, the unexplored or insufficiently explored territory. For that to happen, the gaps must be left, and the territory must exist—i.e., the canon writers must not spell too much out, but there must be somewhere to start from and something to build on."[13] I would argue that the same is true of credible literary scholarship. Literary scholars also speculate in the gaps left by literary texts, yet must ground their analysis in the text itself.[14]

Without laying claim to scholarly expertise, many writers of Austen fan fiction have also reflected on their process and purpose. Diana Birchall, author of *The Compleat Mrs. Elton*, writes that "a new understanding of Austen's works can be gained by the unorthodox method of writing pastiche."[15] She explains that examining *Emma* closely in order to craft her own novel, she gained new insight into Austen's method of writing, especially of drawing character. Recasting the plot from the viewpoint of a minor character—in this case, Mrs. Elton—Birchall claims, "we are enabled to see the story afresh, and gain insight into Austen's method of genius."[16] This strikes me as a primary goal of literary criticism: to illuminate authorial design, including her use of point of view. Discussions with other writers of Austenesque novels reveal similar aims. In an interview with Gabrielle Malcolm, Amanda Grange explains that she thinks of her fiction "as a kind of literary archaeology; piecing together of fragments scattered throughout the novels to create a different, previously unseen, side to each character."[17] Grange insists that her focus on the male perspective offers "something new, but at the same time something which is firmly rooted in Austen's characters."[18] Meanwhile, Jane Odiwe says that her ideas for plots "have come about because Jane Austen's books left me asking questions. I always start with the characters, thinking about what we know about their personalities, imagining motives for their behaviour and what makes them tick."[19] She expresses her hope that "if my books influence in any way, they lead readers back to Jane's books, and give them a different perspective they might not have considered before."[20] This sentiment is echoed by Juliet Archer, in an interview with Laurence Raw: "I think it's wonderful when one of my readers comes back to me and admits that she has been inspired by one of my works to go back and read Austen afresh."[21] Good literary scholarship accomplishes the same end: it returns the reader to the original text with a new interpretive lens. While the writers surveyed above dwell primarily on character, Edward H. Carpenter is interested in *topics* that Austen leaves out of her novels—from poverty to prostitution—and suggests: "Yet they are there at the back of the texts, even though the focus of them might be limited. I think it's important to bring that idea out in my work."[22] This is precisely what literary scholars do, as well; bring out aspects of Austen's world, such as its social context, that are glimpsed at the margins of her texts.

While in recent years popular approaches to Austen have gained traction among literary scholars, the question remains of which responses and reworkings are valid or worthwhile—especially when the "missing scenes" fanfic writers concoct turn out to be sex scenes. As Alice Chandler notes, nineteenth-century convention dictated that sexual activity be implied rather than described; and "The trouble with covert implication is that we cannot be sure if the implication is really there or if we have simply imagined it."[23] Admittedly, Austen fans have let their imaginations run wild. Yet in

Everybody's Jane: Austen in the Popular Imagination, Juliette Wells makes a compelling case for attending to "the fecundity of the popular imagination as well as the peculiar, and apparently unstoppable, pull of Austen upon that imagination."[24] Wells cautions against dismissing nonacademic responses to Austen as "misreadings," arguing that if we hold them up to academic standards or deny their validity, "we will not appreciate fully what Austen means to readers today."[25] While acknowledging the effort it takes for literary scholars like herself to suspend judgment, Wells provides an unbiased survey of all varieties of Austen adaptations, including "hybrids" that spice up Austen's novels with explicit sexual content. Wells notes that "Unique to our era is the impulse to infiltrate Austen's novel with—or depending on your point of view, open them up to—sex and erotica."[26] She doesn't favor either view here, entertaining both possibilities: that the sex is an additive, or is already there, for readers (and writers of fan fiction) to expose.

In "Fifty Shades of Mr. Darcy: A Brief History of X-rated Austen Adaptations," Devoney Looser further explores Austen's dual image as "Prim Austen and Porn Austen," with an emphasis on the porn.[27] Looser informs us that while Austen-inspired erotica is currently experiencing a "boom," this trend has been growing steadily, and has a longer history than we might be familiar with.[28] Looser urges us to examine what "the most blatantly sexed-up Austens mean," as they affect the way we read "prototype Austen" today.[29] As she notes, "Sexed-up adaptations encourage us to imagine that illicit activity lurks around every character and corner, every nook and cranny, and every sly line of Austen's originals. Such things are no doubt sometimes there, but are they *everywhere*?"[30] Like Wells, Looser finds it more productive to leave the question unanswered. Nevertheless, it's the question I want to address. Focusing on one novel, I want to see how the erotica can impact one's reading of "prototype Austen." What can the "sexed-up" versions of *Emma* tell us about the sex we read in or read into the novel? Can it show us where the illicit activity truly lurks? Or does it lay bare our own not-so-scholarly desires?

Because of my academic training, my expectations were initially shaped by what scholars have "encouraged us to imagine" about the erotics of *Emma's* missing scenes—or what they have *discouraged* us from imagining.[31] Academic treatments of Frank and Jane have, for the most part, deflected attempts at finding erotic pleasure in their subplot. For instance, Rachel Brownstein, who declares *Emma* the "least romantic" of Austen's novels, warns us that our search for the novel's sexual secrets will be unrewarded.[32] Brownstein notes that the reader, like Emma, craves knowledge about Jane's secret love life; but the novel refuses to comply. While Austen "teases us with lurid hints" about Jane's supposed affair with Mr. Dixon, we never discover how an upstanding girl like Jane succumbed to a secret engagement with a morally suspect fellow like Frank, or why he staked everything on a penniless girl like her.[33] Brownstein asserts that the novel "deliberately evades information about the sexual life at the core of its plot, a plot that's compelling and powerful to the degree that the information is withheld."[34] Brownstein connects this evasion to changes in the British novel from earlier, more racy women-centered novels like those of Eliza Heywood. In Austen's time, says Brownstein, a lady novelist writing a moral novel about moral young ladies must not betray knowledge of sexual matters.

Other critics, by contrast, find *Emma* rife with sexual subtext, yet adamantly deny its erotic appeal. In *Austen's Unbecoming Conjunctions: Subversive Laughter, Embodied History*, Heydt-Stevenson unpacks Austen's "hybrid, code-switching language" to reveal the erotic innuendo pervading her novels.[35] She contends that Austen's risqué references "foster erotic delight, critique patriarchal ideologies, and offer a reevaluation of Austen's literary achievements and the place of the woman writer in the Romantic era."[36] Yet she finds no "erotic delight" in the sexual allusions surrounding Frank and Jane. While she doesn't dwell extensively on their subplot, she decodes the slang associated with Frank, connecting it with scandal and seduction. For example, Frank's trip to London for a haircut suggests an illicit visit to a woman.[37] As for Jane's aura of sexual intrigue, Heydt-Stevenson reads it as a projection of Emma, who is "disenfranchised" from her own body and must displace it onto other women.[38] In her reading, Jane is humiliated and victimized by Frank, who is basically a scoundrel. Judith Wilt is among the critics who go still further in their condemnation of Frank Churchill, associating him with sexual menace rather than attraction. Wilt denounces "the seducer figure Frank Churchill, who went after the most upright female mind in creation and caused it to stoop, who aroused it erotically first in secret meetings and then, darkly, in public demonstrations, with another woman, of his power to charm."[39] In her reading, Frank's gift of the pianoforte is figured as an act of sexual violence: "Conceive then the astonishment, the terror, the self-loathing of a Jane Fairfax . . . when a Frank Churchill rises from the audience and lays a hand on the instrument."[40] Similarly, Celia A. Easton, examining the "rhetoric of sexual assault, expressed by words of aggression that silence and disempower women" in *Emma*, charges Frank with committing "verbal assault on his secret fiancée." [41] Any sex that binds this pair is clearly not consensual.

A handful of critics acknowledge mutual desire, yet still convey ambivalence about the secret lovers. Nicholas Preus, for instance, argues that the subplot of Frank and Jane is central to Emma's growing sexual awareness, and that for Emma, sex is "a fundamental truth of the self."[42] Since this truth can't be spoken outright, but only intimated through "allusions and codes," Frank and Jane's erotic history provides the secret language by which sexuality is expressed in the novel.[43] Preus identifies the pianoforte that Frank gives to Jane as a "sexually coded object"; "an emblem of the relationship that Frank and Jane shared at Weymouth, the substance of which is sexual attraction."[44] Jane herself represents "an active, adult sexuality that Emma senses but has not attained yet."[45] Preus also identifies Jane's illness, evidenced by her pallor, as an emblem of her sexuality. When Emma and Frank gossip about Jane's complexion, the subtext of the gossip is "the connection between Jane's paleness and Frank's presence at Weymouth; and the hidden meaning of that experience is divulged as an illicit, possibly physical sexual activity."[46] In Preus's reading, the mystery of Frank and Jane's erotic relationship unsettles the lives of their neighbors: "Everyone's life, in one way or another, is disrupted or at least touched by the illicit sexuality of Jane and Frank."[47] Although they are united at the end, their bond has an insidious quality.[48]

Mary Ann O'Farrell is the rare critic who, in identifying Jane's blushing response to Frank as "a site of pleasure" does allow for "erotic delight" in the Jane-and-Frank subplot.[49] As O'Farrell explains in *Telling Complexions: The Nineteenth-Century English Novel and the Blush*, "discovering that pleasures are to be taken with the pains of blushing, Austen recovers a sense of the body in manners. Her erotics of mortification works the perverse conversion of the sign of manners into the sign of desire."[50] While O'Farrell refers to *Emma* only briefly, her analysis of the blush in Austen's other novels clearly applies here. O'Farrell demonstrates how Austen conflates "for pleasure's sake the blush of embarrassment with the flush of arousal."[51] This enables the reader to interpret Jane's blushes not as marks of humiliation, but of sexual excitement. In addition, O'Farrell makes the inviting claim that "Austen's blush can do whatever she wants it to do, can mean whatever she wants it to mean. This freeing detachment permits the restoration of Austen's blush to its erotic preeminence."[52] Austen's rendering of Jane's body permits us to imagine that body's story in pleasurable ways.

Overall, the mostly killjoy critical response to Frank and Jane left me dissatisfied. I realized that I would not find all that my imagination craved among the academics. As a scholar-fan, I could not fully ignore what my peers had to say. Yet while my professional identity wouldn't allow me to be "ignorant," I could still be "partial" and "prejudiced," as Austen boasted herself to be in "The History of England."[53] I decided to hold onto those readings that validated my libidinous response to Frank and Jane, and place those that did not to the side. Preus had pointed to "illicit . . . sexual activity" and O'Farrell "the flush of arousal." I now turned to the fan fiction, which I trusted would deliver what these scholars had detected but not described. For while it is the job of academics to analyze, it is the vocation of fans to dramatize. Since fans read and write for pleasure, I believed that they would provide the pleasure that the scholarship withheld. Privileging the fan side of my scholar-fan persona, I approached the fan fiction with high hopes. What, I wondered, do fans of *Emma* imagine, or believe, is hidden in Highbury? Do they, like me, find Frank and Jane hot stuff? Admittedly, the majority of Austen fans do not consider *Emma* her most erotically suggestive novel, any more than Rachel Brownstein does. Simple math bears this out. The "Comprehensive Guide to Austenesque Novels," on the Austenesque Reviews website currently lists only 64 *Emma*-inspired novels, compared to the thousands of *Pride and Prejudice*-related titles.[54] A mere seven of these titles foreground the story of Frank and Jane. And while temporarily trading scholarship for fandom, I expected to discover the juicy secrets of Frank and Jane, I made a more shocking discovery than I ever anticipated. There weren't any!

The writers who reimagined *Emma* from Jane's perspective uniformly denied that their heroine could be ruled by desire. Taking the novels of the last three decades in chronological order, my survey began with Joan Aiken's *Jane Fairfax: The Secret History of the Second Heroine in Jane Austen's Emma* (1990).[55] In this variation, I found no trace of the sexual passion that I believed must underlie Jane's rash agreement to enter a secret engagement. In fact, Jane is attracted to everyone *but* Frank. In the beginning, Jane feels sorry for Frank, whom she finds ingratiating and over-eager to please. It then turns out she has been cherishing romantic fantasies about Knightley since her childhood. These fantasies give way to an infatuation with Mr. Dixon. That's right, Emma is correct in this version; only the truth is far more chaste than Emma imagined. After the boating mishap, Dixon declares his love to Jane, but she renounces him so that he will marry Miss Campbell. On the rebound, she agrees to an engagement with Frank, but regrets it once she returns to Highbury and sees Knightley again. Jane repines that, in the unlikely event Knightley should one day propose, she would have to turn him down because of her commitment to another, "and another, she could not in her innermost heart deny, of lesser quality than Mr. Knightley."[56] She starts warming to Frank only because he provides a lively contrast to all the bores of Highbury. When Jane and Frank are finally reconciled at the novel's end, she looks at him and thinks: "He was not Matt Dixon. He was not Mr Knightley. (With an internal smile at herself she acknowledged that she must now renounce that childish daydream once and for all.) But he was a dear, kind fellow, he was himself, and he loved her. And she loved him too; yes, she did, in spite of all. Together they would do well enough."[57] With this tepid conclusion, Aiken seems determined to suck all the juice out of her "secret history" of Jane and Frank. Evidently for Aiken, the story of Frank and Jane does not hold much erotic allure. Her novel is an apologia for Jane's bad choice rather than a celebration of her passion.

Frank fares nearly as badly in the next book I read, Joan Ellen Delman's *Lovers' Perjuries, Or, the Clandestine Courtship of Jane Fairfax and Frank Churchill* (2007). In fact, Delman feels compelled to justify Jane's conduct with a subplot. This is the cautionary tale of Jane's older friend, Margaret Devere, who was estranged from *her* lover for fifteen years because she would *not* consent to a secret engagement. This justification suggests that Jane's actions are, in Delman's view, implausible; attraction alone could not account for them. Moreover, Jane's fondness for Frank stems from his generosity to his elderly governess, Mrs. Nesbit, as well as his kindness to animals; "he was always taking care of some injured mouse or abandoned nestling."[58] Delman domesticates Frank rather than playing up his charisma. Not only does Delman downplay his appeal, she magnifies his flaws. Jane sees early evidence of "what she believed to be the great defect of his character: deviousness, she could only term it. It was a flaw which she had always considered of the greatest sort."[59] She has reservations about Frank from the start, and is slow to fall in love with him. The scenes in which passion seems unavoidable, Delman pointedly avoids. Imitating Austen, for instance, she declines to relate the words of Frank's proposal. And when Frank writes Jane a passionate letter, Delman withholds it from the reader, describing it as a letter "of such warmth as would make this author blush to copy it down for your perusal."[60] But what, then, is the point of such a retelling? Where is the "clandestine" material promised by Delman's title? Rather than reward her readers' prurience, Delman insists that there *are* no sexual secrets to uncover.

I had reason to expect more from a contemporary retelling of *Emma*, as the twenty-first-century setting should, I thought, offer more opportunities for sexual encounters. After reading Samantha Adkins's *Suspiciously Reserved: A Twist on Jane Austen's* Emma (2012), with Jane's story transported to modern-day Canada, I learned that, sadly, it did not.[61] Despite the title, the revelation of this novel is that there is nothing *at all* suspicious about Jane. She's just a virginal schoolteacher. While Frank is introduced as a ladies' man, he proposes to Jane before there is even any foreplay. He needs his aunt's money to bankroll his career as a musician; hence the secret engagement. Because of the contemporary setting, Frank seems even weaker than in the original, and his need for secrecy harder to credit. Adkins attempts to save Frank from being a complete loser by ultimately revealing a second, nobler reason for sponging off his aunt—he has been supporting an orphanage in Haiti with her money. This revelation could hardly be called sexy. Once again, the twist was on me. Like Delman and Aiken, Adkins seemed to be telling me that my hunt for the secret of Jane and Frank's passion was misguided.

Despite this series of letdowns, I held out hope that the more recent the retelling, the more explicit it was bound to be. I therefore picked up Ronald McGowan's *The Secret Journal of Miss Jane Fairfax: Weymouth to Highbury* (2015) with great optimism. I was further encouraged by the title's promise of secrecy, as well as the back cover blurb: "If you ever wondered exactly what Jane Fairfax, Frank Churchill and the mysterious Mr. Dixon got up to at Weymouth the summer before events in Emma, now is your chance to find out."[62] In this novel there *is* some funny business going on. However, it's not between Jane and Frank, but between Jane and Mr. Dixon, who is "something of a rake."[63] The predatory Mr. Dixon squeezes Jane's thigh under the table, attempts to fondle her when nobody is looking, and tells her lewd anecdotes. Frank benefits by the contrast, as "his face showed that he, at least, felt the impropriety of such remarks."[64] In this version, Frank rescues Jane when she falls off the boat, fleeing Dixon's sexual advances. The sexual antics depart with Dixon to Ireland, where he impregnates the servants and plots to lure Jane into a threesome. Jane narrates all this in a witty and knowing tone, though there is no hint where the virginal and sheltered Jane might have picked up her sexual knowledge. When Frank declares his passion and proposes in a carriage, her acceptance is jocular and the details are omitted: "we collapsed together into helpless laughter, and other things, until the chaise stopped at Guildford."[65] The couple's stolen meetings during their secret engagement are not fleshed out to this reader's satisfaction. Their words are "few enough, and banal enough" when they meet in London.[66] Later, we are told, "the humdrum world of Highbury, I fear, does not lend itself to clandestine romances"[67] When they are briefly alone at Aunt Bates's, Jane insists, "I will not record what passed between the two of us in the few moments of privacy that we now secured."[68] As for Frank's whispered words when they are out walking, "I will not record them. Who wants to be faced, years later, with a word-by-word account of all the embarrassing things that lovers say to each other, however gratifying they may have been at the time?"[69] Presumably, the readers of this novel would. If not, what is the point of the novel-as-secret-journal? While allowing slightly more risqué doings between Jane and Frank than other fan fiction, McGowan's interpretation of Jane's character highlights her sophistication and intelligence rather than her lust.

Having exhausted the stock of contemporary *Emma*-inspired novels, I finally decided to give the first such title a try.[70] According to Austenesque Reviews, Noami Royde Smith's 1940 *Jane Fairfax* was in fact the first *Emma* retelling ever published. Surprisingly, it bore the greatest resemblance to McGowan's, the last. In both novels, Frank's virility is diminished by the displacement of sexual power onto a secondary male character; in this case, Colonel Campbell. Frank, by contrast, becomes the safe, sexually nonthreatening male. As a child, Jane witnesses the predatory Colonel's attempts to seduce the governess; when she is older, Mrs. Campbell discovers her husband's sexual interest in Jane herself. Frank, meanwhile, is introduced as a harmless flirt; "none of the many pretty girls whom he had distinguished had shown any sign of dying of a broken heart on his account."[71] He has even had two marriage proposals rejected. Nonetheless, this early retelling of the pair's romance has more erotic energy than those that follow. There is even something like love at first sight. When their eyes meet, Jane "had the strangest sensation of having known Mr. Churchill for a very long time . . . the idea was so strong that it robbed her of the power to do anything but smile and bend her head as he bowed towards her."[72] This sense of erotic attraction is sustained through various scenes in which Frank and Jane gaze at one another. Even before his proposal, Jane admits to herself her secret attraction to Frank: "It was because he was never out of her thoughts—never far from the secret heart she must not allow to be so foolish—that she had felt the beat of that heart quicken and a warm blush flood her cheek just now."[73]

As in all the subsequent retellings, however, Jane's consent to the secret engagement is not an act of passion. The details of the scene are obscured, but Smith depicts Jane as confused, even coerced. She protests, then admits her love, pressured by Frank's relentless questioning. Jane subsequently renounces the engagement, then renews it during a surprise reunion. Despite her strong feelings, Jane succumbs to the force of Frank's will rather than his sex appeal: "She was his, and knowing it, he was already assuming the right to her obedience; taking it for granted that his wish must be her law, superseding every other obligation."[74] While the couple's desire is evoked in Smith's novel, it is overshadowed by the dynamics of Frank's proposal. Having concluded my survey of the fan fiction, I had to accept the authors' consensus on the secret engagement. Despite the many decades that separated them, all were united in their conclusion: Jane's conduct was *not* motivated by sexual desire, and Frank was *not* sufficiently desirable to inspire it. If these authors shared a project, it was to rehabilitate Jane's reputation, justify her conduct, and deny Frank's erotic appeal. Their need to explain and rationalize reveals their shared perplexity at Austen's pairing of these characters.

Although the fan fiction refused to grant what I desired, a version of the "missing scenes" that would square with *my* erotic interest in the lovers, I had one last hope: the explicit erotic mashups, or "sex-insert fanfiction."[75] Two series, the Clandestine Classics and the Wild and Wanton Editions, combine Austen's original texts with soft-porn additions. I began with the Clandestine Classics *Emma*, coauthored by Katie Blu.[76] In this version, Emma and Knightley are carrying on from the get-go. The graphic sexual encounters between Emma and Knightley made me look forward to Jane and Frank's arrival in town, and all the hot scenes I would finally witness. Imagine my surprise, then, to find that Blu added absolutely nothing to the Jane and Frank subplot. The flirtation between Frank and Emma is made a bit more explicit, but Blu leaves all the Frank and Jane material strictly as is. I then turned to the Wild and Wanton edition of *Emma*, coauthored by Micah Persall.[77] While it is not otherwise identical to Blu's Clandestine Classic, Persall's mashup treats Frank and Jane in exactly the same way. Nothing whatsoever is added. What, I wondered, did these omissions mean? Did the authors find Frank and Jane so unsexy they weren't worth bothering with at all?[78]

This possibility left me feeling chastened and full of self-doubt. *None* of the fans in my survey, not even the professional sex-inserters, supported my feelings about Frank and Jane. I had declared myself a scholar-fan, and immersed myself in the world of fan fiction, because I believed it would provide the delights I could not openly seek in academia. I observed that fans were good readers, interpreting texts critically, while creatively. And if all their work conveyed the same message, that I was *wrong* about Frank and Jane, then it seemed to mean one thing: I was a uniquely bad reader. My attempt to be a scholar-fan had resulted only in a double failure, for

I had failed both as a scholar and as a fan. I wanted to have my way with Austen's novel; to make it yield something that wasn't there. Even the fans had rebuked me.

Yet there was another way to explain Blu and Persall's decision not to write any sex scenes for Frank and Jane: Austen has made them so sexy already, that there is simply nothing to add. This explanation not only accords with my personal, pleasurable experience of *Emma,* but with my close readings of both mashups. As I read, I marked the texts, putting brackets around erotic additions and underlining suggestive phrases that were in the original novel. Increasingly, I found myself having to check Austen's novel to see if certain lines were original or not. I began suspecting everything that seemed risqué, everything overtly physical, was an addition. When I found it was not, I was surprised. In one early, subtle instance in the Clandestine Classics version, Knightley is seen "moving his chair closer" to Emma.[79] Since Blu so often adds these suggestive stage directions, I was sure it was her addition, but it wasn't. A more glaring example is when Emma tells Knightley about the gossip regarding him and Jane: "Mr Knightley was hard at work upon the lower buttons of his thick leather gaiters, and either the exertion of getting them together, or some other cause, brought the colour into his face."[80] At first, I was certain this was one of Blu's insertions, but the words were Austen's. How did I never remark on this moment before? One might argue that Blu diminishes the power of the original details by cramming in too many, and too crass interpolations. Yet these very additions heightened my awareness of erotically charged gestures I might otherwise have overlooked.

Although no explicit erotic content was added to Jane and Frank's story, the expectations raised by the mashups had the same effect in the scenes where they appear. Titillating references to Jane and Frank surprised me afresh, despite my familiarity with the novel. What seemed the most overtly sexed-up language comes from Austen's own pen: allusions to Jane "sucking in the sad poison," her "dangerous pleasure," her "blush of consciousness" and "blush of guilt."[81] The language of the original seems all the more suggestive when juxtaposed with the salacious additions of the mashups. This is the case, certainly, if one reads Jane's blushes the way O'Farrell does, as a sign of arousal. Interestingly, both Blu and Persall make the sexual attraction between Knightley and Emma explicit from the beginning, scrapping any element of suspense or surprise; yet they keep the secret of Frank and Jane's relationship until the moment when Austen herself reveals it. When Jane receives her pianoforte, for instance, the reader of the mashups is no wiser than the reader of *Emma* regarding its origins. Watching Jane at her instrument, Emma observes that "with all the deep blush of consciousness, there had been a smile of secret delight"; that Jane was "apparently cherishing very reprehensible feelings."[82] Blu's and Persell's reluctance to add anything suggests, perhaps, that this scene is sufficiently provocative as it is.

What the erotic mashups alerted me to most was the keen attention Austen pays to Jane's body. Her coloring, her temperature, her eating habits, her headaches: we are constantly made aware of Jane's bodily condition and its vicissitudes—all of which are responses to Frank. The most overtly erotic scene in the novel occurs when Emma finally meets Jane and Frank as acknowledged lovers. Echoing his comments on Jane's complexion earlier in the novel, Frank delineates his lover's sensual attributes for Emma's delectation. "Did you ever see such a skin?" he asks. "Such smoothness! Such delicacy!"[83] He commands Emma to "Look at her. Is not she an angel in every gesture? Observe the turn of her throat. Observe her eyes, as she is looking up at my father"; "I am resolved to have some ornament for the head. Will not it be beautiful in her dark hair?"[84] He reads Jane's response to his words in "her cheek, her smile, her vain attempt to frown. Look at her."[85] He provokes her and she upbraids him; but she does so with a smile. Once again, Austen's depiction of Frank and Jane is so replete with eroticism that there is nothing left to add. At least, it is in *my* reading. Having trawled the fan fiction and scholarship alike for corroboration, I'm aware that mine is the minority position.[86] Yet returning to the text itself, I am more confident that what I sense is there, is there. I *feel* the electricity between Frank and Jane. And I appreciate the brilliance of Austen's craft, which keeps me seeking what she has hidden so provocatively.

As a scholar-fan who didn't get quite what she wanted from the scholars or the fans, I found myself thinking about *Emma*'s first readers, who were neither. What did *they* want from the novel? What did they make of Frank and Jane? In *Reading Austen in America*, Juliette Wells documents responses to the 1816 Philadelphia edition of *Emma,* the first Austen novel to be published in the United States. The anonymous borrower of an extant library copy, who made notes on all the characters, pronounced Emma "intolerable" and Knightley only "tolerable"; yet declared Frank "delightful" and Jane "enchanting."[87] One of the very first readers in this country was positively pro-Frank—and doesn't "delightful" imply attractive? The American reader's view, however, clashes with those of Austen's friends in England. As Austen reports in "Opinions of *Emma,*" Miss Sharp was "dissatisfied with

Jane Fairfax," and Mr. and Mrs. Leigh Perrot "Pitied Jane Fairfax—thought Frank Churchill better treated than he deserved."[88] They seem to anticipate the Frank-haters and Jane-apologists of the next two hundred years. What intrigues me most, however, is Fanny Knight's statement that she "Should like J.F.—if she knew more of her."[89] Austen's niece sensed that there was more to know—a "secret history" to her aunt's characters. Like today's fan fiction writers and readers, scholars, and scholar-fans, Fanny Knight believed that there was something hidden in Highbury. This "more" to the story was felt *then*, and it remains a fertile area to be explored. Perhaps Fanny Knight didn't wish to know more about Jane's sex life, as I do. She might have been satisfied by the *Emma*-inspired novels in my survey and agreed with their assessment of Jane and Frank. As for the reader who wants more steamy material, who knows? If the variation I desire has yet to be written, perhaps it is up to me to write it.[90]

Notes

1. In this essay I am using Sheenagh Pugh's broad definition of fan fiction "as writing, whether official or unofficial, paid or unpaid, which makes use of an accepted canon of characters, settings and plots generated by another writer or writers." *The Democratic Genre: Fan Fiction in a Literary Context* (Brigend: Seren, 2005), 25.
2. I read only book-length, print fiction, which is known as "profic," or professional fiction, written for money, as distinguished from unpaid online "fanfic." Pugh, *Democratic Genre,* 11.
3. Cornel Sandvoss, "The Death of the Reader? Literary Theory and the Study of Texts in Popular Culture," in *Fandom: Identities and Communities in a Mediated World,* ed. Jonathan Gray, C. Lee Harrington, and Cornel Sandvoss, 2nd ed. (New York: New York University Press, 2017), 29–30.
4. John Wyver, "The Many Lovers of Miss Jane Austen," in *Global Jane Austen: Pleasure, Passion, and Possessiveness in the Jane Austen Community,* ed. Lawrence Raw and Robert G. Dryden (New York: Palgrave Macmillan, 2013), 78. While the term "aca-fan" has been attributed to Henry Jenkins, he denies coining the term. "*Textual Poachers,* Twenty Years Later: A Conversation between Henry Jenkins Suzanne Scott," in *Textual Poachers: Television Fans and Participatory Culture* (London: Routledge, 2013), viii.
5. Matthew Hills, *Fan Cultures* (London: Taylor & Francis Group, 2002), Introduction, ProQuest EBook Central.

6. Hills, *Fan Cultures,* Introduction.
7. Hills, *Fan Cultures,* Introduction.
8. James Edward Austen-Leigh, *A Memoir of Jane Austen* (Harmondsworth: Penguin, 1985), 376.
9. Austen-Leigh, *Memoir,* 376.
10. Pugh, *Democratic Genre,* 19.
11. Pugh, *Democratic Genre,* 43.
12. Pugh, *Democratic Genre,* 57.
13. Pugh, *Democratic Genre,* 92.
14. At least in theory. Devoney Looser remarks: "It has a been a critical commonplace to imagine a life for Emma beyond the ending of the novel." Citing fan fiction writer Emma Tennant alongside recognized Austen scholars, Looser opines that "All of these imaginist enterprises put us in a position similar to Emma's—grafting our critical desires onto fictional women." "'The Duty of Woman by Woman': Reforming Feminism in Emma," in *Emma,* by Jane Austen, ed. Alistair M. Duckworth (New York: Bedford/St. Martin's, 2002), 591. Notable here is that Looser treats the work of academic scholars and fan fiction writers as equivalent, whether it be in offering real critical insights or simply projecting their own fantasies onto a text.
15. Diana Birchall, "Eyeing Mrs. Elton: Learning Through Pastiche," *Persuasions On-Line* 30, no. 2 (Spring 2010), http://www.jasna.org/persuasions/on-line/vol30no2/birchall.html.
16. Birchall, "Eyeing Mrs. Elton."
17. Amanda Grange, "Fan Appreciation no. 1: Amanda Grange, Novelist," interview by Gabrielle Malcolm, in *Fan Phenomena: Jane Austen,* ed. Gabrielle Malcolm (Bristol: Intellect Books, 2015), 37.
18. Grange, "Fan Appreciation," 38.
19. Jane Odiwe, "Fan Appreciation no. 3," interview by Gabrielle Malcolm, in *Fan Phenomena,* 105.
20. Odiwe, "Fan Appreciation," 108.
21. Juliet Archer, "Rewriting Austen: Two Interviews with Juliet Archer and Edward H. Carpenter," interview with Lawrence Raw, in *Global Jane Austen,* 277.
22. Edward H. Carpenter, "Rewriting Austen," 279.
23. Alice Chandler, "'A Pair of Fine Eyes': Jane Austen's Treatment of Sex," *Studies in the Novel* 7, no. 1 (spring 1975): 89.
24. Juliette Wells, *Everybody's Jane: Austen in the Popular Imagination* (London: Continuum, 2011), 6.
25. Wells, *Everybody's Jane,* 7.
26. Wells, *Everybody's Jane,* 177.

27. Devoney Looser, "Fifty Shades of Mr. Darcy: A Brief History of X-rated Austen Adaptations" Salon, July 16, 2017, https://www.salon.com/2017/07/16/fifty-shades-of-mr-darcy-a-brief-history-of-x-rated-jane-austen-adaptations/. An expanded version of Looser's article appears in this volume as "Erotic Austen."

28. Looser, "Fifty Shades."

29. Looser, "Fifty Shades."

30. Looser, "Fifty Shades."

31. For a discussion of sex (or its absence) in Austen's fiction generally, see Alice Chandler, "'A Pair of Fine Eyes': Jane Austen's Treatment of Sex"; Jan Fergus, "Sex and Social Life in Jane Austen's Novels" in *Jane Austen in a Social Context*, ed. David Monaghan (Totowa: Barnes & Noble Books, 1981), 66–85; Susan Morgan, "Why There's No Sex in Jane Austen's Fiction," *Studies in the Novel* 19 no. 3 (Fall 1987): 346–356.

32. Rachel Brownstein, *Why Jane Austen?* (New York: Columbia University Press, 2011), 197.

33. Rachel Brownstein, *Why Jane Austen?*, 233.

34. Rachel Brownstein, *Why Jane Austen?*, 234.

35. Jill Heydt-Stevenson, *Austen's Unbecoming Conjunctions: Subversive Laughter, Embodied History* (New York: Palgrave Macmillan, 2005), 27.

36. Heydt-Stevenson, *Unbecoming Conjunctions*, 28.

37. Heydt-Stevenson, *Unbecoming Conjunctions*, 176.

38. Heydt-Stevenson, *Unbecoming Conjunctions*, 177.

39. Judith Wilt, "The Powers of the Instrument: Or Jane, Frank, and the Pianoforte," *Persuasions* 5 (1983), http://www.jasna.org/persuasions/printed/number5/wilt.htm.

40. Wilt, "Powers."

41. Celia Easton, "'The Encouragement I Received': *Emma* and the Language of Sexual Assault," *Persuasions On-Line* 37, no. 1 (winter 2016), http://jasna.org/publications-2/persuasions-online/vol37no1/easton/. Another anti-Frank critic is Patrick McGraw, who sees Frank as a "rash and impulsive" Romeo figure whose "imprudence harms the woman he loves." "'The World Is Not Theirs': The Plight of Jane Fairfax in Emma," *Persuasions* 37 (2015): 221. Lynda A. Hall acknowledges that Frank is attractive and charming, yet "self-serving"; he "gets everything he wants; he has had his fun at the expense of the one he loves the most." "Jane Austen's Attractive Rogues: Willoughby, Wickham, and Frank Churchill," *Persuasions* 18 (1999): 190.

42. Nicholas E. Preus, "Sexuality in Emma: A Case History," *Studies in the Novel* 23, no. 2 (Summer 1991): 202.

43. Preus, "Sexuality," 204.

44. Preus, "Sexuality," 204–5.

45. Preus, "Sexuality," 204.
46. Preus, "Sexuality," 206.
47. Preus, "Sexuality," 210.
48. John Wiltshire also highlights Frank and Jane's secret in his reading of *Emma,* arguing that moments of overheard conversation allow Austen "to thread other strands through a narrative that otherwise channels the consciousness of the main character, and might risk precluding or excluding any knowledge of the intimate lives of others." *The Hidden Jane Austen* (Cambridge: Cambridge University Press, 2014), 129. Wiltshire's focus, however, is not on sex.
49. Mary Ann O'Farrell, *Telling Complexions: The Nineteenth-Century English Novel and the Blush* (Durham: Duke University Press, 1997), 3.
50. O'Farrell, *Telling Complexions,* 9.
51. O'Farrell, *Telling Complexions,* 21.
52. O'Farrell, *Telling Complexions,* 50.
53. Jane Austen, "The History of England," in *Juvenilia,* ed. Peter Sabor (Cambridge: Cambridge University Press, 2006), 176.
54. The list appears to have been last updated in 2019. It does not include online fan fiction.
55. I was not able to obtain a copy of the one example from the 1980s, Charlotte Grey's *The Journal of Miss Jane Fairfax* (1983).
56. Joan Aiken, *Jane Fairfax: The Secret History of the Second Heroine in Jane Austen's Emma* (New York: St. Martin's Griffin, 1990), 176.
57. Aiken, *Jane Fairfax,* 246.
58. Joan Ellen Delman, *Lovers' Perjuries, Or, the Clandestine Courtship of Jane Fairfax and Frank Churchill* (self-published, 2007), 87.
59. Delman, *Lovers' Perjuries,* 62.
60. Delman, *Lovers' Perjuries,* 274.
61. Samantha Adkins, *Suspiciously Reserved: A Twist on Jane Austen's* Emma (self-published, 2012).
62. Ronald McGowan, *The Secret Journal of Miss Jane Fairfax: Weymouth to Highbury* (self-published, 2015).
63. McGowan, *Secret Journal,* 17.
64. McGowan, *Secret Journal,* 33.
65. McGowan, *Secret Journal,* 137.
66. McGowan, *Secret Journal,* 156–7.
67. McGowan, *Secret Journal,* 238.
68. McGowan, *Secret Journal,* 181.
69. McGowan, *Secret Journal,* 241.
70. I did not read Dee Madore's *The Tense Future of Miss Jane Fairfax* (2018), which is a time-travel novel and is available only in digital format.
71. Noami Royde Smith, *Jane Fairfax* (London: Macmillan, 1940), 137.

was no good: I would start automatically writing a synopsis in my head while reading, and would soon toss it aside because it felt "too much like work." I could still read nonfiction for pleasure, especially history, biography, and memoirs; but after pushing through my daily portion of cartoonish entertainment, it was only Jane Austen's novels that gave refreshment to my tired eyes and jaded spirit. In this I was hardly unique, though I did not know it at the time. My obsession was simply that of any true Janeite.

In 1985, *Persuasions,* the literary journal of JASNA, featured a contest for writing in Austen's style. So, steeped in that very thing, I gave them a bit of Miss Bates, and won. The novel experience of hearing the well-known voice of Miss Bates talking to me, dictating what I should say, was such exhilarating fun that I thought I might try a whole book in my best ersatz Austenspeak. How ironic to scorn the hordes of imitators of *Lord of the Rings* and *Harry Potter*, only to become an imitator myself! But so it was. My novel *Mrs. Darcy's Dilemma* was published by a small English press in the 1990s, but this was still too early to benefit from the thunderous enthusiasm following the 1995 Colin Firth BBC dramatization of *Pride and Prejudice*, and my novel wasn't published in the United States until the age of sequels was in full flower, a decade later. By then there were tens, then hundreds, and by now probably thousands of spin-off stories based on the works and characters of Jane Austen. They ranged from imaginative mashups to a whole new romance genre mainly revolving around Lizzy and Darcy.

My own stories were not romances. One reason for this is that my views on Austen and sex are entirely conventional and old-school. I believe she had either no, or very little, sexual experience personally, was not a lesbian, nor did she practice incest with either her sister or a brother. Her writing shows that she undoubtedly knew what it was to love and to feel passion; and I will go so far as to say that I believe her wit extended to distant but unmistakable off-color jokes—the rears and vices, the slit petticoat, the fair but frozen maid. It was not a romantic character or passionate scene that opened my mind to the possibility of writing pastiche. It was my study of the way the novels were written. Studying her influences and her purposes in order to better understand Jane Austen's art, taught me something about her methods, which were precisely planned and deliberate, even when appearing most airy and effortless. Like the unschooled Elizabeth Bennet, educated by roaming in her father's library (and what a great ironic moment when Lady Catherine assumes that the gloriously ignorant Mrs. Bennet must have been "quite a slave" to her daughters' education!), my study was unconventional in mode, but I am convinced was as much of value as many a more formal, academic process (*PP* 164).

It was none other than Mrs. Elton, of all characters, who opened a new door for me, making me realize certain subtleties of her creator's technique. Mrs. Elton is one of the greatest and most maliciously drawn of Austen's comic characters. The man with the best judgment in the book, Mr. Knightley, shows us how to think about her. We are masterfully led by his pronouncing sentence upon her: "Harriet Smith has some first-rate qualities, which Mrs Elton is totally without. An unpretending, single-minded, artless girl—infinitely to be preferred by any man of sense and taste to such a woman as Mrs Elton" (*E* 331). Intrigued, I examined what we know about the character, both before her marriage and afterward. This led to a series of stories, *In Defense of Mrs. Elton*, which initially appeared on the popular Austen-L and Janeites.com literary listservs and was afterwards published as a book. I also took the opportunity to indulge my own fancy to the extent of taking her on a trip to North America, in my novel *Mrs. Elton in America*. (Poor Mr. Elton gets scalped by Indians, and their son grows up to be cabinet minister to Abraham Lincoln.)

While formulating my defense of Mrs. Elton, I began by examining the novel *Emma* with a view to pastiche. This was most productive, for it resulted in my recognizing Jane Austen's subtle ways of framing a character. In all senses of the word "framing," because Jane Austen is not kind to poor Mrs. Elton. I noticed the layered and clever way in which Jane Austen cunningly set about making Mrs. Elton "the daemon of the piece," and saw that if you cut away Austen's editorial presentation, it becomes possible to view Mrs. Elton in quite a different light (*MP* 448).[4]

In presenting Mrs. Elton in the way she does, Jane Austen is deliberately being a "partial [and] prejudiced . . . historian."[5] (Mrs. Elton's misdeeds are social crimes, not actual ones, and she does far less damage than Emma does herself. Calling Miss Fairfax "Jane," urging her to look for a job, and always fishing for compliments, is not in the same league as trying to manipulate people's lives, as Emma does. But Jane Austen paints Mrs. Elton darkly so that Emma might appear light.

Emma is no saint, but in my view, Mrs. Elton is no sinner. What is it that she does that invites such general scorn and dislike? Why does Jane Austen hold her up to such opprobrium? When she and Emma first meet, Mrs. Elton proposes that they unite to form a "sweet little" musical society, and Emma is outraged (E 277). Mrs. Elton keeps talking, as if nervously, trying to impress Emma about her sister's big house, Maple Grove, but Emma just gets more and more disgusted at everything she says. She keeps putting her foot in it, the woman can't say anything right. Yet it didn't seem to me that poor Mrs. Elton was doing anything so terribly wrong. Emma's bad opinion of the new arrival might be one of Emma's own misjudgments, but the narrator indicates that Emma's opinions of Mrs. Elton are in fact right, "exactly so," as Mr. Elton says. "Emma was not required, by any subsequent discovery, to retract her ill opinion of Mrs. Elton. Her observation had been pretty correct. Such as Mrs. Elton appeared to her on this second interview, such she appeared whenever they met again—self-important, presuming, familiar, ignorant, and ill-bred" (E 281). *That* is Jane Austen telling us what she means for us to think. Emma is frequently conceited and presumptuous herself, yet Jane Austen approves of Emma, makes her a heroine who learns and grows, while Mrs. Elton is condemned to stay just the same at the end of the book as at the beginning, obnoxious and reviled.

By this time, I was showing alarming symptoms of identifying with Mrs. Elton—enough to sympathize, defend her, and study her. The reasons for this may hark back to my own hometown, New York City, from where I was transplanted. I recognized in Mrs. Elton a spiritual New Yorker, with characteristics of vigor, brashness, and take-charge action, almost a Regency Bella Abzug. But Mrs. Elton is a transplant, with a transplant's personality, an outsider whose manners are not quite assimilated, a stranger in a strange land. Mrs. Elton comes from Bristol, "the very heart of Bristol" (E 183).

Emma sneers at Mrs. Elton's origins in an arrogant, socially superior way. Why she is so scornful, is a small but important detail. What did it mean to Austen's contemporary readers to know that Mrs. Elton is from Bristol? Bristol in Jane Austen's day was a major port of the slave trade; and *Emma* was written only a few years after the abolition. Jane Austen was pro-abolition, and she had a technique of forwarding her opinions covertly. Mrs. Elton's tradesman father was of only moderate income, not enough to suspect him of profiting from the slave trade. Mrs. Elton lived with, and perhaps kept house for, her lawyer uncle. Lawyers do not rank high socially in Austen. Bingley's sisters look down on the Philipses, John Knightley is anything but "in society," and everyone looks down on the lawyer John Shepherd in *Persuasion.* But coming from a lawyer's household, Mrs. Elton has acquired a certain type of social facility: she knows people, she makes contacts, she's a networker.

I think we can clear Mrs. Elton of direct association with slavery. But Jane Austen has subtly put it in our minds that there may be a taint of slave trade association in her past, as there is of trade in her background. And Mrs.

Elton seems to show defensive consciousness of this. In the famous passage in *Emma* which refers to the slave trade, she tells Jane Fairfax: "Oh! My dear, human flesh! You quite shock me; if you mean a fling at the slave-trade, I assure you, Mr. Suckling was always rather a friend to the abolition" (*E* 300). As Margaret Kirkham observes, "The woman whose fortune has put her in a position to play the part of a patroness is a Bristolian. No wonder she is sensitive about the slave-trade."[6] At the time Mrs. Elton was growing up in Bristol, it was still going on and would have been a vital subject of discussion. Kirkham says, "Bristol had been dissociating itself from the slave trade." And that is what Mrs. Elton does. No wonder she is wild to leave Bristol, and very glad indeed to marry a respectable clergyman. We may see her as uncertain, embarrassed, and therefore defensive and strident. She's ashamed of her family's roots and yet mouths rhetoric that she, socially precarious and pretentious, is certainly not going to follow up on. Bragging in the way people do who are ashamed of their origins, Mrs. Elton is a more complex character than she may at first seem.

It's interesting to consider that Mrs. Elton is the only person, in any Jane Austen novel, to actually speak out in a modern way in favor of women's rights. This is advanced and unexpected in a commonplace woman who is no Mary Wollstonecraft. But when Mr. Weston admits to opening his wife's letters, Mrs. Elton chaffingly criticizes him. She says, "No, indeed, I shall grant you nothing. I always take the part of my own sex. I do indeed. I give you notice. You will find me a formidable antagonist on that point. I always stand up for women" (*E* 306). Unfortunately, she finishes this ringing statement by effacing it with trivia, in a way which is deliberately satirical; Mrs. Elton's fine protestations of women's rights go for nothing. Yet where does she get them? For Mrs. Elton is not a woman to originate an idea of her own.

In her worldly life, she clearly was exposed to ideas. Ideas, anti-abolitionist, and also feminist, were circulating in Bristol. Hannah More kept her school there, and Mary Wollstonecraft lived for a time in Bristol. The winds of change and of women's rights may not yet have reached the stodgy backwater Highbury, but they had obviously penetrated Mrs. Elton's consciousness, making her a more modern woman than Emma. She does not venture to make women's rights statements unadorned; she conceals them in chat about Selina's sheets, for she is no reformer. But the ideas are there. Janet Todd points out, "Considering how disliked the notion of Mary Wollstonecraft was by the 1800s, it seems that any strident feminist rhetoric would have to be placed in the mouths of fools or villains."[7] So it's interesting that this character, with a half-baked mishmash of new ideas in her head, is one of Jane Austen's characters of whom the author most strongly disapproves. Does this mean Jane Austen was against women's rights? She would have thought of them in different terms than we do, but she repeatedly showed instances of the inequities of woman's lot. She used covert demonstrations, not firebrand rhetoric. The fiery speeches, she leaves to be casually flaunted by a mindless character whose flaw is that she does not know how to behave.

But then again, neither does Emma. Mr. Knightley observes that Mrs. Elton may pay attention to Miss Fairfax that no one else will pay her, but it's never mentioned that no one pays attention to Mrs. Elton. Only Mr. Woodhouse has an old-fashioned sense of what is right. "A bride," he says, "is never to be neglected" (*E* 280). But Emma, the doyenne of Highbury society, gives her no warm and friendly welcome, even though she is the vicar's new wife, whom Emma will associate with forever. How cold, and how unforeseeing it is of Emma not to be a little more gracious! Yes, Emma should have formed a musical society with Mrs. Elton! Yes, she should have allowed her to happily show how ice should be used in the Highbury card parties! But Emma was too proud and vain. Later when Mr. Knightley chastises her for being unfeeling to Miss Bates, he reminds her that others "would be entirely guided by your treatment of her"(*E* 375). Yes, and those same people are also led by Emma's bad behavior to Mrs. Elton. So I was not able to dislike Mrs. Elton simply because she has "manners which had been formed in a bad school" (*E* 272). That is not her fault, and I thought her doing her best by her own lights, only to be received with cold civility. For Mrs. Elton is different from anyone else in Highbury. She has spent more time in the great world than Emma. Emma feels threatened by the first approach of this vigorous outside force, and her instinct is to repress and squash her.

By thinking about a minor character in *Emma*, examining the story from her point of view, and cutting away Austen's editorial perspective, we can see that Mrs. Elton's behavior is open to a more sympathetic interpretation. Thus we are enabled to see the story afresh, and gain insight into Austen's methods of genius. Jane Austen purposely makes Mrs. Elton obnoxious, to make Emma seem less obnoxious. Emma is, Jane Austen said, "a heroine whom no one but myself will much like."[8] How better to make her more likeable, than to give her an even more dislikeable foil? Both characters possess unpleasantly controlling qualities; one amends herself, the other does not. In seeing both good growth and bad example, we can face these qualities in ourselves if we have them, as perhaps Jane Austen felt she did herself, in part. We can then reflect on whether we should try to change or not: if we want to be like bad Mrs. Elton or good Emma.

Mrs. Elton is a small study but she is a window into all of Jane Austen, and knowing a small thing well—a little bit of ivory—*can* teach you more about everything: the world in a grain of sand. Can this approach be done with other characters? Could you see *Mansfield Park* from Mrs. Norris's point of view, *Persuasion* from Mrs. Clay's, *Northanger Abbey* from General Tilney's, *Pride and Prejudice* from Wickham's, *Sense and Sensibility* from Lucy Steele's? Why not? We may, as Emma says, make some discoveries.

In the same spirit of fictional inquiry, I recently set about applying pastiche-writing techniques to see how Lady Catherine de Bourgh developed into the formidable monster she was and to think about what Jane Austen was doing in satirizing her, the representative arrogant aristocrat. My "investigation," however, was different from my analysis of Mrs. Elton. Instead of focusing on Jane Austen's methods of portraying Lady Catherine, I tried to imagine what kind of person she might have been before we meet her in *Pride and Prejudice*. What kind of impact might she have had, if more rounded information about her life had been provided? Would she still be a formidable foe to Elizabeth? For Jane Austen presents Lady Catherine as a brilliantly brazen one-sided figure on a brass shield, a larger-than-life character, whose personality is powerful enough to give weight to the plot of the light, bright and sparkling *Pride and Prejudice*.

In order to demonstrate a little of the "fleshing out" process I tried to employ on Lady Catherine, I fear I must break my silence on the subject of sex. For it was in writing about Lady Catherine that a scene concerning sex swam up, unbidden, from the depths of my perverse unconscious. This scene occurs on the wedding night of Darcy and Elizabeth, but instead of taking place in their bedroom, it is in Lady Catherine's, as she recalls her own wedding night:

> *Images rose up in her mind, unbidden. Sir Lewis had emerged from the closet, his knees knobbly in his nightshirt, and he clambered onto the cold satin sheets. Lady Catherine lay stolidly in the center of the bed and did not move. "My dear, will you make room for me?" he bleated timorously. "Certainly not,'" she answered. "Do not you know that a gentleman never approaches his lady on the wedding-night, or indeed, ever, until and unless he is invited? And I do not recollect giving you the invitation."*

> *A little later, following a hint from her brother that if Sir Lewis died with the marriage unconsummated, unknown heirs might appear to challenge her widow's*

possession of Rosings, Lady Catherine, reluctantly and with infinite distaste, allowed Sir Lucas to have his fumbling way; the puling sickly Anne was the result; and the father faded away soon after, like a gentleman spider eaten by his lady, and not regretted by her in the slightest. Now, she lies alone: As a full, majestic, bright, jubilant winter moon rose at midnight over Pemberley, it rose over Rosings too; but it only gleamed in on an aged widow in her own majestically caparisoned bed, which reflected white in the moonlight, like a galleon. Lying awake, Lady Catherine allowed her thoughts to drift to her benighted nephew and his bride. Would the new Mrs. Darcy be likely to know how a lady managed her husband on the wedding night? Humph! she thought. That coarse girl, how could a knowledge of proper behavior be expected from her? Why, they were probably behaving like barn-yard animals at this very moment . . .

No. She would not think about such things. Resolutely she turned over, away from the window, and closed her eyes, to sleep the dreamless and undisturbed sleep of the just.

Having thus daringly and only half-willingly arrived at the topic of Jane Austen and sex, I will not attempt to imagine any more such scenes in the bedrooms of Jane Austen's characters, or of the author herself. That would be rude in every sense; and I would choose to maintain decorum in my speculations that take me into the world of continuation and pastiche, a world in which I have made some discoveries, and feel most at home.

I will only go so far as to observe that Jane Austen made many approaches to the subject herself, from which it is possible to make deductions about her own feelings, and how they affected her moral and creative choices. For Austen certainly knew what it was to love, and to feel passion. Were her portrayals of people who experienced "the pleasing plague" (*MP* 292) gained only by distant observation? She knew the ungovernable passions of a bouncing teenager like Lydia, and how she and Wickham "were only brought together because their passions were stronger than their virtue" (*PP* 312). Or Maria Bertram, whose "high spirit and strong passions" were made known to her father "only in their sad result" (*MP* 464). Women, in Jane Austen, who give into their passions, are punished severely for it. Maria, "who had destroyed her own character" (*MP* 463), was sent into a "No Exit" exile with Mrs. Norris; while Lydia's fate is hinted at: "with such an husband her misery was considered certain" (*PP* 309).

As a young woman, the Jane Austen we see in her letters flirted and had crushes just like girls today. The difference is that if nowadays girls indulge their passions and make sexual experiments, it's commonplace, and largely free of danger; loss of virginity is unlikely to ruin anybody's life. Future livelihood and reputation are unaffected, and marriage does not unavoidably produce either enormous families or death in childbed. The eighteenth century may have been a licentious age, but mostly pertaining to the aristocracy and the poor, not for a gentry class clergyman's daughter. For Jane Austen the moral rules were absolute and whatever passion burned she would not, could not risk a sexual coupling, the results of which might make her a social outcast. Tradition dictates that she was disappointed in love—Tom Lefroy cut off from her, a story about a lost love at the seaside, a few other dim possibilities—but it is unknown at what point in life she knew her disappointment would be permanent, and she would be as Harriet in *Emma* exclaims: "But still you will be an old maid—and that's so dreadful!" (*E* 85). In that same novel is Austen's study of Miss Bates, as poignant an old maid as can be found in fiction. When she created Miss Bates, Jane Austen had already resigned herself to the certainty that she herself would be of her unmerry band—yet Miss Bates is nothing if not gallantly merry. Jane herself joined her sister, whose fiancé had died, and they were left to endure together stoically. But Jane had a nature different than Cassandra's; a happier temper, humor that could never be entirely repressed, and no wish to "dwell on guilt and misery" (*MP* 461). Reasonable and just, she refused to let disappointment ruin her life: "if one scheme of happiness fails, human nature turns to another; if the first calculation is wrong, we make a second better: we find comfort somewhere," she wrote (*MP* 46). Her writing provided another "hold upon happiness." Jane Austen must have been happy, giving her heroines the joy of perfect unions, each perfectly tailored to the heroine in her own way (just as all her fairies had faces of their own) and if it was compensation for what she herself missed in this life, happy marriage with the benefit of united bodies as well as souls, then her loss was to the benefit and joy of future generations.

Notes

1. Jane Austen, April 1, 1816, in *Letters of Jane Austen*, vol. 2, ed. Edward, Lord Brabourne (Richard Bentley and Son, 1884), 350.
2. Jane Austen, *Pride and Prejudice*, vol. 2 of *The Oxford Illustrated Jane Austen*, ed. R. W. Chapman, 3rd ed. (Oxford: Oxford University Press, 1933 repr. 1988), 57. Subsequent references to the novel will appear in parentheses with the abbreviation *PP.*

3. Jane Austen, *Emma*, vol. 4 of *The Oxford Illustrated Jane Austen*, 355. Subsequent references to the novel will appear in parentheses with the abbreviation *E*.

4. Jane Austen, *Mansfield Park*, vol. 3 of *The Oxford Illustrated Jane Austen*, 448. Subsequent references to the novel will appear in parentheses with the abbreviation *MP*.

5. Jane Austen, *Minor Works*, vol. 6 of *The Oxford Illustrated Jane Austen*, ed. R. W. Chapman (Oxford: Oxford University Press, 1954 repr. 1988), 158.

6. Margaret Kirkham, *Jane Austen: Feminism and Fiction* (Brighton: Harvester, 1983), 132.

7. Janet Todd, email to author, August 24, 2007.

8. James Edward Austen-Leigh, *A Memoir of Jane Austen,* ed. R.W. Chapman (Oxford: Clarendon, 1967), 157.

Part Three

Austen on Stage, on Screen, and Online

Chapter Eight

In Search of
Colin Firth's Bum

Nora Nachumi

The title of this essay refers to the hours I spent searching the 1995 BBC *Pride and Prejudice* for the above-referenced bum, a derriere I was convinced I had seen in viewings past.[1] Unfortunately, I was mistaken. No such shot exists; what I was remembering was an amalgamation of several scenes in which Darcy, as played by Colin Firth, *should* have been naked. Firth himself reported that, in one scene at least, he would have bared all had the BBC allowed the original screenplay to be filmed unrevised.[2] Instead, when Firth's Darcy dives into a lake to cool his passion for Elizabeth Bennet, he does it clothed. That scene, which is not in the novel, helped ignite "Darcymania," an obsession so potent that it has itself become the subject of novels and films. No such response greeted the 1995 adaptations of *Persuasion* or *Sense and Sensibility* or Patricia Rozema's 1999 adaptation of *Mansfield Park*. Compared to these films, the 1995 adaptation of Austen's third novel is libido on toast. Drawing over eleven million viewers in Britain alone, the mini-series raises a question: how does one translate the erotic energy in Austen's novels to screen?

To some, the question might seem preposterous; one might as well ask how to transform iron to gold. Charlotte Brontë found little ardor in Austen's novels. Writing to George Henry Lewes, she describes *Pride and Prejudice* as a "carefully cultivated garden, with neat borders and delicate flowers; but . . . no open country, no bonny beck."[3] To W. S. Williams, she declares that the "Passions" were unknown to Austen, who was "a complete and most sensible lady, but a rather incomplete, and rather insensible (not senseless) woman."[4] Notwithstanding her genius, Bronte seems, in regard to Jane Austen, to have been a bit narrow-minded and insensible herself. Passion is present in Austen's novels, but it is not expressed in the teeth-gnashing, head-banging mode of a Rochester or Heathcliff. Her characters rarely—if ever—voice the depth and intensity of their desires. And that is what makes her novels so sexy. The erotic energy in Austen's novels requires repression; it is generated in the gaps between what the protagonists feel and what they can say or do about it given the social mores with which they live.

This poses a challenge when it comes to translating the erotic energy in Austen's novels to screen. In the novels, Austen's narrative voice makes the protagonists' private experience clear to the reader. With the exception of *Clueless*, however, film adaptations of Austen's novels eschew voice over narration. Instead, they use a variety of cinematic techniques to depict the thoughts and emotions that Austen's protagonists attempt to repress. Often, however, this comes at a cost. A look at the strategies employed by the 1995 adaptations of *Persuasion, Sense and Sensibility*, and *Pride and Prejudice* as well as the 1999 *Mansfield Park*, demonstrates the difficulty of translating sexual tension in the novels to screen. Of course, no adaptation could, or should, be "just like the book." Of the four, however, only the strategy employed by *Pride and Prejudice* succeeds in conveying the full force of the protagonists' attraction without substantially altering the novel's concern with the nature and dangers of desire itself.

6•

Austen wrote *Persuasion* as she was dying and, of the six novels, it most fully embodies a sense of physical longing. Until the end of the story Anne Elliot disguises her love for Wentworth—whose proposal she had rejected almost eight years before the story begins. She is, however, acutely aware of his physical presence. Whenever Wentworth is near, Anne's attention is focused, not only on his words but on the sound of his voice; she derives meaning from his facial expressions and the way that he moves. When he gives up his seat at the piano so she can play, his "cold politeness and ceremonious grace, were worse than anything."[5] Anne is convinced that he no longer cares; nevertheless, she remains attuned to even the subtlest gestures. Although determined to disguise her emotions, she is always aware of his presence and with whom he is talking. His body is like a book she cannot put down.

Throughout the novel Anne's thoughts and emotions are linked to her physical sensations. Despite her best efforts, she cannot stop her body from responding to Wentworth's. Upon discovering that she might see him again, for example, she is forced to "seek the comfort of cool air for her flushed cheeks"; as she strolls through her favorite grove, she imagines that, in a few weeks, he might walk there as well (*P* 25). Even projected, his presence arouses emotions that incite a physical response. Once Wentworth arrives, as John Wiltshire observes, Anne's struggles "to come to terms with the momentary encounters and challenges of his presence are represented as moral or ethical struggles to be 'rational' or 'sensible' but also as 'nervous' excitements, physiological responses of energies half repressed but now aroused and heightened in blushes and agitations."[6] When Wentworth relieves Anne of the nephew who clings to her back her "sensations on the discovery" are so strong as to render her "perfectly speechless" (*P* 80). Her body takes over, manifesting in a physical sense the feelings she cannot say aloud. It is also Anne's body that tells him she returns his affection when, accompanied by her cousin, she meets the captain at the end of the novel. As he stands irresolute, undecided whether to stay or pass on, Anne commands herself to receive his look, "and not repulsively. The cheeks which had been pale now glowed and the movements which had hesitated were decided. He walked by her side" (*P* 242). Neither can speak openly in public but their body language is clear.

Written by Nick Dear and directed by Roger Mitchell, the 1995 film adaptation of *Persuasion* does not grant us similar access to Anne's private thoughts and sensations; its failure to do so speaks to the difficulty of finding a cinematic equivalent to Austen's narrative style.[7] In the novel, Anne's subjective experience organizes the text. "Especially after the cold distanced beginning to the novel . . . the intimacy with which Austen approaches Anne's consciousness appears to be something extraordinary" observes Marilyn Butler.[8] One way this is accomplished is through Austen's use of free indirect speech, which, as Norman Page remarks, provides "insight into Anne's consciousness" in a manner that is the "fictional equivalent of a dramatic soliloquy."[9] Free indirect discourse renders Anne's thoughts; it creates a sense of interiority that works to align our perspective with hers. Her physical responsiveness to Wentworth's proximity is the end result of an interior turmoil that we have witnessed directly.

The film, in contrast, works in reverse. As viewers we obtain information about Anne's thoughts and emotions through external signs. However, the necessity of concealing her feelings renders Anne less than entirely transparent. We see this during her first encounter with Wentworth, when the camera signals her panic by zooming in on her face. Except for a slight widening of the eyes, her expression stays neutral. Only a shot of her hand, slowly tightening its grip on a chair, signals her intensely emotional response to the scene. The narrative, in contrast, conveys Anne's subjective experience of the encounter: "her eye half met Wentworth's; a bow, a curtsey passed; she heard his voice—he talked to Mary, said all that was right; said something to the Miss Musgroves, enough to mark an easy footing; the room seemed full— full of persons and voices—but a few minutes ended it" (*P* 59). Austen's use of free indirect discourse makes Anne's confusion—her inability to do anything but feel her emotions—perfectly clear. At the same time, the rhythm of the narrator's voice creates a sense of urgency, and in doing so, encourages us to experience a sympathetic response to Anne's tension. Nothing so dramatic occurs in the film.

Instead, the film accords primacy to the externals. In the novel, Anne's mousy demeanor functions as a temporary mask, concealing her inner beauty to those who are as imperceptive as they are self-involved. Wentworth's ability to desire Anne for her character—for her mind and her heart—is what makes him a hero. And because we see Wentworth almost exclusively through Anne, we forgive those instances when he treats her coldly. In the first two thirds of the film, however, we don't see this Wentworth but a man whose behavior towards Anne suggests profound disapproval and a deep-rooted dislike. As a result, Anne's desire for him in the film seems more masochistic— and less understandable—than it does in the novel.

&◦

The opposite is true in the 1995 adaptation of *Sense and Sensibility*.[10] In the novel the heroines marry men who are simply not hot. Elinor's yearning for Edward Ferrars—who is neither handsome nor charming—is made comprehensible through Elinor's private appreciation of his character. Conveying Colonel Brandon's suitability as a partner to the seventeen-year-old Marianne is an even more difficult task, and its success debatable. What is a poor filmmaker to do? Through the strategic use of horses and a willingness to revise the men who ride them the film turns up the heat. Its success, however, creates a conundrum: granted, no movie can—or should—be "just like the book." But in this case the difference is significant because Austen's novel warns against embracing romantic cliches. We see this most clearly, perhaps, at the end of the novel, when the narrator remarks on Willoughby's "incivility in surviving [the] loss" of Marianne.[11] Romantic conventions, the narrator asserts, require that he at least "[flee] from society, or contract an habitual gloom of temper, or [die] from a broken heart" (*SS* 379). Austen's comment not only calls attention to the way novels shape unrealistic expectations about "true love" but demonstrate how they also can deflate them.

Written by Emma Thompson and directed by Ang Lee, the film adaptation of *Sense and Sensibility* actually celebrates the conventions of romance that the novel condemns. The book ends as it begins, by foregrounding the relationship of Elinor and Marianne. The movie, in contrast, concludes with the wedding of Brandon and Marianne and—in direct opposition to the novel—emphasizes Willoughby's sorrow. In the book, we are told, Willoughby "lived to frequently enjoy himself" (*SS* 379). Thompson's screenplay concludes with Willoughby on a white horse, "on the far edge of the frame," watching the wedding procession making "its glorious way from the church."[12] "As we draw back further still," Thompson writes, Willoughby "slowly pulls the horse around and moves off in the opposite direction."[13]

That Willoughby rides the white horse of a hero suggests that Thompson clearly understands Austen's intentions regarding the way Willoughby ought to appear (in one instance, the screenplay describes him as "looking about as virile as his horse").[14] However, the fact that Brandon's black charger is equally virile points to a crucial difference between the novel and film. "Making the male characters effective was one of the biggest problems" in adapting the novel, Thompson reports.[15] "Edward and Brandon are quite shadowy and absent for long periods."[16] In a movie that ends up celebrating romance, this is a serious problem.

Thompson's solution was to "keep [the men] present even when they're off screen."[17] In the movie, Edward is played by Hugh Grant, a man Thompson describes as "repellently gorgeous."[18] As Colonel Brandon, Alan Rickman is definitely more macho than anyone who wears a flannel waistcoat should be. He is frequently filmed with a gun or on a horse and his disheveled appearance as Marianne lies ill out-Byron's Willoughby: "Give me an occupation," he murmurs to Elinor, "or I shall run mad."[19] After this, the screenplay asserts, "[h]e is dangerously quiet."[20] This is much sexier than Austen's Brandon who, "with a readiness that seemed to speak the occasion, and the service prearranged in his mind . . . offered himself as the messenger who should fetch Mrs. Dashwood" (*SS* 311).

Indeed, the movie works hard to create the impression that Brandon is the dark horse in the race for Marianne's hand. To do this the screenplay revises the novel so that Brandon's later actions mirror Willoughby's earlier ones. Both ride powerful horses, both carry an incapacitated Marianne through the rain; and both read poetry to her with heartfelt conviction. Austen, in contrast, is notoriously reluctant to describe love scenes of any kind. In the novel, the courtship of Marianne and Brandon is described thus: "[w]ith such a confederacy against her, with a knowledge of his goodness, with a conviction of his fond attachment to herself, which at last, though long after it was observable to everybody else, burst on her—what could she do?" (*SS* 378). Thompson's movie works, but it does so by celebrating the very tropes that Austen's novel refutes.

&◆

Patricia Rozema's adaptation of *Mansfield Park* goes even further; this movie entirely ignores the novel's ambivalence regarding romantic and sexual desire.[21] The novel tells the story of Fanny Price, a perceptive, feeling young woman whose passive demeanor belies her great moral strength. For most of the novel, Fanny conceals her love for her cousin Edmund, watching in pain as he courts Mary Crawford, a woman whose charming exterior masks her moral corruption. Along the way, she challenges the authority of her dictatorial uncle, Sir Thomas Bertram, by rejecting a proposal from Mary's rich brother, Henry. Ultimately Fanny's refusal of Henry is justified when he becomes embroiled in an adulterous affair with Edmund's sister, Maria. Mary's casual response to her brother's misconduct horrifies Edmund, who, after a suitable length of time, bestows his affections on Fanny, where they belong.

And so concludes the least satisfying union in Austen's six novels. For *Mansfield Park* has the task of making sexual desire understandable, attractive, and yet—in the end—unappealing if incompatible with virtue. Fanny Price can't hold a candle to Mary in terms of allure. The contrast is evident in their methods of riding. Fanny learns on an old grey pony. "Ah! Cousin," she says, "when I remember how much I used to dread riding, what terrors it gave me to hear it talked of as likely to do me good. . . . and then think of the kind pains you took to reason and persuade me out of my fears, and convince me that I should like it after a little while, and feel how right you proved to be."[22] Mary Crawford, in contrast, is an excellent horsewoman: "active, fearless, and though rather small, strongly made, she seemed formed for a horsewoman; and to the pure genuine pleasure of the exercise, something was probably added in Edmund's attendance and instructions, and something more in the conviction of very much surpassing her sex in general by her early progress, to make her very unwilling to dismount" (*MP* 67). Intentionally or not, these passages link learning to ride to more amorous pursuits. As one might expect, Edmund enjoys riding with Mary so greatly that he neglects Fanny, who sits at home waiting for her own turn on the horse.

In Rozema's film, Fanny is an excellent horsewoman and Edmund's attraction to her is evident from the start. In one early scene, Fanny and Edmund run hand in hand to the stables. "The two of them ride full gallop," the screenplay instructs: "Edmund rides splendidly. Fanny, riding in a side saddle, bounces around a bit too much but the spirit is willing. Slow motion on their flushed cheeks, on Edmund's thighs gripping the horse, on the horse's nostrils, on the wind in the trees."[23] When they finally slow down, Edmund compliments Fanny on her leap and her wild constructions; "Oh yes," she replies. "I'm a wild beast. I'm sure Sir Thomas would agree."[24]

Rozema thus begins an analogy that she extends through the film that equates Fanny, as a marriageable young woman, with the animals and the slaves on Sir Thomas's plantation. In what is probably the most overt example in the film, she has Fanny flee Sir Thomas (who has just proposed a ball in her honor) for the stable. "I'll not be sold off like one of your father's slaves," she declares to Edmund.[25] Then, after borrowing Edmund's saddle, she mounts her horse and charges off, astride, through the rain. Poor Mary Crawford does not stand a chance. Independent and attractive, Rozema's Fanny is fully embodied and Edmund, fortunate. On screen, at least, he can marry a virtuous woman and still experience erotic desire.

❧

So can Fitzwilliam Darcy in the 1995 adaptation of *Pride and Prejudice*.[26] Like the film versions of *Sense and Sensibility* and *Mansfield Park*, the miniseries effectively conveys the intense attraction between the protagonists. Unlike them, however, it does so without sacrificing Austen's concerns with the nature and dangers of erotic desire. Its success stems, in part, from the novel which, when compared to the others, is the most amenable to adaptation in this regard. For example, the dangers of acting on passion ungoverned by reason are illustrated most clearly by Lydia Bennet. Unlike the two Elizas or Maria Bertram, her story is not tragic; instead, it is sad and a little absurd. Elizabeth Bennet, moreover, is neither mousy nor quiet. Unlike Elinor Dashwood, Fanny Price, or Anne Elliot, she does not need to conceal her love for the hero. For the first half of the novel, she detests Darcy, and she assumes he dislikes her as well. His attraction to her is certainly grudging. His initial proposal of marriage, coming as it does in the middle of the novel, dwells on "her inferiority—of it being a degradation—of the family obstacles that judgment had always opposed to inclination."[27] What the protagonists must learn before they can be together is that they themselves have faults; their union is ideal not because they are well suited for each other initially, but because they make each other better people by the end of the novel.

Motivation to change stems from the sexual tension between Elizabeth and Darcy. They are easily the two most intelligent people in the novel and their interactions are characterized by a sophisticated level of exchange that sets them apart. As Darcy informs Elizabeth when she plays the piano at the home of his aunt, Lady Catherine de Bourgh, "we neither of us perform to strangers" (*PP* 176). This comment, occurring before Darcy's initial proposal, declares them alike. It is an expression of intimacy, one that acknowledges that he regards Elizabeth as a complex human being, rather than the simple object that he would like her to be.

In this sense, Darcy's comment also indicates the primary thrust and parry between his gaze and Elizabeth's. In scene after scene, they attempt to define each other based on what they observe. This dynamic is especially apparent when Darcy refuses to join Elizabeth and Miss Bingley in taking a turn about the drawing room at Netherfield Park. As he explains, he prefers to watch: "You either choose this method of passing the evening because you are in each other's confidence and have secret affairs to discuss, or because you are conscious that your figures appear to the greatest advantage in walking—if the first, I should be completely in your way; and if the second, I can admire you much better as I sit by the fire" (*PP* 56). Darcy here claims an interpretive, authorial power that is explicitly tied to his role as an observer.

And this is where it gets interesting, for Elizabeth refuses to be defined by his gaze. Instead, she claims her own interpretive power. When Miss Bingley refuses her suggestion that they ignore Mr. Darcy, Elizabeth enters into the dialogue, a move requiring Darcy to account for himself. For a moment, his gaze is turned inward. "My temper I dare not vouch for" he admits, "my good opinion once lost is lost forever" (*PP* 58). "That is a failing indeed!" cries Elizabeth. "Implacable resentment is a shade in a character. But you have chosen your fault well.—I really cannot laugh at it. You are safe from me" (*PP* 58). Darcy, however, is anything but safe. In claiming her right to laugh at those who surround her, Elizabeth asserts her right to have a mind of her own. The recognition is perilous to his assumptions; he is relieved when their dialogue ceases, for "he began to feel the danger of paying Elizabeth too much attention" (*PP* 58).

Figure 8.7. A representative sampler courtesy of a Google search for "Romance Novel Covers" (February 26, 2022).

he trying to mask his emotions. As a result, we are more intimate with Darcy than is Elizabeth.

The miniseries' ingenious use of visual perspective—and not just the perspective that Darcy is eye candy—also helps to explain why the series is sexy. What is arousing is not Colin Firth's bum, but Darcy's desire for Elizabeth Bennet. "In the world of romance," Hopkins asserts, "women authors have delighted in creating male characters who crave the love of the heroines with an intensity which, we may fear, real men rarely experience."[38] For Hopkins, it is the intensity of Darcy's love for Elizabeth that fuels our libidos because it "is that need that we most want to believe."[39] Is that the case? Would we be so aroused if someone in real life craved our love so intensely? Hopkins suggests that we would if that person were like Darcy. However, that assertion raises another question: why do we care about Darcy's passionate desire for someone who isn't us? The answer calls attention to a crucial difference between the adaptation and Austen's original. In the novel, the reader's perspective primarily is aligned with Elizabeth's. In the miniseries, the contrast between different points of view is what generates heat.

Take, for example, the sequence of shot-reverse shots depicting an early exchange between Elizabeth and Darcy at Lucas Lodge (Figures 8.8 and 8.9). While Darcy is speaking, the camera frames Elizabeth; we look down on her from just behind his right shoulder. We look up at Darcy from Elizabeth's left shoulder when she replies. These shifting perspectives turn up the heat by

Figures 8.8 and 8.9. Darcy and Elizabeth converse awkwardly at Lucas Lodge, *Pride and Prejudice* (BBC, 1995).

transporting the viewer into the scene. We are shadows, or ghosts, phantoms who know that she sees him as insufferably aloof. We also know that he is transfixed by her face and—given his height—perhaps by the ample view of her décolletage as well.

The use of multiple perspectives also generates tension by delaying the viewer's gratification. Because we know more about Darcy than does Elizabeth, we watch her misread him before he proposes. We know what is in the letter before she reads it, and we know he continues to love her when she thinks otherwise. Likewise, we know that Elizabeth's feelings have changed long before Darcy is in on the secret. This extra knowledge is thrilling, but it makes us more passive than does the book. By aligning our point of view with Elizabeth's, Austen's narrative encourages us—or at least first-time readers—to misjudge characters, events, and exchanges that we have encountered in the first part of the book. It also requires us, like Elizabeth, to become better readers. The miniseries does not make us work nearly as hard. Because we are privy to many perspectives, we know what could and should happen before it occurs. If we accept the premise that the camera works to make us voyeurs, then what we end up with is a miniseries that ups the ante by acting the tease.

Perception, nevertheless, is the means to fulfillment. In both the novel and miniseries, love is kindled not by breasts or bare bums, but by the interior qualities Elizabeth and Darcy develop and discover in each other through close observation. Darcy's scrutiny is triggered by his reluctant-yet-powerful sexual attraction to Elizabeth. "No sooner had [Darcy] made it clear to himself and his friends that she had hardly a good feature in her face, than he began to find it was rendered uncommonly intelligent by the beautiful expression in her dark eyes" (23). He also admits "her figure to be light and pleasing" and is "caught" by the "easy playfulness of her manners" (23). Elizabeth's reevaluation of Darcy, in contrast, begins during his absence. By the time she meets him at Pemberley, she is aware that she has misjudged him and is able to observe him anew. This may be true in the series as well. Elizabeth, after all, is not privy to those scenes with Darcy and the white shirt, scenes that don't exactly encourage rational thought. However, to viewers those particular scenes are essential, for they show us the sincerity, vulnerability as well as the passion that Elizabeth eventually discovers—and responds to—under Darcy's reserve.

The attention the miniseries pays to perception suggests why the 1995 BBC *Pride and Prejudice* outshines the other adaptations considered here in translating the erotic energy in Austen's novels to screen. Sexual tension in Austen's novels often is generated by the disparity between the protagonists' private, or internal, experience and how they must appear and behave in the public realm. With the exception of Emma Woodhouse, Austen's heroines must disguise their feelings about the men they love or risk disaster, like Marianne Dashwood.[40] The 1995 adaptation of *Persuasion* tries to replicate this struggle, but it does not find an equivalent means to convey the overwhelming intensity of Anne Elliott's internal sensations. *Sense and Sensibility* does not even attempt to convey Elinor's desire for Edward Ferrars or Colonel Brandon's suitability for Marianne as Austen depicts them. Instead, it alters the male leads and, in doing so ends up celebrating the conventions of romance that the novel condemns. Rozema's *Mansfield Park* goes a step farther. By transforming Fanny Price into an exceedingly attractive proto-feminist writer, the adaptation lessens not only the degree of Mary Crawford's allure but the significance of Edmund's decision against her. *Pride and Prejudice*, in contrast, leaves its protagonists comparatively intact. Instead, it gives us a broader, more fluid perspective than we have in the novel. The difference between our understanding of Elizabeth and Darcy and their view of each other generates tension that is akin—though not identical—to the erotic energy in Austen's novel.[41] In both, the characters' mutual disclosure is our release.

Notes

1. The discussion of *Pride and Prejudice* in this chapter began as a talk I gave at a one-day conference entitled "*The BBC* Pride and Prejudice, *Reflections Around a Much-Loved Production,*" at Chawton House, England, September 5, 2015. It then was incorporated into an essay, cowritten with Stephanie Oppenheim, entitled "Sex, Love and Austen: Was It Good For You?" in *Persuasions Online*, 38 no. 1. https://jasna.org/publications-2/persuasions-online/vol38no1/nachumi/. Reprinted with permission.
2. "'BBC Axed Nude Scene': Colin Firth," January 23, 2015, https://toronto-sun.com/2015/01/23/bbc-axed-nude-scene-colin-firth; Becky Fuller, "Colin Firth Talks About His Infamous Lake Scene and Both His Darcy Alter-Egos," *4Your Excitement,* January 23, 2015, https://www.4ye.co.uk/2015/01/colin-firth-talks-about-his-infamous-lake-scene-and-both-his-darcy-alter-egos/;

"Colin Firth's Mr. Darcy 'was meant to be naked,'" *The Guardian,*
October 9, 2013, https://www.theguardian.com/media/2013/oct/09/
colin-firth-mr-darcy-naked-pride-prejudice-bbc/.

3. Bronte, Charlotte, extract from letter 12 January 1848 to G.H. Lewes,
"Charlotte Brontë on Jane Austen, 1848, 1850," in *Jane Austen: The Critical
Heritage Volume 1 1811–1870,* ed. B. C. Southam, Critical Heritage Series
(London: Routledge, 2003), 139, https://search-ebscohost-com.ezproxy.cul.
columbia.edu/login.aspx?direct=true&AuthType=ip&db=e025xna&AN=8908
9&site=ehost-live&scope=site.

4. Bronte, Charlotte, extract from letter 12 April 1850 to W. S. Williams, in
Southam, vol. 1, 141.

5. Jane Austen, *Persuasion,* 1818, *The Oxford Illustrated Jane Austen,* vol. 5, ed. R.
W. Chapman, 3rd ed. (1933, rpt. Oxford: Oxford University Press, 1988), 96.
Subsequent quotations are taken from this edition and will appear in paren-
thetical citations with the abbreviation *P.*

6. John Wiltshire, "*Mansfield Park, Emma, Persuasion*" in *The Cambridge
Companion to Jane Austen,* ed. Edward Copeland and Juliet McMaster
(Cambridge: Cambridge University Press, 1997), 77.

7. *Persuasion,* screenplay by Nick Dear, directed by Roger Mitchell, with Amanda
Root, Ciaran Hinds, Fiona Findlay (United Kingdom: BBC Films; Toul,
France: Millesime Productions; Boston: WGBH/Mobile Masterpiece Theatre;
Culver City, CA: Sony Pictures, 1995).

8. Marilyn Butler, *Jane Austen and the War of Ideas* (Oxford: Clarendon Press,
1990), 277.

9. Norman Page, *The Language of Jane Austen* (New York: Basil Blackwell, 1972),
131.

10. *Sense and Sensibility,* screenplay by Emma Thompson, directed by Ang Lee,
with Emma Thompson, Alan Rickman, Kate Winslet, and Hugh Grant
(United States: Columbia Pictures, 1995).

11. Jane Austen, *Sense and Sensibility,* 1811, *The Oxford Illustrated Jane Austen,*
vol. 1, 379. Subsequent quotations are taken from this edition and will appear
in parenthetical citations with the abbreviation *SS.*

12. Thompson, Emma, *The Sense and Sensibility Screenplay & Diaries* (New York:
Newmarket Press, 1995), 202.

13. Thompson, *Screenplay,* 202.

14. Thompson, *Screenplay,* 100.

15. Thompson, *Screenplay,* 269.

16. Thompson, *Screenplay,* 269.

17. Thompson, *Screenplay,* 269.

18. Thompson, *Screenplay,* 121.

19. Thompson, *Screenplay,* 181. Also see https://youtu.be/mWwA74j1MEw.

20. Thompson, *Screenplay,* 181.

21. *Mansfield Park,* written and directed by Patricia Rozema, with Frances O'Connor, Jonny Lee Miller, Embeth Davidtz and Alessandro Nivola (United States: Miramax, 1999).

22. Jane Austen, *Mansfield Park,* 1814, *The Oxford Illustrated Jane Austen,* vol. 3, 27. Subsequent references to the novel will appear in the body of the essay with the abbreviation *MP.*

23. Patricia Rozema, *Mansfield Park: A Screenplay* (New York: Talk Miramax Books, 2000), 31–32.

24. Rozema, *Screenplay,* 32. See also https://youtu.be/xyWPpT-TuIs.

25. Rozema, *Screenplay,* 63.

26. *Pride and Prejudice,* written by Andrew Davies, produced by Sue Birtwistle, directed by Simon Langton, with Jennifer Ehle and Colin Firth (London: BBC Productions, 1995).

27. Jane Austen, *Pride and Prejudice,* 1812, *The Oxford Illustrated Jane Austen,* vol. 2, 189. Subsequent references to the novel will appear in the body of the essay with the abbreviation *PP.*

28. The question of when Elizabeth becomes sexually attracted to Darcy is a matter of considerable debate. See Elaine Bander, "Neither Sex, Money nor Power: Why Elizabeth Finally Says 'Yes!'" in *Persuasions,* no. 34 (2012): 25–41.

29. See, for example, Lisa Hopkins, "Mr. Darcy's Body: Privileging the Female Gaze" in *Jane Austen in Hollywood,* eds. Linda Troost and Sayre Greenfield (Lexington: University of Kentucky Press), 111–21; Sarah Ailwood, *Jane Austen's Men: Re-Writing Masculinity in The Romantic Era* (New York: Routledge/Taylor & Francis, 2020), 52. See also Henriette-Juliane Seeliger, "Looking for Mr. Darcy: The Role of the Viewer in Creating a Cultural Icon," *Persuasions On-Line,* 37 no. 1 (Winter 2016), https://jasna.org/publications-2/persuasions-online/vol37no1/seeliger/, who argues that the miniseries, like the novel, allows viewers to construct their own images of the character.

30. Sue Birtwistle and Susie Conklin, *The Making of Pride and Prejudice* (New York: Penguin, 1995), 3.

31. Cheryl Nixon, in *Jane Austen in Hollywood,* eds. Linda Troost and Sayre Greenfield (Lexington: University of Kentucky Press), 111–21.

32. The color of Darcy's mount, like Colonel Brandon's, signals its owner's status as the "dark horse" that wins the race in the end. In later scenes his horse is white, a change that confirms his identity as the film's hero.

33. Conversation with the author, *BBC Pride and Prejudice* (conference), September 4, 2015.

34. See also https://youtu.be/FdAFiGlv-s0.

35. See also https://youtu.be/hasKmDr1yrA.

36. Hopkins, "Mr. Darcy's Body," 112.

37. For a more generous estimation of our access to Darcy's perspective, see Ailwood, *Jane Austen's Men,* 51–59.
38. Hopkins, "Mr. Darcy's Body," 120.
39. Hopkins, "Mr. Darcy's Body," 120.
40. In *Emma,* the sexual tension generated by the protagonists' efforts to disguise their emotions is displaced onto Jane Fairfax and Frank Churchill. The pair stands in contrast to—and illuminates—Emma, who is ignorant of her own heart for most of the novel.
41. The primary difference, I would argue, is that Austen's novel trains us to be better readers by wedding our perspective to Elizabeth Bennet's. The miniseries doesn't go this far.

Chapter Nine

Jane Again

Rachel M. Brownstein

In the first year of the third decade of the twenty-first century, when the *fin de siècle* vogue seemed to be over, two new Jane Austen films appeared: *Sanditon,* a BBC mini-series made for the small screen (aired in Britain the previous year), and *Emma.,* a feature designed for the big one. Based on very different Austen texts, one a sketch for a novel she died before completing and the other the most complex of her six masterpieces, neither was strictly speaking an adaptation.

Andrew Davies, the author of the six-part 1995 BBC miniseries of *Pride and Prejudice* that is still marketed as "the most successful TV period drama ever," wrote the script for *Sanditon,* which elaborates on Austen's skeletal story, enriching it with kinky sub-plots and sexy shots. In his hands, the tale of Charlotte Heywood's seaside encounter with the large hypochondriacal Parker family lost a few Parkers and acquired more "adult" content, including male frontal nudity, brother-sister incest, and traumatic child abuse. Davies, born in 1936, had sexed up Jane Austen before, not only in his breasts-up *Pride and Prejudice* but also in a 2008 adaptation of *Sense and Sensibility* for television that deliberately competed with the big-screen Emma Thompson–Ang Lee version of 1995.

The new *Emma.,* in contrast, was written by Eleanor Catton (born in 1985), a prize-winning New Zealand novelist. It is the first film directed by Autumn de Wilde, an American photographer evidently known for her music videos. It is lavish, engaging, and cute, like every adaptation of Austen's novel about the matchmaking heroine who finds love herself, next door. These include Amy Heckerling's brash *Clueless* (1995), set in twentieth-century Hollywood, and the two period dramas that were released the following year, one starring Gwyneth Paltrow and the other with Kate

Beckinsale. De Wilde's film aims to one-up those by astonishing. "Behold a new vision of Jane Austen's comedy," the trailer commands, following an opening shot set in church (where Jane Austen never set a scene), where Bill Nighy's cranky but dapper Mr. Woodhouse objects to the clergyman's pro-nunciation of "innocence." De Wilde, the *auteur* of *Emma.*, archly explained to the press that the period at the end of the title of her film identifies it as a period piece.[1]

The period in question is indeterminate, evocative but certainly not his-torical. The lines of paired red-caped girls from Mrs. Goddard's school that recur in the movie distractingly recall both Ludwig Bemelmans's much-loved children's book, *Madeline*, and the film versions (1990; 2017) of Margaret Atwood's popular dystopian feminist novel, *The Handmaid's Tale*. Like *Bridgerton*, the dressy, implausible television series released at the end of 2020, de Wilde's *Emma.* is an anti-historical romance. It is set in a time and place that never existed, a squeaky-clean English countryside where the satu-rated colors are startling, all the characters caricature themselves, and ebul-lient invisible orchestras burst into eclectic music to comment, presumably ironically, on the action. Replete with ironies, nearly all of them indetermi-nate, it is "true" to neither the past nor Jane Austen's novel. Mindful of ear-lier Austen adaptations, for the most part condescendingly, it riffs, really, on the big book Austen dedicated to the Prince Regent in 1815.

❦

The first modern Jane Austen film adaptation is the black-and-white *Pride and Prejudice* of 1940 starring Greer Garson as Elizabeth and Laurence Olivier as Darcy. It is pure Hollywood: watch two sets of bonneted ladies in crinolines, in two horse-drawn carriages, race for the prize at the rumor of a possible husband. The *fin de siècle* vogue that took off some forty years later was very different, inflected by earnest educational Masterpiece-Theater-style television: in living color, it emphasized big houses, lawns, and shrub-bery, more accurate period costumes and hair, toned youthful bodies, and more gorgeous horses. It peaked early, with Davies's miniseries of *Pride and Prejudice* (1995), the opening of which engagingly gives away the Jane game of the period as Jennifer Ehle (Elizabeth) reads in voice-over, with intelli-gent emphasis, the long, loaded, famously ironic first sentence of Austen's most loved novel. The witty narrator and the sly heroine and behind them the English spinster of long ago who wrote the novel are conflated, and with them sexiness and girlish savvy, realistic womanly wisdom and the world-turned-upside-down of comedy, in which rich men are the rightful property of poorer people's daughters. Literature, as we used to say, and life.

For college-educated women in the 1990s, the confection of literary, visual, erotic, and narcissistic pleasure was heady: more than a few of them would soon be shopping for shoe-roses to wear to a Regency masquerade ball. As if they all lived together in an English country village, they exchanged juicy gossip about the stars: that pert, dark-eyed Ehle was or had been in fact the lover of Colin Firth, that her mother was the actress Rosemary Harris, made the television series more fun and more real. Austen's re-readers were enchanted and flattered by recalling the words and loving their music, identifying with Elizabeth and Jane Austen and the lively-looking actress and joining the most knowing and best-ever elite coterie. This smoother, more graceful, more romantic miniseries trumped the 1980 *Pride and Prejudice* with a script by the feminist writer Fay Weldon. Colin Firth in his wet shirt was the icing on the already delicious cake.

In the gay feminist nineties, in reading groups and graduate seminars, Jane-related giddiness merged with earnest and fashionable womanly solidarity. We were all of us in love with Elizabeth: bring on Catherine and meddling Emma, give us tender Anne, and Jane! No, not Jane Fairfax, silly: Jane Austen, the greatest woman writer ever, was her own best heroine. We wanted more about her life, why it wasn't fabulous, like Elizabeth's. Biographers and scholars, and writers of romance in the U.K. and America, publishers and filmmakers and advertisers, along with manufacturers and marketers of bobblehead dolls and bookbags, note paper and dishtowels, successfully vied for profits, the likes of which poor pewter-loving Jane Austen never dreamed of.

You could argue that the *fin de siècle* Austen vogue focused the cultural anxieties of the sixties and seventies—maybe also helped blow them away. Certainly, the vogue was nourished by the women's movement and academic feminism, and, in the background, the student movement and quarrels about the canon, increased interest in ethnic and gender identities, the politicization of literary studies, and the new interest within the academy in film and popular culture. People asked, Why Jane Austen, alone of all her sex, rather than, say, Frances Burney or Maria Edgeworth or Mary Wollstonecraft or Eliza Haywood or Sarah Fielding, all recently reprinted? Was it because she was not a political writer? Was Jane Austen, like so many of her admirers, an advocate of retrograde ruling-class values, which begins to explain her exceptional status in a literary canon devised by dead white men? The new Penguin paperbacks with old-fashioned portraits of rosy-cheeked, dewy, genteel English girls on their covers suggested as much. Ten years after it was aired, Joe Wright's gritty *Pride & Prejudice* (2005), starring beautiful Keira Knightley, took issue with Davies's vision of the novel by taking Elizabeth's story outdoors onto the farm and into the weather. Anthony Lane, in *The New Yorker,* described it as "Brontified."[2]

In 1940, Laurence Olivier had played not only Darcy but also Heathcliff, in the movies: films based on literary classics eased the elision of English women writers into one another. Some young women preferred Wright's version of *Pride and Prejudice* because it was more "realistic." Literature or life? Andrew Davies started out as a schoolteacher; Emma Thompson, while writing the script for *Sense and Sensibility*, went up to Cambridge to consult the don with whom she had read Jane Austen at Newnham.

❧

You could also argue that its roots in bookishness anchor the emphasis on knowingness, in Jane Austen movies. Jane Austen wrote for readers familiar with the sentimental romantic novels of their time, which she imitated while sending them up. She read her manuscripts aloud to her sister and their little circle or coterie of female friends, and the books sparkle with private jokes those young women would have giggled at: *Northanger Abbey* describes Catherine Morland's father as "a very respectable man, though his name was Richard"—an in-joke that makes no sense to anyone, now.[3] Jane Austen moviemakers since the 1990s have been chummily, flatteringly confident that viewers will get their allusions and references: in Autumn de Wilde's *Emma.*, Mr. Knightley's housekeeper is a Mrs. Reynolds—which you will recognize is the name of Mr. Darcy's housekeeper, in *Pride and Prejudice* (and arguably an allusion to the artist and theorist Sir Joshua Reynolds). They also take for granted that we are in the know about the people who made the movie. *Emma.* portrays Isabella Knightley as an anxious shrew reminiscent of stressed moms in hip sitcoms of today, like the married sister of the heroine in *Fleabag,* the daring British television romcom starring Phoebe Waller-Bridge, whose real-life sister is listed in the credits for de Wilde's movie. When Isabella hisses, "Husband, comport yourself!"[4] to long-suffering John Knightley we laugh at her old-fashioned language while recognizing her dreadful type.

De Wilde's film plays with and against the notorious gentility and politeness of Austen's blameless novels and of earlier Austen movies. When Austen's Emma suspects Mr. Knightley of wanting to marry Harriet, the narrator startlingly specifies that "it darted through her, with the speed of an arrow, that Mr. Knightley must marry no one but herself."[5] In the new film, there is no arrow, but we do suddenly see blood when Emma has this insight: it is Emma's, and from the nose, and shockingly red, and more than a little disgusting—also comical and oddly beautiful. *Sanditon,* more repellently, rejects prettiness by lingering on the disgusting maggots in a rotten pineapple and the sagging flesh of aged Lady Denham. Perhaps a related impulse to corrective naturalism is behind its emphasis on careers for women in city planning and the hospitality industry.

Virginia Woolf speculated, about Austen, that had she lived longer she would have turned her attention away from country villages and moved outward (following *Persuasion*) to the shore of the ocean and the wider world beyond. Andrew Davies's amplification of Austen's late sketch seems to have been inspired by this suggestion. Boldly, it introduces into a Jane Austen movie not only sexy nude male bathers but also attractive working-class characters who literally play ball with the gentry on the seashore. More notably, there is a love story about a Black couple. The West Indian heiress Miss Lambe is merely mentioned in Austen's sketch as "half mulatto, chilly and tender"[6] but in the film she becomes a character—Black, beautiful, and hot-blooded—who loathes her upper-class guardian and is ardently attached to a charming lover who happens to be a working revolutionary. These attractive young lovers can't wait to get out of Sanditon. The viewer sympathizes: there is too much going on there, and the focus is unclear.

•

The in-group or coterie of Austen's admirers has become bigger and less divided over the years. Rudyard Kipling, in 1924, had distinguished between literary-minded admirers and those pious patriotic British "Janeites" who imagined the sainted spinster as the essence of home and England, like one of their own maiden aunts. Later critics scrupled to distinguish between romantic readers gobbling love stories and subtler ones who read Austen as if she were, say, Henry James. These days, an arch devotion to faux-Jane unites the parties. The emphasis of contemporary Jane-o-mania is that we are all of us in the know about Jane Austen. That she was like us.

•

Other artists will always want to imitate Jane Austen's tidy plots and memorable characters, who already seem like people in a play. Not to mention the brilliance and energy and control of her novels. But the very different films of 2020 suggest that the Jane Austen movie as a knowing romcom, the genre that has developed since 1940, might be finally exhausted. It's high time for popular culture to be done with "the most perfect artist among women," as Woolf called her, now that "women" and "artist" and "perfect"—Mr. Knightley worries that word nicely, in *Emma*—are all contested categories.[7] Davies's *Sanditon* is much too eager to please; Autumn de Wilde's *Emma.* is about only style, which the works of Jane Austen, cinematic appearances to the contrary, are not. If the "period piece" seems closer to Austen in spirit than Davies's earnest *Sanditon,* it is because it mocks itself, as Austen's novels mocked while miming the sentimental novel. Deliberately or by accident, both these films may be telling us to get back to the pleasures of the texts.

Notes

1. Flora Carr, "*Emma.* director Autumn de Wilde explains the film's unusual punctuation," *Radio Times,* February 14, 2020, https://www.radiotimes.com/movies/emma-title-full-stop-period/.

2. Anthony Lane, "Parent Traps: *Pride and Prejudice* and *Bee Season,*" *The New Yorker,* Nov. 6, 2005, https://www.newyorker.com/magazine/2005/11/14/parent-traps.

3. Jane Austen, *Northanger Abbey,* in *The Oxford Illustrated Jane Austen,* volume 5, ed. R. W. Chapman, 3rd ed. (Oxford U.K: Oxford University Press, 1933 repr. 1988), 13.

4. *Emma.,* directed by Autumn de Wilde, screenplay by Eleanor Catton (Working Title, 2020).

5. Jane Austen, *Emma,* vol. 4, *The Oxford Illustrated Jane Austen,* 408.

6. Jane Austen, *Minor Works,* vol. 6, *The Oxford Illustrated Jane Austen,* ed. R. W. Chapman (Oxford UK: Oxford University Press, 1954 repr. 1988), 421.

7. Virginia Woolf, "Jane Austen," in *The Common Reader* (New York: Harcourt, 1925), https://www.gutenberg.org/files/64457/64457-h/64457-h.htm.

Chapter Ten

Touching Scenes

Austen, Intimacy, and Staging *Lovers' Vows*

Elaine McGirr

It is February 2011. I am on research leave from my teaching position at Royal Holloway, spending the spring as a Fellow at Chawton House Library, researching Jane Austen's relationship with private theatricals and preparing a play to be performed in June, which will be the capstone event to the Chawton House Library Garden Party. Normally, Fellows would be resident at Chawton, housed in the glorious renovated Stables, living and working together like an extended party at a country house, or a small acting company.

I am not living in the Stables. I drive through the English countryside most mornings, commuting down to Chawton from my home in Richmond, about forty-five miles away. Although slightly sad to be missing out on the intimacy and experience of living at Chawton, I do not mind the drive; the scenery is beautiful once I leave the motorway, and I enjoy watching the snowy canopy slowly give way to snowdrops and the green buds of approaching spring. I remind myself that this commute was my choice, a compromise to create some semblance of work-life balance: I have a toddler at home who has Feelings about my not being there to read to her every single night, so a residential Fellowship was out of the question. It was this or nothing. So I have traded the intimacy of the Stables and intellectual community for the intimacy of snuggling into a tiny toddler bed with a stack of Julia Donaldson books, an impressive array of stuffed animals, and a two-year-old. It's a tricky balance—especially fitting into the toddler bed with toddler and her army of teddies—but it's just about manageable.

I sit in the hush of the Library Reading Room, looking at the Austen family's dramatic adaptation of *Sir Charles Grandison*, Richardson's massive triple-decker novel. The piece was preserved because it is in Jane Austen's handwriting, but the slight play, largely about the attractions of cucumber sandwiches, was almost certainly a family production, dictated to or transcribed by a doting Aunt Jane. This private theatrical was clearly a project for and by the family's very young people: it is full of barely suppressed laughter and in jokes, and was clearly a joy to create, even if it was never performed. The Austen *Grandison* is far from a literary or dramatic masterpiece, but it is a brief glimpse of domestic harmony, of the intimacy of close-knit family. Turning Richardson's 2,000⁺-page moralising novel into a *petit pièce* about snacks is the kind of burlesque of form and matter Austen would have appreciated, I am sure. It reminds me of the affectionate satire of *Northanger Abbey* as well as *Mansfield Park's* avowal that private theatricals are "nothing but pleasure, from beginning to end."[1] Yet try as I might, I am struggling to concentrate or draw much inspiration from the *Grandison* playlet: the repeated descriptions of food begin to make me feel unwell. When I leave the reading room, the smell of lavender permeating the House, used in potpourri and in scented, Austen-branded toiletries, overwhelms me. I retch. *Grandison* is forgotten.

I am pregnant. Again. I struggle with gravidarum hyperemesis again. I am sick. Again and again and again. My body is not my own. My mind can only focus on complete stillness, fighting to keep the violent nausea at bay.

ᛞ

I spend that spring trying to balance my academic productivity with my body's reproductivity. This research leave is my first in three years, and I cannot afford to waste it if I want to progress in my career. And I still have a toddler with Feelings—who was very clear that she wanted a puppy and NOT a baby sister or brother. I am also a wife, a friend, a daughter, and a sister. But for now, I can only concentrate on being a good academic and trying to become a mother again. Everything else gets pushed to one side. It is a kind of balance, albeit a very lopsided one. I spend hours in my car, alone, but not alone; the nausea reminding me of the pregnancy even when I try to concentrate on other things. Then, about thirteen weeks into the pregnancy, I begin to bleed. Again. The previous year, on Mothering Sunday, I had suffered a miscarriage that had led to haemorrhaging, emergency surgery, transfusions, and uterine scarring. My doctors had warned me that this new pregnancy might not "take" as a result. I assume the worst. My body will go back to being mine alone. I can concentrate on writing and research. I can focus on my daughter and my husband. I can concentrate on Jane Austen rather than impending maternity.

But the worst does not happen. The bleeding stops and the scan picks up a strong fetal heartbeat. The sonographer thinks I started out with twins but lost one. She wishes me cautious hope for the remaining fetus. My doctors advise bedrest but admit that there's little they or I can do to ensure the remaining fetus holds on. So I return to work—to play, playing, and Austen's private theatricals.

&

I take the sonographer's cautious hope back with me to Chawton House and continue working on my play, a pastiche of Austen's *Mansfield Park* and Elizabeth Inchbald's *Lovers' Vows*, the play the young people in Austen's novel choose for their private theatricals, for the acting out of their own passions. As I write and read more about Austen family theatricals, about Jane's cousin, Eliza de Feuillide, who supposedly inspired the character of Mary Crawford, I am struck anew and more viscerally by the seriousness of play and the dangers of courtship—to reputation and to life. Of the closeness of childbirth, with its attendant dangers, to courtship, with its attendant pleasures. I think about the time and attention demanded by both courtship and child-rearing and wonder about Austen's refusal to marry. When she changed her mind about marrying Harris Bigg-Wither, was it a positive choice to keep her own needs and wants central, rather than having to rebalance her life in favour of a husband and children? I wonder if being a doting aunt was the compromise she struck between her domestic and her professional identities. I wonder if limiting the number of identities she needed to maintain allowed her to experience them more fully, or if she regretted choosing maiden aunt and author over loving wife and mother.

I think about all this as I prepare a talk on "conjugal lust" in eighteenth-century comedies, describing licensed sexuality within marriage, the cultural encouragement married women were given in the eighteenth-century to initiate and enjoy sex, not only for reproduction, but also to reaffirm marital love and pair bonding. I think about the eighteenth-century euphemism for pregnancy: "pledge of [our] love." My hand frequently strays to my belly, seeking confirmation that my own pledge is still there. My academic CV traces my lived experience: the essay on conjugal lust is followed by a book about mothers. I am maintaining my precarious balance, trying to make my many roles speak to and through each other. It is exhausting, but, like fitting into the toddler bed, it is just about manageable.

My continuing morning (and afternoon and always) sickness, my hypersensitivity to smell, and my continuing anxiety about my pregnancy make me bad company. I do not socialise with the other Fellows. I spend as much time as possible alone, outdoors. But of course, I am not alone. I am with child. It is a strange experience, being both lonely and never alone.

🐾

Time passes. It is June. I am now visibly pregnant. I am still sick, but no longer quite so anxious; the pregnancy is well established and while I might still feel like death warmed over, the fetus is thriving. I am also rehearsing my play with a small six-person company of theatre students, all aged between 19–24, not unlike the characters in Austen's *Mansfield Park*. *Staging Lovers' Vows* is set in promenade throughout Chawton's house and gardens, moving from the Wilderness through the Courtyard to the Servant's Attic and the Great Hall. The six weeks we spend rehearsing creates its own Fellowship, its own intimacy. We discover, like Edmund Bertram, the "excessive intimacy . . . the *more* than intimacy—the familiarity" that necessarily arises during private theatricals (*MP* 153). However, this "*more* than intimacy" is also the appeal of theatricals for the young people in the novel. This includes Edmund himself, who uses the threat of a "young man [but] slightly known to any of us" as justification for taking a part that would allow him to act a love scene with the woman he hopes to marry (*MP* 153). In other words, Edmund's concern is not about the dangers of theatrical intimacy, but of an intimacy that excludes him. Exclusion becomes a running anxiety for my young company.

As director, dramaturg, and tutor, I am of the company but also not: I instruct and critique rather than play. I am also separated by my personal status: to the young actors I am old, married, and pregnant. Theirs are the concerns of courtship; mine of childbirth. Because they are young, they do not yet see the connection between them. So although I am excluded—from their socialising, their group chats, their anxieties about grades and dates and jobs—I do not mind. The same cannot be said for the actors, who all feel excluded at various points, locked out of the easy intimacy they assume the others enjoy.

While I have taught most of these students before, this project is part of an optional summer season for students who take part for experience, rather than university credit. The lack of grades is meant to break down some of the hierarchy between teacher and student and create a more inclusive company. But I am still in charge. And I am still old, and married, and pregnant. These marks of difference mean that I am not only their director, but also their confidante and confessor. As the weeks of rehearsal mount, my young actors take turns to seek me out to complain, to worry, to seek reassurance.

We move our rehearsals to Chawton and start to familiarize ourselves with the site. Patterns and pairings have established themselves in the small company, just as they have in the novel we are dramatizing. My attention is largely taken up with the trio who have taken on the love triangle of Fanny Price, Mary Crawford, and Edmund Bertrand. Celine, Rose, and Jack are all accidentally Method in their connections to their characters: Jack, who plays Edmund, is self-conscious, anxious, and worried that the woman he admires—Rose—is too "fast" for him; Rose, who plays Mary, is confident and un-self-conscious but not above flirting to gratify her vanity; while Celine, my Fanny Price, is struggling with finding herself not the centre of attention. The two scenes the three have together bring out their conflicting emotions and remind me that we all have multiple parts to play.

Interruption 1: *Staging Lovers' Vows* in the Wilderness

EDMUND. . . . . Go into the law! With as much ease as I was told to go into this
    wilderness.
MARY. Now you are going to say something about law being the worst wil-
    derness of the two, but I forestall you; remember, I have forestalled
    you.
EDMUND. You need not hurry when the object is only to prevent my saying
    a *bon mot*, for there is not the least wit in my nature. I am a very
    matter-of-fact, plain-spoken being, and may blunder on the borders
    of a repartee for half an hour together without striking it out.

[*general pause in conversation*]

FANNY. [*timidly*] I wonder that I should be tired with only walking in this
    sweet wood, but the next time we come to a seat, if it is not dis-
    agreeable to you, I should be glad to sit down for a little while.
EDMUND. My dear Fanny [*immediately drawing her arm within his*] how
    thoughtless I have been! I hope you are not very tired. Perhaps,
    [*turning to Miss Crawford*] my other companion may do me the
    honour of taking an arm.

MARY. Thank you, but I am not at all tired. [*taking arm*]

EDMUND. [*to Mary, turning away from Fanny*] You scarcely touch me. You
do not make me of any use. What a difference in the weight of a
woman's arm from that of a man! At Oxford I have been a good deal
used to have a man lean on me for the length of a street, and you are
only a fly in the comparison.

MARY. I am really not tired, which I almost wonder at; for we must have
walked at least a mile in this wood. Do not you think we have?

EDMUND. Not half a mile.

[*Fanny breaks off and goes to sit down. Edmund and Mary do not notice her absence*]

MARY. Oh! you do not consider how much we have wound about. We have
taken such a very serpentine course; and the wood itself must be
half a mile long in a straight line, for we have never seen the end of
it yet, since we left the first great path.

EDMUND. But if you remember, before we left that first great path, we saw
directly to the end of it. We looked down the whole vista, and saw it
closed by iron gates, and it could not have been more than a furlong
in length.

MARY. Oh! I know nothing of your furlongs, but I am sure it is a very long
wood; and that we have been winding in and out ever since we came
into it; and therefore when I say that we have walked a mile in it, I
must speak within compass.

EDMUND. We have been exactly a quarter of an hour here. [*takes out watch
and consults it*] Do you think we are walking four miles an hour?

MARY. Oh! do not attack me with your watch. A watch is always too fast or
too slow. I cannot be dictated to by a watch.

EDMUND [*notices Fanny*]. I am afraid you are very tired, Fanny. Why would
not you speak sooner? This will be a bad day's amusement for you, if
you are to be knocked up. Every sort of exercise fatigues her so soon,
Miss Crawford, except riding.

[*Edmund and Mary sit either side of Fanny and continue to talk across her*]

MARY. How abominable in you, then; to let me engross her horse as I did all
last week! I am ashamed of you and of myself, but it shall never happen again!

EDMUND. Your attentiveness and consideration make me more sensible of
my own neglect. Fanny's interest seems in safer hands with you than
with me.

MARY. That she should be tired now, however, gives me no surprise; for there is nothing in the course of one's duties so fatiguing as what we have been doing this morning—seeing a garden and great house, dawdling from one room to another—straining one's eyes and one's attention—hearing what one does not understand—admiring what one does not care for.—It is generally allowed to be the greatest bore in the world, and Miss Price has found it so, though she did not know it.

FANNY. I shall soon be rested. To sit in the shade on a fine day, and look upon verdure, is the most perfect refreshment.

MARY. I must move. Resting fatigues me.—I have looked across the ha-ha till I am weary. I must go and look through that iron gate at the same view, without being able to see it so well. [*She starts away. Edmund follows*]

EDMUND. Now, Miss Crawford, if you will look up the walk, you will convince yourself that it cannot be half a mile long, or half half a mile.

MARY. It is an immense distance. I see that with a glance.

[*They depart, still arguing flirtatiously, without a backward glance for Fanny*]

FANNY. [*to audience*] The season, the scene, the air, were all favourable to tenderness and sentiment. Without studying the business, however, or knowing what he was about, Edmund was beginning, at the end of a week of such intercourse, to be a good deal in love; and to the credit of the lady it may be added that, without his being a man of the world or an elder brother, without any of the arts of flattery or the gaieties of small talk, he began to be agreeable to her. She felt it to be so, though she had not foreseen, and could hardly understand it; for he was not pleasant by any common rule: he talked no nonsense; he paid no compliments; his opinions were unbending, his attentions tranquil and simple. There was a charm, perhaps, in his sincerity, his steadiness, his integrity, which Miss Crawford might be equal to feel, though not equal to discuss with herself. She did not think very much about it, however: he pleased her for the present; she liked to have him near her; it was enough. [*sighs.*]

Jack, who plays my Edmund/Anhalt, struggles with Austen's language and with his own sense of being an outsider in the company, whose friendship circle—and group chat—often excludes him. Like Edmund, he might "blunder on the borders of a repartee for half an hour together without striking it out"

(*MP* 94). Unluckily for Jack, the others do not see this failure of wit as evidence of manly forthrightness. Only as an absence of wit. During our dress rehearsal, I find Jack sitting in the (aptly named) Blue Room at Chawton, moping. Jack discovers himself to be more introspective and self-aware—but also more melodramatic—than the character(s) he plays. He confesses his growing attraction to Rose, who plays Mary Crawford/Amelia, and his realization that even with all the benefits of the "more than intimacy" of playing opposite each other, Rose does not return his feelings. He describes the difference in their characters—differences not unlike those of the characters they play: Jack is serious and studious. He does not drink and dislikes clubs and parties; Rose is only in the play "for a laugh" and to justify staying on at uni for the summer and not returning to her family home. She uses her independence to go to all the clubs and parties Jack avoids. Jack, using the play as his guide, had hoped opposites would attract. Rose's continued indifference has crushed him. Dramatically—as only a twenty-one-year-old drama student can—he worries that this proves no one ever will or ever can love him. He contemplates quitting the production rather than performing with Rose ever again.

Two cups of tea and much sympathy later, Jack is ready to return to the wilderness for the play's opening scene. But his heartbreak is hard to hide when he and Rose rehearse their love scene. The attic scene is Jack's longest and most emotionally fraught. It is also where he has to confront the fact that his acting partner misrecognises his earnestness for acting, just as he had previously misrecognised her play for real feeling.

Interruption 2: Rehearsing Lovers' Vows

ANHALT. I beg pardon if I have come at an improper hour; but I wait upon you by the commands of your father.

AMELIA. You are welcome at all hours. My father has more than once told me that he who forms my mind I should always consider as my greatest benefactor. [*looking down*] And my heart tells me the same.

ANHALT. I think myself amply rewarded by the good opinion you have of me.

AMELIA. When I remember what trouble I have sometimes given you, I cannot be too grateful.

ANHALT [*to himself*]. Oh! Heavens!—[*to Amelia*]. I—I come from your father with a commission.—If you please, we will sit down. [*He places chairs, and they sit.*] Count Cassel is arrived.

AMELIA. Yes, I know.

ANHALT. And do you know for what reason?

AMELIA. He wishes to marry me.

ANHALT. Does he? [*hastily*] But believe me, the Baron will not persuade you—No, I am sure he will not.

AMELIA. I know that.

ANHALT. He wishes that I should ascertain whether you have an inclination—

AMELIA. For the Count, or for matrimony do you mean?

ANHALT. For matrimony.

AMELIA. All things that I don't know, and don't understand, are quite indifferent to me.

ANHALT. For that very reason I am sent to you to explain the good and the bad of which matrimony is composed.

AMELIA. Then I beg first to be acquainted with the good.

ANHALT. When two sympathetic hearts meet in the marriage state, matrimony may be called a happy life. When such a wedded pair find thorns in their path, each will be eager, for the sake of the other, to tear them from the root. Where they have to mount hills, or wind a labyrinth, the most experienced will lead the way, and be a guide to his companion. Patience and love will accompany them in their journey, while melancholy and discord they leave far behind.— Hand in hand they pass on from morning till evening, through their summer's day, till the night of age draws on, and the sleep of death overtakes the one. The other, weeping and mourning, yet looks forward to the bright region where he shall meet his still surviving partner, among trees and flowers which themselves have planted, in fields of eternal verdure.

AMELIA. You may tell my father—I'll marry. [*Rises.*]

ANHALT [*rising*]. This picture is pleasing; but I must beg you not to forget that there is another on the same subject.—When convenience, and fair appearance joined to folly and ill-humour, forge the fetters of matrimony, they gall with their weight the married pair. Discontented with each other—at variance in opinions—their mutual aversion increases with the years they live together. They contend most, where they should most unite; torment, where they should most soothe. In this rugged way, choaked with the weeds of suspicion, jealousy, anger, and hatred, they take their daily journey, till one of these also sleep in death. The other then lifts up his dejected head, and calls out in acclamations of joy—Oh, liberty! dear liberty!

AMELIA. I will not marry.

ANHALT. You mean to say, you will not fall in love.

AMELIA. Oh no! [*ashamed*] I am in love.

ANHALT. Are in love! [*starting*] And with the Count?

AMELIA. I wish I was.

ANHALT. Why so?

AMELIA. Because he would, perhaps, love me again.

ANHALT [*warmly*]. Who is there that would not?

AMELIA. Would you?

ANHALT. I—I—me—I—I am out of the question.

AMELIA. No; you are the very person to whom I have put the question.

ANHALT. What do you mean?

AMELIA. I am glad you don't understand me. I was afraid I had spoken too plain.

[*IN confusion*].

ANHALT. Understand you!—As to that—I am not dull.

AMELIA. I know you are not—And as you have for a long time instructed me, why should not I now begin to teach you?

ANHALT. Teach me what?

AMELIA. Whatever I know, and you don't.

ANHALT. There are some things I had rather never know.

AMELIA. So you may remember I said when you began to teach me mathematics. I said I had rather not know it—But now I have learnt it gives me a great deal of pleasure—and [*hesitating*] perhaps, who can tell, but that I might teach something as pleasant to you, as resolving a problem is to me.

ANHALT. Woman herself is a problem.

AMELIA. And I'll teach you to make her out.

ANHALT. You teach?

AMELIA. Why not? none but a woman can teach the science of herself: and though I own I am very young, a young woman may be as agreeable for a tutoress as an old one.—I am sure I always learnt faster from you than from the old clergyman who taught me before you came.

ANHALT. This is nothing to the subject.

AMELIA. What is the subject?

ANHALT. —Love.

AMELIA [*going up to him*]. Come, then, teach it me—teach it me as you taught me geography, languages, and other important things.

ANHALT [*turning from her*]. Pshaw!

AMELIA. Ah! you won't—You know you have already taught me that, and you won't begin again.

ANHALT. You misconstrue—you misconceive every thing I say or do. The subject I came to you upon was marriage.

AMELIA. A very proper subject from the man who has taught me love, and I accept the proposal. [*curtsying.*]

ANHALT. Again you misconceive and confound me.

AMELIA. Ay, I see how it is—You have no inclination to experience with me
"the good part of matrimony:" I am not the female with whom you
would like to go "hand in hand up hills, and through labyrinths"—
with whom you would like to "root up thorns; and with whom you
would delight to plant lilies and roses." No, you had rather call out,
"Oh liberty, dear liberty."
ANHALT. Why do you force from me, what it is villainous to own?—I love
you more than life—Oh, Amelia! had we lived in those golden
times, which the poets picture, no one but you—But as the world
is changed, your birth and fortune make our union impossible—To
preserve the character, and more the feelings of an honest man, I
would not marry you without the consent of your father—And
could I, dare I propose it to him. [*breaks off*]

*

Mary Crawford/Amelia's flirtatious speeches—such as her playful demand
that her tutor teach her love as he taught her geography—are why Fanny
(and others) thought *Lovers' Vows* "exceedingly unfit for private representation" (*MP* 140). But these playful speeches, performed beautifully by Rose,
are also what gave Jack hope that she, like him—and like *Mansfield Park's*
Mary Crawford—was acting in earnest, using role play to speak what was
indecorous (or too scary) to say in *propria persona*. Jack used this strategy as
his character(s) extolled "the good in marriage" to Rose/Mary/Amelia, gently
taking her hand. Coming back to this scene after his crushing realization
that Rose was "only acting" may have been hard for Jack, but it did lend his
performance even more pathos, and, perhaps to the discerning eye, foreshad-
owed the novel's conclusion, when Edmund realizes that Mary Crawford's
lightness must separate them forever.

Interruption 3: Solus

FANNY. We promised ourselves nothing but pleasure from beginning to end
when we embarked upon our play. But so far from being satisfied
and all enjoying, everyone seems to require something they have
not, and gives discontent to the others. Everybody has a part either
too long or too short; nobody will attend as they ought; nobody
will remember on which side they are to come in; everybody will
complain, but nobody will allow themselves to need any amend-
ment. The whole is never rehearsed, but Maria and Henry Crawford

rehearse this first scene so needlessly often that I am in constant terror of complaints from Mr Rushworth.

But there are pleasures: Henry Crawford acts well—do you not think?—he has more confidence than Edmund, more judgment than Tom, more talent and taste than Mr Yates. I may not like him as a man, but I must admit him the best actor, although Mr Yates will exclaim against his tameness and stupidity, and Mr Rushworth watches him with a very black look . . . Maria also acts well . . . too well . . .

✿

Another day, another crisis of confidence. This time it is Celine, who plays Fanny Price. Celine's personality is the opposite of Fanny's: confident almost to a fault, vivacious and ambitious. However, there are still shadows of the novel's relationships in my actors' interactions: just as Fanny is jealous of Mary, Celine hates Rose, who is a good actress "without even trying!" Celine was desperate to be cast as Fanny, who serves as the play's narrator and links the worlds of the novel, the play, and Chawton itself as she leads the audience from scene to scene. But after weeks of workshopping, she complains "I thought I was the lead character, but I'm more like a prop!" Celine has been sitting, unobserved, in the background as I worked with Jack and Rose on the long "East room" scene excerpted above, trying to help them use their *Lovers' Vows* characters to unlock their *Mansfield Park* characters. Celine's role in this scene is to sit and watch. She feels left out and grows bored and fretful.

Watching the other actors in the company develop their characters, Celine begins to doubt her own talents and ambition to act professionally. I placate, praise, and pet her into a better frame of mind, reminding her that her character has to bridge the nineteenth and twenty-first centuries, while the others merely have to move between their characters from novel and play, characters that are designed to speak to and through each other. Pleased with this assurance of exceptionality, Celine returns to rehearsal. Privately, I compare Celine's silent presence to my bump—visible, but unobtrusive; present, but unremarked. I have stopped worrying about the pregnancy and am now worrying about finishing this project or anything else before the baby comes. As the pregnancy advances, I am finding it harder to balance my two selves: the old, married, pregnant me keeps obtruding on the director and dramaturg. The careful balance between my professional and domestic worlds is collapsing.

But the day of the performance comes, and it goes off without too many disasters. Jack's black mood only makes his Edmund more clerical and priggish, setting off Rose's playful Mary Crawford beautifully. Celine comes into her own with a live audience and thoroughly enjoys being the center of attention again. The unproblematic half of my company continues to be wonderful and all together ensured that the audience did not agree with Mary Crawford that "seeing a great house, dawdling from one room to another—straining one's eyes and one's attention—hearing what one does not understand—admiring what one does not care for . . . is . . . the greatest bore in the world" (*MP* 95-96). The performance over, the company disbanded—the young actors back to their homes, and me to maternity leave.

&♣

It is 2021. There is a global pandemic, and we have been more or less housebound for a year. I work from home; the children learn from home. I record lectures in my bedroom and cook in the children's schoolroom. The production of *Staging Lovers' Vows* at Chawton seems like a lifetime ago, and I struggle to remember what it was like to work that closely with others, or even to drive through the English countryside. But I also feel closer to Jane Austen and her family, gathered together to put on a makeshift performance of *Sir Charles Grandison*. The pandemic has collapsed the separation between professional and private; the domestic erupts into work with staggering regularity. Like Austen, who wrote while surrounded by the chaos of family life, I need to relearn the rhythms of both family and work and aim for harmony rather than balance. Pandemic life is like that of a country house party—or a small acting company—bubbled together for the duration of a production.

Note

1.   Jane Austen, *Mansfield Park,* vol. 3 of *The Oxford Illustrated Jane Austen*, ed. R. W. Chapman, 3rd ed. (Oxford: Oxford University Press, 1933 repr. 1988), 105. Subsequent quotations are taken from this edition and will appear in parenthetical citations with the abbreviation *MP*.

Chapter Eleven

Jane's Players

Sex and Romance in the Virtual World of Jane Austen

Judy Tyrer

In the land of Norrath in a zone called Sky, a brave group of forty adventurers are thirty-two Earth hours into a seventy-two-hour raid. They have cleared the fourth island of a hive of murderous giant wasps, each the size of three of our hearty band. They banter while their priests resurrect their fallen comrades. It's late at night. Waiting for resurrection is slow. Flirtations and more abound:

> SYLVANAR: "I slip my hand under your armor and slide it up your thigh."
> MORGANA: "MISSTELL!"[1]
> FLUBART: "We are on a raid! FOCUS!"
> ICEIALLANA: "You just told the whole guild, didn't you?"
> SYLVANAR: "I clicked on the wrong tab. Again. Sorry for the misstell, everyone."

Instead of an intimate whisper in Iceiallana's ear, Sylvanar has detailed his actions over the loudspeaker, not only informing the raiding party he happens to be leading, but the entire guild, that his hand is on Iceiallana's thigh and heading steadily North.

Misstells like Sylvanar's can happen on *EverQuest*, one of many Massively Multiplayer Online Role Playing Games (MMORPGs). They are especially common during downtime, periods in which players can socialize while they wait for the server to do what it must. Players' reactions to such misstells vary, as does the degree of open sex in each game. In *World of Warcraft* (WOW), for example, "role play" has degenerated into semi-naked avatars dancing in The Lion's Head Inn, in Goldshire. Those of us who designed *Ever, Jane: The Virtual World of Jane Austen* wanted sex in our game to be a bit more discreet.

A Bit of Background

Ever, Jane is an MMORPG which is perhaps best described as a mashup of EverQuest and Jane Austen's literary works. It was devised as a response to a shift in the MMORPG genre which, as a whole, had increasingly favored action and adventure, at the expense of periods of downtime that EverQuest provided. To me, an avid MMORPG player and lover of Jane Austen, it seemed like an ideal solution to the difficulty of finding good role play in MMORPGs. As a video game developer ready to branch out into my own studio after a wonderful career with Ubisoft, Sony Online Entertainment, and Linden Lab working on Second Life, I thought this would be a good first game. And *Ever, Jane* was born.

I led the team who built *Ever, Jane* and wrote the code and designed the prototype. I was joined by Annabel Smyth, whose ancestors were peers of Jane Austen, and Renee Nejo, who created the art. After the design was complete, we used Kickstarter to get funding for the first two years of development. At that point the team grew to include two more artists, another programmer, and a person to handle customer support. The team managed the game online, with a group of active players, during development. After five years we ran out of money. The team had to break up and, in 2020, the world of *Ever, Jane* closed its doors.

Welcome to Tyrehampton

The world of *Ever, Jane* takes place in Tyrehampton, between 1790 and 1820. The primary village is centered around the village green. It includes three types of housing: two-story terraced houses, three-story townhouses, and large three-story cottages. These were built following blueprints of Georgian homes of the time. In addition to the primary village, we also designed an estate, which is a multistoried home of multiple rooms, including vast kitchens, dining rooms, sitting rooms, and ballrooms along with libraries and a large assortment of bedrooms (Figure 11.1). After the Kickstarter, we added housing and that became our primary focus as it allowed people to buy furniture and personalize their play spaces. The characters in *Ever, Jane* had life spans of five years during which they built legacies, whether they chose to marry or remain single. Players had two options when their characters died. They could be reborn as new characters and start afresh. Or, they could be adopted instantly by their former families and therefore inherit the legacies they had built up in their former lives. We also gave multiple characters to each account. That way our players would not be inconvenienced if their characters died unexpectedly (death was always good for a dramatic storyline). That way characters could be killed off at will. Death never was permanent because we controlled time.

The characters themselves were designed to possess qualities that would serve them well in Jane Austen's time. Instead of traditional MMORPG characteristics such as Strength, Intelligence, and Agility, we included attributes like Duty, Happiness, and Reputation. Instead of skill at combat, we added the ability to use and counter gossip, our weapons of choice, so that a person's reputation could be destroyed should the gossip spread before it was stopped.

Figure 11.1. The Tyrehampton Estate.

We also created stories and actions in keeping with the Regency milieu.[2] Unlike Norrath, a dangerous land of kill or be killed, Tyrhampton was a world of invite and be invited. Instead of large multiplayer cooperative raids, our players attended balls. Instead of embarking on quests, our players would develop individual roles. They might engage in flirtations at funerals or at concerts on the village green. They might participate in love triangles or destroy them with gossip. And where other MMORPGs have guilds, our players joined families, which allowed them to hire servants and adopt children, become engaged, and marry.

Like other MMORPGs, *Ever, Jane* provided its players with opportunities to choose a variety of actions. Upon their arrival, our players discovered that—like Elinor, Marianne, and Margaret (and perhaps, like Jane Austen herself)—their lives had been upended by death. Fortunately, the deceased was not a parent, but a cousin, and our players could choose the degree of disruption caused by the death. Perhaps, while attending the funeral, they would spot a person of interest and begin their first flirtation. How *does* one flirtatiously smile at a funeral? We left that to the player to determine. Other options revolved around village activities. For example, players inevitably would be asked by a shepherd for help in corralling his sheep, who had escaped from a breach in a fence. Although no young lady or gentleman would normally do such a task, we hoped our players would roll up their sleeves and make the best of it for the good of the community. Players also had the choice to collect flowers for a posy for a person of interest and discover the joy, or lack thereof, of gossip while attending a local concert or at a ball.

Our community of players also provided their own stories. We had multiple balls, a Christmas program, and an Easter egg hunt all organized by the player community. There were announcements for banns to be read at the church and children were born and christened there as well. In one case the marriage was so successful the two players had banns read and were married in their real-world church (Figure 11.2). They sent us a delightful Christmas card from the wedding.

Sex and Romance

When online romances turn into real-world marriages, as has happened in *Ever, Jane*, one doesn't want to necessarily discourage the practice. After all, we thoroughly encouraged romance in our world. We found the slight brushing

Figure 11.2. The Tyrehampton Church.

of the fingers over a man's ungloved hand while handing him a recent book of poetry far more interesting than the urgent needs of an engorged appendage. But that is just personal taste, I presume. Still, we rather promoted the more subtle forms of romance and erotica. We just preferred more than "hot, steamy, throbbing members" in our role play in *Ever, Jane*. Plus our avatars were never naked.

However, as the game grew, we found ourselves having to negotiate between the expectations of sexually adventurous twenty-first-century players and those who were attracted to the decorous vision of Jane Austen's world as filtered through her Victorian relatives. Ironically, the twenty-first-century MMORPG players who were used to plenty of cybersex were more in line with the actual sexual freedom of the Regency period, where once a male heir was produced, a woman had considerable freedom of choice in her partners so long as she remained discreet. So, while the debauchery would be quite fitting at the Royal Pavilion in Brighton, a palace the Prince Regent had built while he was staying in the seaside resort, not all of our players were quite ready for the notorious goings-on that took place there. Some of our less-knowing players might be shocked.

To preserve the expectations of our more sexually conservative players we required that all debauchery be private. We also enabled a considerable degree of freedom for those who wanted to be more sexually adventurous while maintaining a respectable facade. We included several tactics for keeping players' liaisons discreet. In order to prevent misstells like Sylvaner's, we deviated from standard MMORPG practices in requiring a deliberate change of context for our private chats. We hoped that having to pause to press a big, bright button would prevent our gentlemen from accidentally sliding their hands under a lady's skirt for the entire village to see (Figure 11.3). We were certain no lady in our world would clandestinely slide her hand into a man's pants; but if she did, as long as we didn't know it, we couldn't complain.

For those who wished to play the game with a bit more risk, we offered "whisper," which limited the range in which a player could be heard. Whisper is a feature used in stories involving parties, where one player may need to tell another player a secret but does not want anyone to hear. Unlike Private, which basically takes players out of the world entirely, Whisper reaches anyone within a small hearing range. Some of our players found it a delightful way to communicate, since it involved a little bit of social danger.

For actual trysts, players could sneak off to the upper bedrooms if they were well-born or to lower bedrooms if they were members of the servant class. Rumor had it that our guests woke before dawn so they could return to the proper rooms before the day began. All of the bedrooms were very public, so guests had to beware of any random carriage that might arrive within hearing range and spread scandal to all. One funny glitch that we hesitated to fix was a flying carriage that interrupted guests hoping for privacy in the upper bedrooms (Figure 11.4).

Good Behavior (and the Reverse)

As in Jane Austen's world, the world of *Ever, Jane* required its denizens to follow the rules. To that end, we devised methods of dealing with trolls, a.k.a. players who caused trouble to destroy the fun. Players who chose inappropriate names were required to change them in order to play. We had one stalking incident and that player was banned as well. We also encountered people who would run into the world and just start shouting smut to see if they would get banned (they were). Most of the time our customer-support person in the guise of a nonplayer character called Captain Worthwaite kept order. He was assisted occasionally by the game's players, who enjoyed keeping Tyrehampton smut free. For instance, when an intruder shouted "FUCK

Figure 11.3. The Chat Window.

YA'LL DUDES," he was deflected with the quip, "Excuse me sir, are you from France? I do not recognize your accent. So many Frenchmen these days, fleeing while their heads are still attached to their bodies."

Sometimes, however, even the wittiest of comebacks was insufficient to manage an inappropriately behaved player. Here we relied on history to save us. Although it was never developed, our plan was to ship repeat offenders to a separate, fully functional server called "Botany Bay," inspired by Britain's real penal colony. As we envisioned it, our Botany Bay would resemble Tyrehampton. However, it would lack behavioral restrictions and

Figure 11.4. A Carriage in the Sky.

we would not offer players guidance or support. Instead, it would allow its citizens to behave as they wished. The colony would have been ideal for those players who were disappointed by the fact that, in *Ever, Jane*, they had to stay dressed and could not role-play in the Prince Regent's Royal Pavilion at Brighton. Although these players may have found *Ever, Jane* to be overly rigid, we decided not only to respect Austen's distaste for the Prince Regent but to preserve the world which we believe she would have preferred.

We never wanted to limit anyone's choices for fun, but to prevent one person's idea of fun from infringing on another's. For that we allowed various means of carrying on covertly in Tyrehampton while maintaining a facade appropriate to respectable ladies and gentlemen in Jane Austen's time. Those who wished for a less curated experience were free to go to Botany Bay. And stay there.

Notes

1. Misstell: a message sent to the incorrect recipient in an instant messaging program or online game.
2. The stories were sparse because we were still in development; we hoped to add additional stories down the line.

Chapter Twelve

To YouTube from Gretna Green

Updating Lydia Bennet for the Digital Age

Margaret Dunlap

Lydia Bennet might not be the most beloved character in Jane Austen's *Pride and Prejudice*, but she is absolutely pivotal to the plot. If not for Lydia running off with Wickham, Darcy would not be forced to unbend from his principles to save her, setting in motion the chain of events that leads Elizabeth Bennet to reassess her first impressions and eventually become Mrs. Darcy. But how do you translate Lydia's elopement for an early twenty-first-century American setting?

For me, that quest began in late 2011. I was a young freelance television writer with two produced episodes on my resume, along with a multiyear run as a writers' assistant on several series, all of which had been cancelled before I could be promoted to the writing staff. I had just been laid off after the cancellation of series number four when Bernie Su reached out and suggested we meet at a Los Feliz coffee shop so he could tell me about his latest project. I knew Bernie casually at the time. I was aware he had written and directed several web series that had gotten some attention, and that he was always taking pictures when I saw him at writers' events. The new project he wanted to talk to me about was a collaboration with a guy named Hank from Montana to create vlog-style adaptations of public-domain novels for a young, female audience.[1]

"Oh," I said, "So you're going to do something like *Pride and Prejudice* on YouTube."

Bernie paused. "Actually, we're going to do exactly *Pride and Prejudice* on YouTube. Do you want to write for it?"

I hadn't read *Pride and Prejudice* since college, but I remembered it fondly, and I had watched and enjoyed the BBC miniseries and the 2005 film versions. The project sounded interesting, and I had just been laid off. Crucially, someone was offering me a job that wasn't an over-qualified writers' assistant on yet another soon-to-be-cancelled television show.

Did I want to write for *Pride and Prejudice* on YouTube?

To paraphrase an English novelist who is *not* Jane Austen: Reader, I did.

The Series

For those who are not familiar with *The Lizzie Bennet Diaries*, as the project would come to be known, the series was an experiment in interactive, multiplatform storytelling. The conceit was that Lizzie Bennet—now a twenty-four-year-old grad student who lived with her mother, father, and two sisters (Jane and Lydia) in a small town in modern-day California—was recording a video blog (vlog) about her life as part of her thesis. In the first episode, the big news in the neighborhood is that a rich, handsome, and (most importantly) single young medical student named Bing Lee has just bought a large house on Netherfield Drive. Mrs. Bennet is already gunning for him to marry one of her daughters. Over the course of the next year, with the help of childhood bestie Charlotte Lu, "Lizzie" uploaded a three-to-eight-minute video every Monday and Thursday, updating her viewers with the latest drama in and around the Bennet household.

The show was designed so viewers could follow the entire narrative through Lizzie's twice-weekly videos alone, but Lizzie's vlog was only part of the experience. Fans looking for more—more content, more engagement—could follow Lizzie, Jane, Lydia, and Charlotte (initially, our only on-screen characters) on Twitter, Facebook, and other social media platforms, where the characters tweeted at each other and answered questions from followers, like any other vlogger in the early 2010s.

But just because a character from the novel wasn't on screen, didn't mean that they didn't have a voice in the story. We first revealed this to the audience when Lizzie announced that Jane and Bing were dating by posting a screenshot of her sister's Twitter account that showed @LooksbyJane and @Bingliest were mutually following each other. Anyone who looked up Bing's account found that he was also following @that_caroline and @wmdarcy, who had all been tweeting at each other for weeks, unnoticed by the fandom. As our budget grew, we were able to cast those roles and others, bringing characters beyond our core four to the screen, but throughout the series we continued to use social media to foreshadow new characters and story developments. By the end of the series, the team was maintaining more than forty accounts for various characters on at least a dozen platforms. (After the initial reveal of Bing, Caroline, and Darcy, we had to get sneaky, as fans regularly searched Twitter for handles with any version of *Pride and Prejudice* characters' names. Transmedia Producer Jay Bushman and Transmedia Editor Alexandra Edwards managed to keep Gigi Darcy hidden for months by giving her only one account, on a [now defunct] music sharing site, *This Is My Jam*).

Our characters' interactivity was intended to add a layer of immersion and verisimilitude to the narrative, not to mislead the audience that they were watching unscripted content. While there was and is debate in the transmedia community on this point, I am firmly of the opinion that asking an audience to suspend their disbelief is almost always preferable to lying to them. The former allows a viewer to choose to come along for an adventure; the latter will inevitably leave them feeling resentful and betrayed when the ruse is revealed. On *Lizzie Bennet*, while Lizzie never acknowledged "in character" that she was fictional, every episode included full cast and crew credits in the video description, and out of character promotion and interviews from the cast and crew never tried to obscure the nature of what we were doing.

Still, even though we were frank about the scripted nature of the show, every layer of transmedia content was designed to encourage our audience to interact with fictional characters *as though* they were real people. In fact, it was one of the primary draws of the experience. Our show couldn't compete with television, films, or even higher budget web series in terms of visuals, famous cast, or dazzling special effects, but what we lacked in those areas we made up for in intimacy. Viewers watched the show on their computers, tablets, and phones—screens that are up close and personal. And in every episode, Lizzie looked out of those screens directly *at them*. The cliché is that television asks the audience to invite characters into their living rooms. Our audience carried Lizzie and her sisters in their pockets.

That intimacy was not a one-way street. Whenever I was asked at the time how fans affected the storyline, my stock response was that we were telling a story based on a novel that had been published two hundred years before and whose plot was widely known. There was only so much we could change about where the story was going before fans who were also fans of the book would cry foul. However, in retrospect, just because certain plot elements were set didn't mean that our audience didn't shape our narrative choices. The tension between the demands of the source material and the viewers was particularly evident in the Lydia/Wickham story arc.

The Search for a Modern Scandal

In the novel, Lydia running off with Wickham scandalizes society because it means they're going to have sex. In the most socially acceptable case, they're running off to Gretna Green to get married, *then* have sex. Worst case, they're running off to *not* get married, at which point whether or not they have sex is moot, because everyone will assume they have. Once she's left home without a chaperone, if Lydia does not return a married woman, her reputation will be ruined, her four sisters will be tainted by association, and with any chance of a respectable marriage (and financial survival) up in smoke, when poor Mr. Bennet dies, his surviving daughters will be condemned to perish in a gutter at the end of short, miserable lives of poverty and prostitution.[2]

For a workable modern analogue, the writers needed two things: first, a scandal with real and credible stakes that would resonate for a modern audience; second, because intervening to save Lydia is what triggers the shift in Lizzie and Darcy's relationship, whatever Lydia got herself into, there had to be a plausible way *for Darcy to help her get out.*

Some modern parallels were obvious. If there was ever a twenty-first-century equivalent of Gretna Green, it would be Las Vegas, conveniently within driving distance of our unnamed California town.

So the first story pitch was: what happens if Lydia and Wickham run off to Vegas and get married? Well . . . Lizzie would certainly have strong opinions about her sister making that particular life choice, but a quick and ill-advised marriage in the early 2010s had an obvious and accessible solution: the quick no-fault divorce. No muss, no fuss, no intervention from Darcy required.

Onto the next option: what would happen if Lydia and Wickham ran off to Vegas and *didn't* get married? Unfortunately for our dramatic purposes, to the characters—and to the majority of the audience—that would be even more of a nonevent. A wild weekend in Vegas might be the catalyst for a scandal, but for Darcy to help save the day, Lydia would have to get herself into something beyond standard party-girl shenanigans.

The writers explored more possibilities. What if Lydia got pregnant? It felt tonally in keeping with the original, but we didn't want to imply an unplanned pregnancy—however Lydia chose to handle it—was a life-ruining event for a young woman. Plus, how could Darcy help? Heroically pay for Lydia's abortion? Somehow, that didn't strike the right note.[3] I think we briefly discussed Lydia coming out as a lesbian, but again, we didn't want to send a message that not being straight would ruin a woman's life and her family's reputation.

Finally, Transmedia Producer Jay Bushman brought in the perfect pitch: Wickham would seduce Lydia, make a sex tape of the two of them, then trade on Lydia's internet fame to sell it for the money he hadn't been able to convince Darcy to give him. It had all the elements we were looking for. It was a visceral scandal that would be instantly understandable to our audience. Like the original, it played on power dynamics, sex, public exposure, and on Lydia's vulnerability to Wickham's manipulations. From a plot perspective, it represented an impending disaster where Darcy had the power to step in and helpfully intervene.

It was one of those ideas that everyone knew was right as soon as we heard it. But the space between a good idea and a good story is a long one, and the devil, as always, would be in the details.

Laying the Groundwork

The best plot twist in the world was going to fall flat if the audience didn't care about the characters involved. In this case, our problem was Lydia. From the beginning, the character had been a bit of a lightning rod. Some fans thought she was unspeakably annoying. Others found her a spontaneous breath of fresh air: a shot of exuberant chaos splashed into the lives of her more responsible older sisters. For many viewers who discovered the series in their teens and hadn't yet read Austen's novel—and so encountered Lydia for the first time without preconceptions—Lizzie was aspirational, but Lydia was a peer.

This is where our low budget had an interesting side effect. Four months into production, we were nearing the "Lizzie and Jane get stuck at Netherfield" portion of the story. The show was doing well enough that we had money to add Bing and Caroline to the cast, but because we shot a month's worth of episodes in a single day in one location, Lizzie and Jane were going to be Bing's houseguests for a full month. Our excuse was that Lizzie's mother decided to suddenly renovate the house in an effort to push Jane and Bing into cohabitating for as long as possible. The ploy was a bit of a narrative stretch perhaps, but not out of character for the unseen Bennet matriarch. However, Bernie pointed out a problem: Lydia wasn't at Netherfield. She *couldn't be* at Netherfield if love were going to blossom undisturbed between Bing and Jane. But he was justifiably concerned that the viewers who loved Lydia wouldn't stick with the show if she were gone for an entire month. The solution? We gave Lydia her own YouTube channel and had her make her own vlog while her sisters were away in hopes that would keep her fans hooked. Written by Rachel Kiley, the Lydia episodes were originally intended as a one-off.[4] However, once Lydia had her own platform, why wouldn't she continue to use it? For budgetary reasons, the videos went on pause after the month at Netherfield was over, but Rachel continued posting to Lydia's social media channels, further strengthening the relationship between fans and character.

As the series storyline brought us closer to Wickham's seduction, we realized there was no way our version of Lydia would fall head over heels in love and *not* tell the entire Internet about it. For perhaps the first time in a filmed adaptation, Lydia was going to tell her side of the story.

The Story

It begins with a New Year's Eve trip to Vegas. After ditching her museum-bound friends, Lydia finds herself at a club and decides to make a video for her dormant YouTube channel. Although she claims in her video that she is glad not to be stuck at home, she appears lonely, feeling left behind by her older sisters.[5]

However, over the course of the night, her progressively more inebriated Tweets make it clear she hasn't let those feelings stop her from painting the town red. Eventually, Lydia runs into a familiar face.

GEORGE WICKHAM: Well that's a happy new year if I've ever seen one.[6]

Yup. George Wickham *just happens* to be in town, tweeting and being kinda creepy about it. Viewers watching Lydia's social media that night try to warn her that hanging out with her sister's skeevy ex might not be the best idea, but by night's end, Wickham nevertheless leaves Lydia with quite the impression.

LYDIA BENNET: So that was . . . different. I guess sometimes people surprise you.

Over the next month, while the series' main platform chronicled Lizzie's life as an intern at Pemberley Digital, along with her slowly thawing personal relationship with its CEO William Darcy, viewers following Lydia's channel watched her fall for Wickham, blind to the increasingly problematic ways he treated her in her own videos. When fans reached out on social media, Lydia blew off their concerns.

January 29, 2013:

MARIA RAQUEL SILVA: @TheLydiaBennet your videos are getting sadder and sadder. I always supported you, but this is getting hard to watch. I mean, can't you see he's throwing you against your sisters?
LYDIA BENNET: @_mrsilva That isn't what's happening. He wouldn't do that.

On one level, Lydia had to defend Wickham for plot reasons. If someone talked her into dumping him before he sprang his trap, the end of the main story would collapse, and Lizzie and Darcy wouldn't get their happily ever after. (While Lydia saw herself as the main character of her own story, the series was still centered on Lizzie.) But on a meta level, Lydia's interaction encouraged engagement with the show, no matter what form it took. Lydia didn't block people who told her things she didn't want to hear; she argued. This meant that she was still listening. So fans continued to try and persuade her to change course . . . and kept watching her videos to see what was going to happen next. Eventually, Wickham stepped into the fray:

GEORGE WICKHAM: @TheLydiaBennet. Hey, it's alright. Don't push them away, Lydia. They care about you. People care about you. Let them, okay? Promise me that.
LYDIA BENNET: @TheGWickham But they don't get it. They're being so mean to you. Why? You're more important to me than them. You know that.
GEORGE WICKHAM: I know. I wish things were different, but the world is what it is. I'm sorry.

The reasons for Wickham's apology would soon become evident.

The next day, January 30, 2013, spam comments appeared on several series videos. At first, the fans ignored them. After all, who clicks on links in spam comments?[7] But eventually, someone noticed the posts contained a URL for "www.lydiabennettape.com," which indicated either a remarkably savvy spammer, or that this was actually a story-related clue. Clicking on the link took viewers to a website from a company called Novelty Exposures that advertised: "Hot Lydia Bennet XXX Video: See YouTube Star Lydia Bennet reveal EVERYTHING."[8] The page featured a photo of Lydia and Wickham in bed together, apparently unclothed.[9] Below the photo was a countdown clock and an email link for a preorder mailing list.[10]

Erin Wert was one of the first fans to find the link and spread the word. She described her excitement at discovering a new element of the story, but also added: "I still remember feeling actually awful about posting the website on Tumblr . . . [I] felt like I was really talking about a real person and something terrible that had happened to her. I remember talking [with other fans] about, like . . . does Lydia know about this? What is she thinking?"[11]

What *had* Lydia been thinking? In Jay's original pitch, while Lydia was unaware of Wickham's plans to use the sex tape as a source of revenue, she had willingly made the recording. Ultimately, we made the call that it was better for the story if Lydia had been taped without her knowledge or consent. Many factors went into that decision: it made Wickham a more clear-cut villain, it protected Lydia—and Mary Kate Wiles, the actress who played her—from the potential fury of the Internet and its sexual double standards, and it sent a clear message to the audience about where we wanted them to put their sympathies. Even with the deck stacked as firmly in Lydia's favor as we could manage, Mary Kate remembers the lead-up to the reveal vividly: "I was so nervous [on launch day], which is so funny because there wasn't anything. It was all fake, but I remember sitting by my computer and just shaking, knowing that people were going to start finding it."[12]

Mary Kate wasn't the only one anxiously waiting behind the scenes.

Dropping the Bomb

The sex tape was a huge plot point for our series, and the creative team had been working at a dead sprint in the lead-up to the website reveal. Despite some nerves, the overall feeling was one of excitement. We had been working so hard. We couldn't wait to see what the fans were going to make of our big moment.

Jay Bushman recalled it vividly: "Oh my God. Launch of the sex tape is one of the highlights of the whole experience for me. I was in a coffee shop in Hollywood, and I got a parking ticket because I *couldn't leave.* Because I kept going, 'I should go,' but I just kept refreshing [thinking]: 'I gotta see what happens next. I gotta see what happens next.'"[13]

As we had hoped they would, fans began sending messages to the email address on the Novelty Exposures website almost immediately. The sentiment in this early missive was a common one (Figure 12.1):

Figure 12.1. Screenshot of email received by Novelty Exposures, subject: "WICKHAM I SWEAR TO GOD," sender redacted.

However, we did get a couple along these lines (Figure 12.2):

Figure 12.2. Screenshot of email received by Novelty Exposures, subject: "Sign me up!," sender redacted.

I'm still not sure if messages like this second one were glimpses into the baser parts of human nature or if fans were merely playing along, responding "in character" as someone who would sign up to pre-order a sex tape. Likely, they were a combination of both; however, it does go to show that creators don't have a monopoly on blurring the line between fiction and reality in an interactive experience.

Fans wondered about that blurred line as well (Figure 12.3):

Figure 12.3. Screenshot of email received by Novelty Exposures, subject: "Pre-order list," sender redacted.

For the record, there was (and is) no Lydia Bennet sex tape.

Of course, for all our preparations, the launch didn't go off without snags. Fortunately, one of the features of interacting with an audience in real time is that if your team is on the ball, it's possible to turn mishaps into opportunities. For example, on February 2, three days after the Novelty Exposures website launched, it went down. When fans noticed, they reasonably speculated that Darcy had found Wickham and stopped him. Which of course he was going to do . . . in about four weeks.

Production Designer Katie Moest got the call that something had gone wrong while she was driving. She pulled into a Starbucks parking lot to borrow their free WiFi on her laptop and—once she'd verified the site wasn't up—called the hosting service. As it turned out, the server our plot point was on had been taken down for maintenance and wouldn't be back up for several days. Katie then got to "sheepishly try to explain that I wasn't hosting an adult video site to the very kind tech support guy . . . It was one of the funniest stressful experiences of my life."[14]

While Katie was on the phone, Jay needed to give the audience an excuse to explain what was happening. He scrambled to create a Twitter account for Novelty Exposures and post an update about the outage (Figure 12.4):

Figure 12.4. Screenshot of a Tweet: "@NoveltyXposures, https://twitter.com/NoveltyXposures/status/297943846678052865?s=20.

What had been a technical glitch had now raised the stakes. Bad enough that Wickham had made and planned to distribute an illicit sex tape. But that so many people were interested to the point they crashed the site? Yikes! Poor Lydia!

Eventually, the site came back up; the story was back on track, and we all heaved a sigh of relief. Until the idea of crashing the website surfaced again. Jay recalls: "Somebody in the fanbase started advancing this idea. They were like, 'Hey, Wait a minute. Maybe *we're* the ones who are supposed to save Lydia. Maybe if we get everyone to work together and attack this site like a denial-of-service attack, we can overload it, and then it will crash, and they won't be able to release the sex tape!'"[15]

The fans probably could have done it, and it would have crashed the site. It also would have cost the production hundreds of thousands of dollars we didn't have in bandwidth charges. Plus, for the sake of the plot, we *still* needed Darcy to save the day. Unfortunately, we couldn't fix this problem with a new in-world Twitter account. The only *character* who didn't want the site taken down was Wickham, and no one trying to save Lydia was going to listen to *him*.

In the end, this was one of the places where the decision to acknowledge that our series was fictional paid dividends. For narrative reasons, the team tried to avoid out-of-world explanations for in-world issues. Our philosophy was that it was better for the story to stand on its own, and that viewers should be able to ignore us and still have a fulfilling experience with the show. But many fans were aware of us, and followed the writers, actors, and producers on social media, which meant that we did have that additional "out-of-world" communications channel available. Lacking a plausible in-world alternative, Jay eventually stepped out from behind the curtain, explained to the fans that they had come to a very reasonable (but incorrect) conclusion, and humbly asked them to please not crash our sex tape website. Because we had built a relationship of trust over the previous ten months, they listened. More than that, in the weeks that followed, fans spread the word themselves when new voices who hadn't heard Jay's appeal reproposed the DNS attack plan.

It's a testament to the relationship we had built with the viewers over the course of the series. When we made an implicit promise that if they stuck with us, everything would be okay in the end, they trusted us to deliver. That wasn't a trivial ask.

Our light romantic comedy was taking a very dark turn as Lydia's breakdown played out over multiple weeks. Lydia was raw and hurting. She had always been open and responsive to her viewers, and she didn't let them off the hook. In episode eighty-seven, she explicitly called out viewers who had posted comments on Lizzie's Videos that she needed to get over herself, or that she was "being too dramatic," or who blamed her for Lizzie's choice to leave Pemberley Digital and her burgeoning romance with Darcy.[16] For the first time in the series, Lydia moved the audience's participation from meta-narrative to a central part of the text. In effect, she cast them in the role of a disapproving Regency society, which wasn't necessarily comfortable.

As the clock on the Novelty Exposures website ticked down, Christine Linnell, an entertainment journalist and fan of the series, recalled the building tension in the fandom between those who blamed Lydia's crisis on Lizzie for ignoring her younger sister, and the Lizzie partisans who argued Lydia needed to own her choices. According to Christine, "After the sex tape website dropped, it all intensified, obviously. A lot of us [who were fans of the book] were still feeling protective of Lizzie, but there was also an element of, 'Are we slut-shaming Lydia right now?' Because . . . any time a woman on the Internet gets humiliated, there is a pile-on tendency. The show played into that, with Lydia liking comments of people saying that she was ruining everything for Lizzie."[17]

I suspect that even for fans who knew the book and might have been biased against Lydia because of it, there was a difference between reading about the downfall of a secondary character who existed somewhere between the page and their imaginations and watching that fall in real-time as portrayed by a talented actress like Mary Kate.

For Rachel Kiley, who was still running Lydia's social media accounts, Lydia's "liked" videos were less a way to guilt-trip the audience and more a tool to foreshadow how Lydia was feeling before each episode was released: "I'd also have her drunk tweet and delete stuff, which felt in character and also encouraged fans to be engaged so as to not miss out."[18]

It's not that Rachel (or any of the other writers) were indifferent to the strong emotional reaction that our fans were having to the storyline. But for us, the fact that fans were upset by what was happening to a fictional character, that they were arguing over whether the blame for Lydia's downfall lay at her own feet or her sister's, that they worried about how their own words affected a character whom they knew intellectually was not a real person . . . Well, it was all a sign that we were doing our jobs and doing them well.

Needless to say, the countdown on the Novelty Exposures Website expired to reveal not a sex tape, but the message shown in Figure 12.5.

We're sorry. Due to reasons
beyond our control, we are no longer able to offer this product.

Figure 12.5. Screenshot of the Novelty Exposures logo and
message, http://web.archive.org/web/20130214165118/
http://www.lydiabennettape.com/.

Fans and characters alike heaved a sigh of relief. Lizzie went on to pursue
the mystery of who had stopped Wickham—a search that would lead her to
Darcy, and the series' happy conclusion—and Lydia largely withdrew from
the public eye to heal in privacy. Although she did make a hopeful appearance in the series' conclusion, viewers looking for additional closure or curious about the next chapter in Lydia's life would have to wait for a book:
The Epic Adventures of Lydia Bennet, in which she retold the full story of her
experiences with Wickham, and shared her struggles to put her life and relationships back together afterwards.[19]

Aftermath

One year to the day after Lizzie Bennet first told the world, "My name is
Lizzie Bennet, and this is my life," she posted her one-hundredth, and final,
episode.

I take it as a sign of the show's evolution that while we were nominated
for Best Comedy at the 2013 Streamy Awards, we won the following year for
Best Drama. Our bright confection of a show had grown and changed along

with its characters, which our fans recognized. Christine Linnell remembers: "That [storyline] was my first experience with online discourse about emotional abuse, unhealthy relationships, and consent . . . I had never been involved in that kind of conversation before. And this was all pre-"Me Too," before it became a really mainstream discussion."[20] Mary Kate Wiles recalls: "People reached out and said, 'This reminds me of an abusive relationship that I was in,' or, 'This helped me realize I was in an abusive relationship and get out of it.' . . . I don't think anybody ever goes into creating art going, 'I'm gonna make this art that's gonna help someone through a difficult situation.' And that certainly wasn't what I expected when we started the show, but I'm glad that we got to do that."[21]

When Bernie and I met at that coffee shop in 2011, he didn't know if the show would last beyond the initial twelve episodes Hank had agreed to fund from his own pocket. None of us imagined this experiment in vlog-style storytelling would end up touching on emotionally abusive relationships, revenge porn, and consent, or that the following year we would be on stage at the Emmys accepting a statuette for Best Original Interactive Program.[22] While no creative endeavor is without its missteps, I am proud that—anecdotally at least—our impact on those larger societal conversations has been more positive than not.

Postscript

I wake up each day in my own bedroom, in a home I pay for with money I've earned from an occupation I freely chose. I wear skirts or trousers as the mood strikes me or the weather demands, and for the most part, I don't worry that a social faux pas will forever doom my future prospects. In so many ways, my life as middle-class white-presenting cisgender woman is much freer than it would have been in Austen's time. But I also live in a world where revelations of a consensual extramarital affair can ruin a woman's public life, while men shrug off allegations, even admissions, of sexual assault as a matter of course. Especially men like Wickham who are both handsome and white, or—lacking those advantages—rich and powerful.

Today, as then, we all live with or rebel against the norms and codes of what our societies deem acceptable behavior, sexual and otherwise. If we didn't, I'm not sure a modern *Pride and Prejudice* would resonate.

Notes

1. Hank Green, at the time, most notably of Vlog Brothers fame. https://hank-green.com.

2. If anyone tries to tell you *Pride and Prejudice* doesn't have high stakes, give them my number.

3. The possibility of a Lydia pregnancy and Darcy's involvement with same had also occurred to fans. They theorized Darcy could carry the baby for her, like a seahorse—which is how a certain segment of the fandom came to call themselves "seahorses."

4. Rachel Kiley was a founding member of the Lizzie Bennet writers' room and the one who most defined Lydia's voice on the series. She wrote the scripts for all Lydia's vlogs, and most main series episodes in this arc.

5. The Lydia Bennet, episode 21, "Midnight," January 1, 2013, https://youtu.be/Ne2w9jyi1DM.

6. Tweets referenced here from the fan-created compilation of Lizzie Bennet transmedia content available at: https://sociallyawkwarddarcy.tumblr.com/post/62958207163/download-the-complete-lbd-transmedia-booklet-pdf.

7. Finding the correct level of mediation in new media is a delicate balance.

8. Domain ownership has since lapsed, but an archived version is available at: http://web.archive.org/web/20130212155142/http://www.lydiabennettape.com/.

9. "Apparently," being the key word in this sentence.

10. hotlydiabennetvideo@gmail.com, for the curious. As of this writing, it's still active. It's not checked regularly, but if you want to make our production designer happy, send Wickham a note to tell him how terrible you think his website is.

11. Twitter direct messages to the author, October 7, 2020.

12. Personal interview with the author, September 4, 2020.

13. Personal interview with the author, August 31, 2020.

14. Text messages to the author, October 13, 2020.

15. Personal interview.

16. *The Lizzie Bennet Diaries,* episode 87 "An Understanding," February 11, 2013, https://youtu.be/9LdEPWt0R60.

17. Personal interview with the author, October 11, 2020.

18. Via email to the author, 10/7/2020.

19. Kate Rorick and Rachel Kiley, Simon and Schuster, 2015.

20. Personal interview.

21. Personal interview.

22. Somewhere on the Internet, there's a picture of me holding the show's Emmy while surrounded by animated sparkles. Moral of the story: say yes to the coffee meeting.

Part Four

Austen in Conversations and Contexts

Chapter Thirteen

Erotic Austen

Devoney Looser

"It is a truth universally acknowledged, that a dominant man in possession of a good set of cuffs, must be in want of a much younger, submissive wife" begins *Spank Me, Mr. Darcy* (2013) by Jane Austen and Lissa Trevor.[1] *Pride/Prejudice* (2010) by Ann Herendeen opens with Darcy ("Fitz") and Mr. Bingley ("Charles") in bed together, pleasuring each other and scoffing at the prospect of being married off to eligible women.[2] *Mrs. Bennet Has Her Say* (2015) by Jane Austen and Jane Juska gives us *Pride and Prejudice*'s marriage-obsessed mother's tale of pretending to be a virgin on her wedding night. Mr. Bennet repeatedly utters "Consummate!" while entering her.[3]

Of course, Jane Austen-inspired pornographic fiction exists. There's porn everything, and there's Jane Austen everything. Why wouldn't there be Austenesque erotica? Whether you welcome the phenomenon with open arms, a raised eyebrow, a raised fist, or a guffaw, you don't have to do much digging to discover that twenty-first-century print-porn Austen adaptations have flourished. Although not every kind of porn has penetrated Austen's original plots and characters, there is a wider variety of this material than one might think, especially when coming at the subject through Austen criticism, where treatment of it is sparse. Few of us who "do Austen" as critics have tried to make sense of the proliferation of such horny homages, or, if you'd rather, dirty dishonors. Perhaps it is because such texts may at first seem to require little by way of careful analysis to grasp their appeal or inner workings. Such texts thrive, you might say, because there is a market for them. They work (or don't) by entertaining and/or arousing readers. Case closed.

An earlier, shorter version of this essay appeared in Salon.com, at http://www.Salon.com and remains in the Salon archives. Reprinted with permission.

Yet to stop at dollars and pounds, or sex and sensationalism, would be a mistake. As we try to come to grips with the scope of Austen's legacy, celebrity, and iconicity, we must examine the meanings of even the most blatantly sexed-up Austen-inspired texts. In the first part of this essay, I start close to the present, providing an overview of recent straight-up and send-up Austen erotica, as it circulates in the early twenty-first century. But Austen-inspired smut is not as new as many might suppose, as I show in the second half of this essay. Its origins date as far back as half a century ago, with a disturbingly comic novel, published under a pseudonym, that has an unlikely story of authorship and reception. In the years since that apparently originary 1980 work, the sexy subgenre of Austenesque fiction has become, by comparison to its beginnings, more tame and banal. This essay charts the history of Austen-inspired erotica's explosive growth and greater acceptance.

There are some commonalities that emerge over the course of fifty years of multimedia adaptation. One feature many Austen-inspired erotic texts of this period share is the use of attention-grabbing juxtaposition. Titillating takes are meant to provide a contrast to Austen's staid, polite reputation, whether for laughs or shock value. Where original Austen underplays the direct narration of desire, Austen erotica says more, more, more. In doing so, these porn-inflected Austen-inspired texts may make the original novels seem tamer than they really are. New erotic Austen retellings reinforce the (mistaken) idea that the original versions are sexless or painfully restrained. On the other hand, Austen-inspired porn may also make original Austen seem more sex-obsessed than it is, encouraging its readers to imagine that illicit sex is lurking around every character and corner of the original fiction. That feature may make it difficult for today's readers to conclude that nineteenth-century literary cigars were ever just cigars, to turn a Freudian truism on its head. Austen-inspired porn, in providing these possibilities for under- or over-reading sexuality in the original novels, is sure to have some impact going forward. As a result, even among those skeptical of Austen-inspired erotica's literary quality or value, the significance of the subgenre ought to be acknowledged.

Austen Sells Sex; or, Austen Sex Sells

It may help to begin with a description of the range of texts that fall under what I am loosely calling "Erotic Austen." Those texts taking a serious tone are generally soft-core and print-based, while the comic porn has ranged more widely beyond the page to stage productions and short video. These texts take slight inspiration from Austen, or, for that matter, from Romantic-era sexual practices or from pornography published in the eighteenth and nineteenth centuries.[4] Perhaps predictably, recent authors more often take inspiration and cues from erotica of their own historical moment, rather than from those of the past. Austen porn has proven more often a form of crudely creative anachronism than an attempt to revisit Regency raunch.

Critics were talking about Jane Austen's novels in comparison to porn for at least two decades before there was a first published work of Austen-inspired porn. Calling Austen a purveyor of porn-like fiction dates back to at least 1962. In a panel on Sex in Literature, featuring the day's literary luminaries, novelist Carson McCullers is said to have suggested that Austen's novels deserved to be understood as pornography. The remark was made in front of an audience of a thousand at the Cheltenham Festival, on a panel in conversation with fellow writers Joseph Heller and Kingsley Amis. (Amis had himself recently been accused of writing pornography.) Amis apparently agreed with McCullers's assertion, likening Austen's fiction to porn, saying, "Yes, I see what you mean. It's a sort of pecuniary pornography."[5]

Our understanding of how to read the money-obsessed parts of Austen's fiction have certainly evolved since then. Things have moved well beyond fellow novelists asking whether Austen's rich men and women are eroticized because of their wealth and into a literary marketplace unapologetically capitalizing on the erotic-economic structured into her fiction. One pioneering comic text that did well on this formula was Arielle Eckstut and Dennis Ashton's spoof *Pride and Promiscuity: The Lost Sex Scenes of Jane Austen* (2001). Its authors claim to have discovered a hidden cache of manuscript pages, restoring "original" Austen content of the most scandalous kind. One of the coauthors, Eckstut, describes the book's origins in *The Essential Guide to Getting Your Book Published*. Eckstut (a literary agent as well as an author) reports that her friend made an offhand joke in a taxi about what it would be like if someone discovered Austen's lost scenes. That conversation resulted in "a galaxy of light bulbs" lighting up over Eckstut's head.[6] It's hard not to imagine some of these light bulbs being in the shape of dollar signs.

Whatever motivated the book *Pride and Promiscuity*, it made a splash, was reviewed widely, and sold well.

Pride and Promiscuity has a clever conceit. It begins with two American Austen scholars staying at a Hertfordshire estate, in the style of A. S. Byatt's *Possession*. But it's perfectly clear from *Pride and Promiscuity* that this is a send-up. The authors begin, "We were untangling our cuttings of Greek oregano when an antique wooden box caught our attention simultaneously.[7]" The box turns out to have hidden manuscripts in it, featuring, among other things, letters from Austen. In these long-lost letters, the famous novelist is lamenting her publisher's insistence that she rename her novel *Pride and Prejudice*, from *Pride and Promiscuity*. She is also upset that the publisher has asked her to remove her name from the title page. Subsequent chapters provide the content she was compelled to omit (although not the original novel), telling readers where precisely these sections would have gone in an unexpurgated book, if it were published as the bold, saucy author originally intended. One wonders how directly this early sex-added mash-up inspired the Quirk Books project that would later become Seth Graeme-Smith's bestseller *Pride and Prejudice and Zombies* (2009).[8]

Porn-Austen entrepreneurialism continued in a robust fashion after 2001. A recent addition to the light-bulb-inducing, "Now-why-didn't-I-think-of-that?" Austen porn genre is the *Jane Austen Kama Sutra: A Playful Presentation of Sense & Sensuality* (2016). It features delightfully compromising black-and-white silhouettes, accompanied by double-entendre quotes from Austen's writings. (The book is packaged as authored by Jane Austen but "curated by" Joelle Herr.) It features sexy, suggestive shadow images. In one image, a silhouetted and bonneted woman is seated with her legs open, as her fingers explore her own body. The accompanying quotation is from heroine Elinor Dashwood of *Sense and Sensibility* (1811): "I will be mistress of myself."[9] Another image shows two women, tête-à-tête, as a man behind one of them reaches for her bottom. The accompanying quote is from *Emma*: "Men never know when things are dirty or not."[10] The book's subtitle is "A Playful Presentation of Sense & Sensuality."

Recent comic sexed-up versions of Austen have also ranged beyond illustration and print. One video that became highly successful as YouTube comedy click-bait racked up almost half a million views. The team National Banana produced a Regency-costumed spoof trailer in 2008 for a fake movie titled *Porn and Penetration*. A proper British male's voice-over informs readers, "There was another side to Jane Austen. A side she was forced to keep hidden—until now." The recently discovered novel, *Porn and Penetration*, is introduced with movie trailer snippets of dirty dialogue scenes. One young woman says to a Colin Firth–Darcy-like figure, with the utmost politeness, "I assure you. Your cock shall be sucked, most vigorously." The Darcy-like figure replies to her and another propositioning woman, equally politely, "It t'woud be my honor. And my pleasure." In the rest of the video, Regency ladies make out with each other and matter-of-factly ask servants to deliver them contemporary sex toys, including an anal intruder. The video's young women deliver serious-faced lines, including, "I think you are entitled to a poke in the whiskers." Then an older woman, in the mold of a Mrs. Bennet or a Lady Catherine de Bourgh, delivers a punctuated one-word closing line: "Cock."[11]

Porn-inspired Austen came to the stage as well as to little screens in the first decade of the 2000s. One Austen-inspired play worked in precisely the same coarsely comic vein as the short video, albeit with more thoughtful, sentimental follow-through. Steve Dawson's play *Jane Austen's Guide to Pornography* (2007) mixes the old-fashioned and newfangled in sexed-up Austen, showing where each falls short.[12] The play's innovation is an all-male cast, which means the character of Jane Austen is played by a cross-dressed man. The conceit is to put a twenty-first-century gay playwright in conversation with the ghost of Jane Austen, in order for each to give the other writing advice. The contemporary writer tries to nudge the historical Austen toward writing about passion, while she tries to school the playwright to consider love. Each then watches their fictional character-creations acted out on stage. As a result, each goes through a transformation.

Dawson's fictional Austen ultimately embraces putting explicit sex scenes into her fiction, rather than fearing or refusing them. The play's wish fulfillment message is that today's pornographic playwrights are the rightful heirs to a largely unknowing, but by no means sexually closed, Jane Austen. *Jane Austen's Guide to Pornography* was first performed in Australia and went on to sold-out performances at the Edinburgh Fringe. The *Guardian* gave the play a largely positive review, although it complained about its "predictable nudge-nudge" elements. The reviewer writes that someone must have been thinking, "ooh, let's make Jane Austen say 'enormous cock,' that'll be hilarious."[13] Although Dawson works in every Austen biographical cliché in the book (e.g. she writes in solitude, she doesn't know the male mind, the only men she had conversations with were her brother and father, etc.), some of her advice to the present is told in order to make porn more sentimentally touching. Dawson's Austen tells the contemporary playwright, "don't be afraid to write about sex . . . Challenge every notion of propriety."[14] Dawson ends his play by having the straight nineteenth-century past, through Austen, coach the queer twenty-first-century present on how to better depict love with sex.

Serious, sentimental, Austen-inspired porn, even more than the comic kind, has boomed in print. A glimpse into the profitability of the genre is offered by the experiences of Austen adapter Linda Berdoll. She describes having taken her online fan fiction, *Bar Sinister: Pride and Prejudice Continues* (1999), later retitled *Mr. Darcy Takes a Wife* (2004), into self-published print sales that totaled more than 200,000 copies.[15] The book has been described as "an epic historical romance written in a baroque prose style and liberally studded with energetic sex scenes."[16] Berdoll has since completed several sequels. When she first approached a literary agent, she was told, "Jane Austen and sex? Nobody would be interested in that."[17] Berdoll's Amazon.com author page claims total sales upward of 400,000 copies. Austen porn—like most porn—is big business.[18]

After Berdoll, many other similar projects emerged, whether to contribute to the genre, to try to cash in, or both. One of the most successful among them was Mitzi Szereto's *Pride and Prejudice: Hidden Lusts* (2011). It advertises itself as "The classic that goes all the way!"[19] Upon receiving the promotional materials, *The Los Angeles Times* asked its readers, "Do you want a XXX Jane Austen? Vote in our poll." A thousand readers answered; 40 percent said yes.[20] Countless other works appeared after Berdoll's success.

Among the most notable were Clandestine Classics's soft-core repurposings of Austen's fiction. Clandestine Classics's line of erotic mash-ups are offered at a low cost, because "You only pay for the words our authors have added—not for the original content." In the Clandestine Classics *Northanger Abbey*, coauthor Desiree Holt adds content that has Catherine Morland acquiring a female friend named Virginia. The two girls frequently consult "a thick volume entitled *Sexual Satisfaction for Mature Adults*."[21] The Clandestine Classics *Pride and Prejudice*, by Austen and Amy Armstrong, describes Elizabeth's "positively wicked" thoughts. In her first meeting with Mr. Darcy, his gaze takes in "every inch of Elizabeth's body, from the top of her neatly arranged hair to the toes of her newly acquired slippers." Darcy, we're told, finds Elizabeth's lips "mouth-wateringly fleshy."[22] After the series launched in 2013, it got a great deal of negative press, which presumably moved some copies. Critic William Deresiewicz calls these titles, "a new low in Austen-exploitation, even worse than *Pride and Predator* or *Pride and Prejudice and Zombies*."[23] Whatever else one may think of his assertion, the "new" part doesn't hold up, as we will see shortly.[24]

Like the Clandestine Classics, most serious-toned, contemporary, Austen-inspired porn falls in the subgenre now known popularly as mommy porn (or, in the UK, mummy porn), a label coined in the wake of the bestseller-dom of E. L. James's *Fifty Shades of Grey* (2012).[25] Austen porn tends not to celebrate female masochism to the same degree as *Fifty Shades*, but it shares a female-centered narrative viewpoint, while adding a sheen of normalcy, or perhaps even banality, to what was supposedly previously considered kink. But how new is mommy porn, really? As Australian TV personality Chrissie Swan puts it, "'mummy porn looks a lot like the straight-up normal stuff that's been around forever . . . but . . . it was immediately labeled mummy porn simply because the vast majority of people buying it had a set of boobies."[26] She suspects someone in a corner office noticed women buying it and slapped a new label on it, therefore creating "a whole new condescend-ing genre of literature!" Her quips are a useful starting point in the analysis of the history of Austen porn, as a not-really-all-that-new sort of "chick lit."

Which Came First: The Origins of Austen Porn

Austen-inspired Wild and Wanton editions, Clandestine Classics editions, and slash fiction entered the literary marketplace in the 2010s, claiming to be innovative, original adaptations, as we have seen. Claims of supposedly shocking newness were used to sell these texts to readers, by claiming that they were making old-fashioned Austen stories into new-fangled bawdy fic-tion. But Austen porn's proper (or improper) origins date back decades ear-lier than these far better-known twenty-first-century ventures. These earliest texts were simply not visible in the same ways, especially to Janeite readers.

Some scholars mistakenly date the notion of a sexed-up Austen back to a 1992 London *Telegraph* newspaper cartoon that reads, "Jane Austen's Sex Boutique: We're in the Extremely Chaste Sex Shop Guide."[27] In the image, a hunched-over, stereotypical dirty old man in a trench coat, his back to the viewer, peeps into a shop window. The store's slogan appears on an ornate eye-level sign, next to what appears to be a Regency lady mannequin. It was Austen scholar Roger Sales who first brought this cartoon to wider Janeite attention. He argues that the cartoon's humor derives from its juxtaposing overt sexuality with Austen, whom he describes as the cultural icon univer-sally acknowledged to be its antithesis.[28]

As we have seen thus far, associations of Austen with prudery have expe-rienced rapid growth and change in the past two decades. For those who imagine Austen as a prim, uptight pedant, and who think of sex shops as vulgar, dirty fun, putting the two things together might equal surprising hilarity. But as more readers and viewers become accustomed to associating Jane Austen with overt sexuality (porn), alcohol (as in the recently released Austen-branded Bath Gin), or the horror genre (vampires, zombies, etc.), that set of associations must shift wider cultural expectations. These racy texts and objects serve to normalize Austen's proximity to sex, booze, and blood. It's interesting to speculate on whether linking licit and illicit Austens will continue to be readable as funny material, if and when such jokes lose their shock value. It stands to reason that the more that the figure of Austen is associated with sex, the less she will seem to audiences to represent its antithesis. (The flip side to this, of course, is that sex shops and porn, too, have become far more bourgeois and more accepted cultural spaces.)

But if we are serious about predicting Erotic Austen's future, then we ought to start by more accurately describing not only its recent but its more distant past. In the beginning, Austenesque porn was created differently. Austen-inspired porn's apparent origins were in a work of pseudonymous mass-market fiction, Grania Beckford's *Virtues and Vices* (1980).[29] Incredibly, this twice-published, retitled novel wasn't even packaged by author or publisher as Austen-inspired. Yet it is both a direct send-up of Austen's fictional techniques and of late twentieth-century popular pornographic fiction. This likely first work of Austen-inspired erotica approaches literary and pornographic conventions in ways that are both comic and serious, humorous and satirical, although it is also a disturbing text. What makes it interesting as well as disturbing is that Beckford's *Virtues and Vices* employs some of the same fictional techniques that Austen herself brought to the history of the novel in her juvenilia and early fiction. Both Austen and Beckford used their own fiction to expose and ridicule popular patterns in previous fiction, through outrageous exaggeration employed for would-be comic effect.

Beckford's 287-page novel carries the title, *Virtues and Vices: A Delectable Rondelet of Love and Lust in Edwardian Times*. Here Beckford takes up Austen's *Persuasion* (1818) as its inspiration, rather than other, better-known titles and characters. Beckford's *Virtues and Vices* retains many of *Persuasion's* character names and plot elements, substituting an Austen-sounding alliterative title. Its most significant changes are to its mode of narration and historical setting, which is moved forward a century, from Regency to Edwardian England. Rather than unfolding in Austenian third-person, free-indirect discourse, Beckford's story is told from multiple first-person perspectives, with a plot that's entirely sex-driven, including encounters that are horrifying and despicable. Literally everyone in the novel is having sex with everyone else—men, women, and children. With far more vices than virtues, the novel features Austen-inspired pedophilia and incest. These acts move this early porn Austen effort very far away indeed from contemporary mommy porn. Beckford's novel makes today's *Fifty Shades*-inspired, Austen-derived sado-masochism gender violence seem garden-variety stuff by comparison.

Yet Beckford was clearly going for humor in *Virtues and Vices*, well beyond its Austen-echoing title. The book flap copy describes the novel as a sophisticated comic romance.[30] For the hardcover edition, a longer blurb, from the author herself, features what might almost be read as an updated defense of the novel, in its echoing the manifesto style of Austen's narrator in *Northanger Abbey*'s chapter five. Beckford provides her own endorsement, authoritatively stating, "The most erotic books are the worst novels, being self-indulgent, gratuitously dirty, or plotless. The best novels are the least erotic, since sex is apt to become an occasional and subordinate episode. What waits to be written is a very erotic book which is also a good and original novel." An unsigned response following Beckford's statement adds, "Readers will agree that the author has filled this gap herself with *Virtues and Vices*." That may be wishful thinking, but it is certainly an audacious claim for a derivative book.

In the pages of the novel itself, the use of first-person narration means that, unlike on the book jacket copy, no moralizing narrator ever intrudes. The point of view shifts to tell the story from different characters' perspectives, which makes discerning tone a challenge. There is unquestionably comedy here, derived from Austen-inspired humorous details, which are spread throughout. Although *Pride and Prejudice*'s Mr. Darcy and Elizabeth Bennet have become the most porn-repurposed characters of Austen's oeuvre, Beckford's pornographic mash-up begins instead with an older sexed-obsessed couple at its center, Austen's Sir Walter Elliot and Lady Russell. Spendthrift Sir Walter Elliot is made into a rake and renamed Sir Wilfred Elliott. He's said to have a bedroom of wall-to-wall mirrors. The detail of a bemirrored Kellynch is indeed from Austen's original, but the mirror-saturated bedroom is Beckford's embellishment. We learn about this feature of Sir Wilfred's bedroom from his neighbor, the widow Lady Russell, who retains her name from Austen's original. Lady Russell has had a close-up look at these mirrors and at Sir Wilfred. She describes cavorting with him in his bedroom, where she observes him admiring the reflection of his own member in his many mirrors as they have intercourse. It's a well-chosen detail, told from Lady Russell's perspective, infusing porn elements into a male character defined in the original Austen by his overwhelming vanity.

Other chapters, too, take small details from Austen's novels and amplify them into darkly comic sexual exploits. The chapter in the voice of Louisa (renamed Lucinda) Musgrove describes her doing it with Wentworth in cliched, florid, and would-be poetic language, perfectly pitched to the impulsive immaturity of Austen's callow original. Mrs. Clay is revealed not to be Mr. Shepherd's relative at all but his former lover. Lady Russell has an affair with "Kevin" Wentworth, who is a very discreet lover, which is necessary, because Lady Russell is also sexually involved with Angela (Anne) Elliot. The oldest Elliot daughter, Edwina (renamed from Elizabeth in the original) describes being sexually abused by her father. She shows no understanding of his criminality, describing a game in which she nurses him like a baby at her own bosom. In his first-person sections, Sir Wilfred describes enjoying a woman partner's playfully connecting his beloved "baronet" title to what she calls his prodigious "bayonet" genitals.

As these examples suggest, few of the sex scenes in *Virtues and Vices* are invested with seriousness, although some must fail to raise comfortable laughter. The book is designed to make readers deeply disconcerted. It opens with a limerick epigraph from Edward Lear's *More Nonsense*, providing the apparent inspiration for its title: "There was a young person of Kew, / Whose virtues and vices were few; / But with blameable haste, she devoured some hot paste / Which destroyed that young person of Kew."[31] The novel ends with a reference to "beautiful shamelessness."[32] In the pages between are not only narrated comic (and repulsively would-be comic) sex scenes but knowing references to all manner of literary texts, including those by Rudyard Kipling, William Thackeray, Charles Dickens, Gustave Flaubert, and others.[33] Amidst all of this allusiveness, Jane Austen is never referenced.

Newly added sexual climaxes abound in Beckford's adaptation, but a few original narrative climaxes are retained from Austen's original novel as well. For example, Lucinda Musgrove has an unfortunate accidental fall that necessitates her long recovery, echoing Louisa Musgrove's accident on the stairs at Lyme Regis. Because Beckford's novel is transposed to Edwardian times, the injured girl convalesces in a hospital bed, with her broken leg hoisted up in a plaster cast. Pimps Captain Benwick and Captain Harville pay her a visit in the hospital, where she gamely has sex in this supine, half-hanging patient-position, with both men, simultaneously.

Since the book's publication in 1980, few readers have known what to make of it. The minimal critical response from previous Austen scholars is dismissive. One exception is Marilyn Sachs, who calls this "bawdy retelling of *Persuasion*" "the most remarkable of all the sequels."[34] Deidre Lynch labels

Virtue and Vices as "soft-core porn," which doesn't quite capture the spirit of the thing.[35] Natalie Tyler's description is exactly the kind of prim critical response that would later serve to launch a proliferation of comic Erotic Austens. Tyler writes, "This off-color, salacious tale of ribaldry . . . is not likely to amuse many readers. Lady Russell is a nymphomaniac, and Wentworth is her boy toy. Mrs. Clay sleeps with *everyone*."[36] Susannah Fullerton describes it as "all so tasteless and unnecessary."[37] But Austen critics who voice such (perfectly valid) opinions also miss part of the point. Beckford's novel is aiming for burlesque, or, arguably, satire.

It is possible to read Beckford's novel as parodying both Austen *and* porn. If so, it may be seen as in the spirit of Austen's *Northanger Abbey*, mirroring its relationship to the subgenre of Gothic fiction. In the juvenilia, too, Austen was using prevailing generic conventions to various eyebrow-raising effect. Sometimes she was writing burlesque, such as in her rowdy *Jack and Alice*, with its unrepentant male and female gamblers at a masquerade party who must be "carried home, Dead Drunk."[38] It may be read as send-up and reenactment of literary conventions, piling them on for effect. *Virtues and Vices*, like *Northanger Abbey*, may set out to compel its most thoughtful readers to recognize the constructedness—and often constructed silliness—of its form. *Northanger Abbey*, through its updated Gothic villain General Tilney, might be said to reveal the banality of evil. What you conclude of that may be up to you, as Austen's morally ambiguous last lines to that novel make clear. *Virtues and Vices*, too, puts on display the features of perverse, unequal, manipulative, and abusive sexuality, told from the perspective of those who are describing purported pleasures. What you conclude of that is also up to you, especially because the chapters' alternating first-person narrators cannot be considered reliable moral guides. Taken together, *Virtues and Vices* might prompt a reader to ask precisely where pornographic pleasure reading moves from banal to satirical to problematic, especially absent the author's tacking on any tidy moral lesson at story's end.

All of this is perhaps more a sophisticated analysis than Beckford's novel deserves. *Virtues and Vices* was packaged as mass market fiction, even if it used the signaling word "sophisticated" in its marketing materials. That reviewers were not wise to its purported cleverness is demonstrably clear. Not one of the standard reviews published in 1980–81 noticed that Beckford's novel was a rewriting of Austen or *Persuasion*. Indeed, only one reviewer, in *Publishers Weekly*, recognized that the novel was aiming for comedy, as claimed on the book flap copy. *Publishers Weekly* describes *Virtues and Vices* as a "delightfully foolish erotic spoof, a romp through the bedchambers of an

English family." The reviewer concludes that it's "not stinging enough to be called satire, nor provocative enough to be called porn" but that it's "good, light-hearted fun."[39] Although this may not demonstrate a deep familiarity with the full contents of the book, it does show that the reviewer grasps the would-be humor in Beckford's prose.

Other reviewers show less discernment—or perhaps just less patience. In her review in *Best Seller*, Nan S. Levinson begins, in an astonishing review, "Forewarning! This is not a review. It's rebellion. I REBEL!! I don't have to read stuff like this." She continues in a screed that deserves quotation at length:

> In all my years (decades!) of reviewing I have read every word of every book that I have reviewed. I felt an obligation not only to the reader of my review but also to the author . . . I did read approximately halfway through this book.
> Pornography itself quickly becomes boring but add minutely graphic lessons in incest, eroticism, licentiousness, etc. . . . nausea is incipient. . . . By comparison [novelist Joseph] Wambaugh is conservative. Since the publisher and Grania Beckford feel that she has filled the gap in literature by writing *Virtues and Vices* which they consider 'a very good erotic book which is also a very good and original novel,' they might exploit her 'ironic wisdom' further by producing a handbook.
> I know there is a mass market of pornography. I think that in the final analysis I dislike the fact that St. Martin's Press no longer feels a responsibility to the sensibilities of the audiences which has supported it unquestionably in the past.[40]

It's interesting that the reviewer herself employs sarcasm here and that both genre and publisher become central to her deeply negative assessment. But it is also astonishing that the reviewer does not seem to understand that "original" as it is used by Beckford and/or the publisher has a double meaning. Beckford is certainly original, in that Austen-inspired porn was previously unheard of. But Beckford's fiction is also not original, as an Austenesque retelling. *Virtues and Vices* is, among other things, a kind of copycat novel. I would not want to discount the possibility that readers and reviewers like Levinson have legitimate grounds for outrage. Beckford sets out to be provocative and without shame. Judgments may vary as to what degree the novel is admirably or disgustingly shameless—or both. Still, it is strange that Jane Austen was so tangentially linked to Beckford's book for so many years after it was first published and that even Austen critics, immediately and long after, have apparently been so incurious about its characters, methods, or author.

Who was Grania Beckford, against whom her first reviewers so strenuously rebelled? The marketing copy for *Virtues and Vices* describes her as a divorcée "born thirty-six years ago in Ireland" and a "citizen of the world." Beckford adds, in her own voice, "I live out of a suitcase, with a portable typewriter, off alimony, and under a cloud." The publisher adds, in the third person, "She has a wide knowledge of history with a special love for the luscious Edwardian epoch." Her previous novel, *Touch the Fire* (1979) is then mentioned, approved of by a reviewer as a kind of "*Upstairs, Downstairs*, porno-style."[41]

As it turns out, however, Grania Beckford wasn't the pseudonym of a liberated woman. Beckford was one of the many pen names of the late Roger Erskine Longrigg (1929–2000).[42] It seems important to stop here, for just a moment, to say how perfect it is that the author who appears to have been Jane Austen's first pornographer was a man whose given names were "Roger" and "Longrigg." Roger Longrigg was a prolific fiction writer of some fame and infamy. He published 55 books of genre fiction under at least seven pseudonyms, male and female. He first burst onto the literary scene, having successfully duped audiences into believing he was a female teenager named Rosalind Erskine, publishing a novel about boarding schoolgirls turning their school's gym into a brothel in *The Passion Flower Hotel* (1962). That novel, a bestseller, was later made into a musical. A German film version of it gave Nastassia Kinski her first role. Longrigg's ruse of being a teenage girl-author lasted for three years, before his cover was blown. His deception apparently didn't damage his literary career; he merely went on to other pseudonyms.

Author-chameleon Longrigg knew his Austen. Yet apparently neither Longrigg nor publisher St. Martin's Press thought marketing *Virtues and Vices* as Austen-inspired porn was a good idea. Interestingly, *Virtues and Vices* passed up a second chance to reveal its connection to Austen's *Persuasion*, when it was republished under a new title, *Catch the Fire*, in 1981. The original cover of *Virtues and Vices* used a wedding-ring-wearing young woman on its cover. She was in bed, under white sheets, in a white lace nightgown falling off one of her shoulders, demurely looking away from the viewer. By contrast, Longrigg's new cover for *Catch the Fire: A Smouldering World of Erotic Passion* is more explicit. It features a 1980s updating of an Edwardian merry-widow-wearing temptress, using a pink parasol to cover her nether region. Its back-cover copy provides a subtle nod to Austen's original title through the use of the word "persuasion." The marketing copy also refers slyly to Austen-inspired content, with its reference to "Kellynch Hall—the magnificent country seat of the Elliott family, where the life of elegance and leisure hides in a molten tide of naked desire." The Gothic send-up marketing blurb concludes, "Catch the heat of true love and gentle persuasion engulfed by evil machinations, the languorous fin de siècle world of the

English aristocracy caught up in a conflagration of lust."[43] The word "persua-sion" is buried into the sentence like an Easter egg, but there is precious little true love or gentle persuasion in this Austenesque novel.

Longrigg/Beckford's *Virtues and Vices*, and its repackaged and retitled *Catch the Fire*, are compelling oddities in Jane Austen's reception history. What author or publisher today would dream of producing a sexed-up ver-sion of Austen's fiction that entirely omitted the mention of her name? In the years after the recent *Pride and Prejudice and Zombies* film (2016) came to the screen alongside a tie-in Hot Topic lingerie line—when sexy Austen seems nearly ubiquitous and very marketable—we need to flag the fact that the apparent originator of porn Austen did not directly mention her as a source of literary inspiration. Reviewers apparently failed to notice the con-nection independently. There is no evidence that a wider readership grasped it then either.

Although today's Austen-inspired porn sets out to offer what's suppos-edly "missing" in the original, the apparent first work of Austen porn by Beckford-Longrigg seems to have had different aims and, in some ways, loftier ones. Uncovering the history and circumstances of *Virtues and Vices* allows us the opportunity to measure the distance that porn Austen—and we have traveled since. Is Austen-inspired porn, then or now, cause for worry or celebration? That may depend on who your Jane Austen is—or on what she and her fiction are to you. But as we consider the impact of porn on proto-type, we would do well to remember that the general pattern over time for sexed-up, adapted Austen has involved a movement from covert, envelope-pushing, offensive burlesque to openly adapted, mildly iconoclastic erotica. As Austen porn has become more prevalent, it's become less audacious. Its future may well be as just another accepted, even ho-hum, kind of literary tribute to (or literary opportunism on) the classic novelist. If so, that would be in line with many other subgenres and media that have come before, from Austen-inspired romances and mysteries to book illustrations, dramatiza-tions, and films.

Jane Austen wrote, in a May 24, 1813, letter to her sister Cassandra, "If I am a wild Beast, I cannot help it."[44] For better or worse, the Erotic Austen phenomenon compels us to open ourselves up to new ways of reading—and laughing at—that line.

Notes

1. Jane Austen and Lissa Trevor, *Spank Me, Mr. Darcy* (Riverdale, NY: Riverdale Avenue Books, 2013), 1.
2. Ann Herendeen, *Pride/Prejudice: A Novel of Mr. Darcy, Elizabeth Bennet, and Their Forbidden Lovers* (New York: Harper, 2010), 1–6.
3. Jane Juska, *Mrs. Bennet Has Her Say* (New York: Berkeley Books, 2015), 1–3.
4. Lynn Hunt, ed. *The Invention of Pornography, 1500–1800: Obscenity and the Origins of Modernity* (Cambridge: MIT Press, 1993).
5. Zachary Leader, *The Life of Kingsley Amis* (New York: Pantheon Books, 2007), 485.
6. Arielle Eckstut and David Henry Sterry, *The Essential Guide to Getting Your Book Published* (New York: Workman Publishing, 2010), xx–xxii.
7. Arielle Eckstut and Dennis Ashton, *Pride and Promiscuity: The Lost Sex Scenes of Jane Austen* (New York: Fireside Books, 2001), ix.
8. Jane Austen and Seth Grahame-Smith, *Pride and Prejudice and Zombies* (Philadelphia: Quirk Books, 2009).
9. Jane Austen and Joelle Herr, *The Jane Austen Kama Sutra: A Playful Presentation of Sense and Sensuality* (Kennebunkport, ME: Cider Mill Press, 2016).
10. Austen and Herr, *Jane Austen Kama Sutra.*
11. National Banana Classics. "Porn and Penetration" (video). YouTube. 31 May 2008. https://www.youtube.com/watch?v=oz3jg-HVB2E.
12. Steve Dawson, *Jane Austen's Guide to Pornography* (Craigieburn, Victoria: Lulu Publishing, 2015).
13. Alison Flood, "Pornography and prejudice: Jane Austen's dirty talk is a sweet affair." *The Guardian* (7 Sept 2009), https://www.theguardian.com/stage/theatreblog/2009/sep/07/jane-austen.
14. Dawson, *Jane Austen's Guide to Pornography,* 83.
15. Linda Berdoll, *The Bar Sinister: Pride and Prejudice Continues* (USA: Well, There It Is, 1999). Republished as Linda Berdoll, *Mr. Darcy Takes a Wife: Pride and Prejudice Continues: A Novel* (Naperville, IL: SourceBooks, 2004).
16. Deborah Yaffe, *Among the Janeites: A Journey Through the World of Jane Austen Fandom* (New York: Mariner Books, 2013), 72.
17. Yaffe, *Among the Janeites,* 74.
18. "About Linda Berdoll," *Linda Berdoll Author Page,* Amazon. com, n.d. https://www.amazon.com/Linda-Berdoll/e/B001JS1Y98?ref=sr_ntt_srch_lnk_1&qid=1602552825&sr=8-1.
19. Mitzi Szereto, *Pride and Prejudice: Hidden Lusts* (Berkeley, CA: Cleis Press, 2011).

20. Carolyn Kellogg, "Do you want a XXX Jane Austen? Vote in our poll." *Los Angeles Times* (7 June 2011), http://latimesblogs.latimes.com/jacket-copy/2011/06/dirty-jane-austen-or-not-poll.html.

21. Jane Austen and Desiree Holt, *Northanger Abbey: Clandestine Classics* (Great Britain: Total E. Bound Books, 2012).

22. Jane Austen and Amy Armstrong, *Pride and Prejudice: Clandestine Classics* (Great Britain: Total E. Bound Books, 2012).

23. William Deresiewicz, "Jane Austen Porn: We're All Guilty" (blog), *Huffington Post* (9 August 2011), http://www.huffingtonpost.com/bill-deresiewicz/jane-austen-porn-were-all_b_874349.html.

24. A rival series to the Clandestine Classics is the Wild and Wanton editions. Its publicity materials for *Pride and Prejudice* by Annabella Bloom and Jane Austen claim, misleadingly, "Unfortunately, we've never been able to see Elizabeth and Fitzwilliam *in flagrante delicto*—until now." See Annabella Bloom and Jane Austen, *Pride and Prejudice: Wild and Wanton Edition* (Avon, MA: Adams Media, 2011).

25. E. L. James, *Fifty Shades of Grey* (New York: Vintage Books, 2011).

26. Chrissie Swan, *Is it Just Me? Confessions of an Oversharer* (Collingwood, Victoria: Nero Books, 2015).

27. Quoted in Juliette Wells, *Everybody's Jane: Austen in the Popular Imagination* (New York: Continuum, 2011), 181.

28. Roger Sales, *Jane Austen and Representations of Regency England* (New York: Routledge, 1994), 33.

29. Grania Beckford, *Virtues and Vices: A Delectable Rondelet of Love and Lust in Victorian Times* (New York: St. Martin's Press, 1980).

30. Beckford, *Virtues and Vices.*

31. Beckford, *Virtues and Vices.*

32. Beckford, *Virtues and Vices,* 287.

33. Beckford, *Virtues and Vices,* 152–53.

34. Marilyn Sachs, "The Sequels to Jane Austen's Novels," *The Jane Austen Handbook,* Ed. J. David Grey (London: Athlone Press, 1986), 376.

35. Deidre Lynch, "Sequels," *Jane Austen in Context,* ed. Janet Todd (Cambridge: Cambridge University Press, 2005), 160.

36. Natalie Tyler, *The Friendly Jane Austen: A Well-Mannered Introduction to a Lady of Sense and Sensibility* (New York: Viking, 1999), 276.

37. Susannah Fullerton, *Celebrating Pride and Prejudice: 200 Years of Jane Austen's Masterpiece* (Minneapolis, MN: Voyageur, 2013), 167. Fullerton's book contains a section describing trends in Austen and pornography.

38. Jane Austen, *Juvenilia,* ed. Peter Sabor. (Cambridge: Cambridge University Press, 2006), 16.

39. Rev. of *Virtues and Vices* by Grania Beckford. *Publishers Weekly* 219 (5 April 1981): 73.

40. Rev. of *Virtues and Vices* by Grania Beckford. *Best Seller* 41 (July 1981): 124.
41. Beckford, *Virtues and Vices.*
42. "Roger Longrigg," *The Times* (London) (16 March 2000): 25.
43. Grania Beckford, *Catch the Fire: A Smouldering World of Erotic Passion* (London: Granada, 1981).
44. Jane Austen, *Jane Austen's Letters,* ed. Deirdre Le Faye, 4th ed. (Oxford: Oxford University Press, 2011), 221.

Chapter Fourteen

The Shadow Jane

Laura Engel

"What should I do with your strong, manly, spirited Sketches, full of variety and Glow?— How could I possibly join them on to the little bit (two inches wide) of Ivory on which I work with so fine a Brush, as produces little effect after much Labour?"

—Jane Austen[1]

AQUA-TINTA PROFILE LIKENESSES
"Likenesses painted on Ground Crystals in a New & Elegant Style producing the Effect of Aqua-tinta Engraving on a beautiful Transparency. & Requiring only one Minute's Sitting by Mrs. Read Portrait and Historical Painter 72, Lamb's Conduit Street."

Jane Read's trade label 1806.[2]

Jane Austen famously compared her work to a carefully crafted miniature, a small, meticulously painted work on ivory. Much has been written about this reference, and about the practice of miniature painting that flourished in the late eighteenth century—a delicate form of painting that Austen must have admired. Another form of miniature, the silhouette, or shadow portrait, also surfaces frequently in discussions of Jane Austen and material culture.[3] There is the famous shadow portrait of Edward Knight, Austen's adopted brother and his new family, and the silhouette profile of Jane herself found pressed in an edition of *Mansfield Park*.[4] These mysterious images reveal the outline of the sitters' face and promise to be an exact likeness of the subject, at the same time that the person's features are obscured in darkness. During Austen's lifetime another unique practice of miniature painting emerged that combined the materials and strategies of silhouette portraiture with the verisimilitude of portrait miniatures. These works contained a range of materials: wax, papier-mâché, paper, paint, and glass to create silhouette miniatures that resembled early photographs. Another Jane, Jane Beetham Read, a woman who lived and worked at exactly the same time as Jane Austen, became one of the most accomplished artists in this genre. The daughter of the silhouette artist Isabella Beetham and Edward Beetham, an actor turned washing machine inventor, Jane Beetham Read was born in 1773 a few years before Austen. She died in 1857 living in eccentric poverty with her daughter Cordelia. Read exhibited fifteen works at the Royal Academy between 1794 and 1814, a time frame that mirrors Austen's authorial career.[5] Her extraordinary works showcase minute details of clothing, hair, and facial features, juxtaposed with mysterious, haunting backgrounds (Figure 14.1).

Read's delicately rendered sitters captured in profile invite the viewer into an eerie realm of clarity and obscurity; they are visible but largely unknown. If we consider Jane Austen and Jane Read to be shadows or silhouettes of one

Figure 14.1. Jane Read, "Unknown woman." Profile painted on glass, 1810–12, 3¼ x 2¾ in./83 x 70mm. Frame: papier mâché, with ormolu matting oval. Courtesy of *Profiles of the Past.*

another, we get closer to envisioning a more complete picture of the working life of women authors and artists in the late eighteenth century. In addition, looking closely at their early works, we may be able to trace the shadowy desires of their past.

The idea that Austen's characters are seen but unknown (sometimes even to themselves) is most prevalent in relation to romance, desire, and potential sexual liaisons in her novels. Emma and Elizabeth must discover that they actually love Knightly and Darcy. Eleanor must keep her love for Edward a secret until the last pages of the story. Marianne's seduction by Willoughby is seen but not entirely revealed (what really happened on that carriage ride??). Anne Elliot and Fanny Price both struggle to understand and resist their passions for Captain Wentworth and Edmund until they are allowed to make their feelings public. These struggles and ambiguities have led scholars and Austen fans to speculate a great deal about Austen's own love life and potential suitors: her one possible love interest Tom Lefroy; her disastrous offer of marriage from Harris Bigg-Wither; and her awkward admirer James Stanier Clarke, who may have drawn an image of her in his friendship book wearing a fashionable gown and holding a muff.[6] Because we have so little to go on in terms of Austen's autobiographical writings (her sister Cassandra likely burned Austen's most intimate letters), readers are left to imagine Austen's inner world through the depictions of her heroines. Similarly, while we have a few striking examples of Jane Read's artwork and a list of her pieces that are now missing, she did not leave any writings behind. Her history has been pieced together largely through biographical materials related to John Opie, the well-known portrait painter who was her tutor and her lover.[7] The story of their romance, both hidden and in plain sight can be imagined through the interconnected threads of their individual artworks. In Austen's case her writings, particularly her early novel *Sense and Sensibility* (first conceived as a fragment "Elinor and Marianne" and later revised, may contain some coded clues about her first experience with romance.[8]

While it is unlikely that Jane Austen and Jane Read ever met one another, their entanglements and artistic trajectories create shadowy parallels. We have no concrete information about Austen's interactions with Tom Lefroy, only her clever correspondence, which hints at the depths of her feelings, but does not fully narrate them. The details of Jane Read's relationship with Opie come from the only biography of him written by Ada Earland in 1911. Although Earland confirms that Opie became attached to Read while he was her tutor and that he proposed to her and was rejected by her father, we have nothing from Read herself about her feelings for Opie. In the absence of an archive of evidence about Austen and Read's ephemeral romantic past what remains is the tangible artifacts of their artistic labor.

Curiously both Janes experienced their greatest romantic liaisons during the same time period, 1794–1799. Austen wrote the beginnings of her first published novel around the time that she met Tom Lefroy, the same moment when Read began exhibiting her paintings at the Royal Academy. The following is a brief timeline illustrating the progression of each relationship.

Romance Timeline for the Janes

1794:   Jane Beetham exhibits at the Royal Academy. John Opie is her tutor and unhappily married to Mary Bunn.

1795:   Austen meets Tom Lefroy during the Christmas and New Year's season. She is working on "Elinor and Marianne," the fragment that will become *Sense and Sensibility.* Jane Beetham exhibits a portrait (now lost) titled "King Lear and Cordelia."

1796:   Austen dances with Lefroy at several balls and writes to Cassandra on January 9, 1796 "I am almost afraid to tell you how my Irish friend and I behaved. . . ." She anticipates seeing Lefroy at his uncle's house in a letter on January 14th and then on the 15th she writes of the day "which I am to flirt my last with Tom Lefroy, & when you receive this it will be over—My tears flow as I write, at the melancholy idea."

1796:   After his wife deserts him for another man, John Opie sues for divorce so that he can be free to marry Jane Beetham. Jane Beetham creates a silhouette of an "Unknown Man" that resembles John Opie's self-portrait.

1797:   Edward Beetham rejects Opie's offer to marry Jane. Jane marries John Read. They have a daughter named Cordelia. Tom Lefroy becomes engaged to the heiress Mary Paul.

1798:   John Opie marries Amelia Alderson (later the novelist Amelia Opie).

1799:   Tom Lefroy marries Mary Paul.

🌿

After her break with Opie and her marriage to Mr. Read, Jane Read stopped exhibiting her works until 1804. Although she continued to write through the 1790's and early part of the nineteenth century, Austen's first novel, *Sense and Sensibility* (based on a fragment she was writing when she met Lefroy) would not be published until 1811. She continued to publish novels until her death in 1817. The last known pieces by Jane Read are dated 1816. We will never know exactly how the disappointment of failed romance affected each Jane, but the gaps in their visible artistic trajectory seem to overlap. Yet, there are important differences between Austen's relationship to Lefroy and Read's with Opie. Austen and Lefroy seemed to have enjoyed only a flirtation, not a full-blown affair. Like Read, Austen had a second offer of marriage, but she declined it and remained single throughout her life. Read married and had a child. Austen has become one of the most famous female authors in the world. Academics and art collectors have only recently discovered Read's work.

Tracing the Silhouettes of Jane Beetham Read and John Opie

We have a sense of Read's captivating beauty from Opie's portrait of her (1793–97) now in the Brompton Consumption Hospital Collection. In the painting Read is positioned in profile (as in a silhouette). She turns halfway towards the viewer, the rest of her face shrouded in darkness. She stares at the spectator with a mysterious calm and a hint of a smile. A simple ribbon in her hair and a strand of pearls suggest that she is a Lady, but not an aristocrat. Her expression is intimate yet reserved; she emerges from the shadows like a knowing ghost.[9] Opie's portraits of other women including the controversial essayist Mary Wollstonecraft and his own wife the novelist, Amelia Opie, are far less striking and personal. Wollstonecraft and Opie are both depicted from the waist up (bust length), dressed in fashionable, but practical white gowns. Their expressions are serious and composed. If you look closely at some of Opie's other works Jane's face seems to appear again. In his painting "Portrait of a Lady in the Character of Cressida," now at the Tate Museum in London, the lovely Cressida closely resembles Opie's depiction of Jane. Inspired by Pandarus' lines in in Act 3, Scene 2 of Shakespeare's *Troilus and Cressida*: 'Come, draw this curtain, and let's see your picture.' The painting debuted at the Royal Academy in 1800, just a few years after Opie and Read's relationship ended when her father rejected Opie's request to marry his daughter.[10] The character of Cressida is an interesting choice for Opie, particularly given the fact that the play was not performed regularly in the later part of the century. The portrait features the moment before Cressida is united with her lover, Troilus, the last time that they will be together in harmony. Cressida is unable to determine her own fate, and is passed around between men through the play, ultimately unwittingly betraying Troilus and suffering the consequences. Perhaps Opie's portrait is an acknowledgment of Jane Beetham's precarious position as a young woman dependent on her father's approval. Portraying Jane as Cressida also signals Opie's continued desire for her.

Although we have fewer surviving examples of Read's work, her beautifully crafted "Portrait of an Unknown Man" ("profile painted on glass, the sitter's features rendered with light stippling." Late 1790s–1800s—Profiles of the Past, image 1557), depicts a gentleman in profile posed against a natural landscape (Figure 14.2). His features are obscured, but his hair and clothing

Figure 14.2. Jane Read, "Portrait of an Unknown Man." Profile painted on glass, the sitter's features rendered with light stippling. Late 1790s–early 1800s, 3¼ x 2¾ in./83 x 70 mm. Frame: papier mâché, Courtesy of *Profiles of the Past*.

are lit from behind. Using minute brushstrokes, Read creates an extraordinary sense of the feel and drape of the fabric of his jacket and cravat as well as the curly, wild texture of his hair. The sitter has a distinctly narrow, long nose and a noticeably receding hairline.[11]

This profile closely resembles Opie's representation of himself in his self-portrait now at the Royal Academy of Art (1801–1802).[12] Curiously, Opie's dramatic self-portrait has the same body position as his portrait of Jane Read. The two figures appear partially turned towards the viewer emerging from a dark background. The effect forces the viewer to focus specifically on the sitter's face, the part that we can see, which also highlights the part of the face that is hidden from us. Does Opie's representation of himself and Jane Read suggest the complexity and secrecy of their multifaceted lives? What does Read's "Unknown Man" silhouette, a small snapshot, keepsake perhaps of Opie, reveal about what she saw in him that is hidden from our view?

Perhaps the most intriguing trace of Read and Opie's passion is Read's lost painting of "King Lear and Cordelia," dated 1795, at the height of her romance with Opie. A work titled "A Lady with a Letter," not dated but listed with other works from the late 1790s, parallels Opie's work "An angry father reproaching his daughter after intercepting a love-letter to her" also known as "The Angry Father" (1801–2) now in the Birmingham Museum (Figure 14.3).[13] The daughter in the portrait resembles Jane Read, with her dark hair and long slender nose. Clearly there are strong connections to the story of Shakespeare's most famous and tragic disagreement between a father and his daughter. Cordelia risks everything to speak her mind and challenge her father's power and position. It seems important to note that Jane Read named her only child Cordelia, and that her daughter was born sometime in between her break with Opie and her marriage to John Read. Is it possible that Cordelia may have been Opie's daughter?

The Shadow Archive of Jane Austen and Tom Lefroy in *Sense and Sensibility*

Austen seems to always be telling us that as readers we can't fully know what to expect from her characters and their passions until we have read to the end of the story. And, for some of the more minor figures, all we have are vague outlines. Mary Bennett, Colonel Brandon's Eliza, Georgiana Darcy, these female characters are all essential to the plot but do not take center stage. Austen doesn't reveal much or anything about their inner worlds. Because we

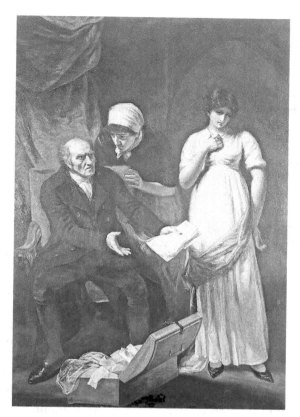

Figure 14.3. John Opie, "The Angry Father or The Discovery of the Clandestine Correspondence." Oil on Canvas,1801-1802, Courtesy of Birmingham Museums Trust, licensed under CC0.

have access to only a fraction of Austen's letters, her fully illustrated fictional counterparts have always been seen as mirrors for the possible gaps in our knowledge about Austen herself. Yet, what if we considered for a moment the dynamic of the silhouette, the shadow profile, as a more accurate way of accessing traces of Austen's emotional world? While many consider *Pride and Prejudice* to be Austen's most romantic novel, *Sense and Sensibility* is the novel that is the most tied to the relationship between visual objects and mistaken/thwarted/impossible romance. Elinor is convinced of her misguided passion for Edward by Lucy's presentation of his miniature; the lock of hair Edmund possesses is not hers but Lucy's, seeming proof of a love that does not exist. Marianne gives Willoughby her hair, but this is not a sign of an official engagement. Even letters are not authentic transparent documents. Willoughby's letter disavowing his former passion with Marianne is written by his new fiancée.

The plot of the novel is itself a kind of coming-of-age primer for what to do and what not to do in potential romantic situations. Elinor presides over the romantic "to do" list. She thinks before she acts; she conceals her true feelings; she presumes the worst even though she has some evidence that Edward loves her. Marianne is the lead actress in the romantic "Don't" category: She acts before she thinks; she assumes that passion always leads to marriage; she thinks the best of people instead of anticipating the worst. Although Austen is clearly endorsing Elinor's approach, she complicates the binary between the sisters by highlighting the ways in which Elinor suffers as much as Marianne does. Concealing and screening oneself has its own price, but in the world of the novel, this pain is rewarded in the end with Elinor achieving a marriage based on love.

In a curious scene later in the novel when the unhappy sisters are forced to meet Edward's mother under the watchful eyes of Lucy Steele, the Dashwoods, and the Middletons, John Dashwood draws our attention to a pair of fire screens that Elinor painted originally at Norwood (her childhood home) now remounted and displayed in the Dashwood's drawing room. Although Colonel Brandon admires them, Mrs. Ferrars rudely ignores them and begins to talk about someone else's artistic talents, which then incites Marianne to exclaim on behalf of her sister, "This is admiration of a particular kind! What is Miss Norton to us? Who knows, or who cares for her?—it is Elinor of whom *we* think and speak" (193).[14]

As with many visual things in Austen's novels, Elinor's screens are passed around and admired or ignored but are not described to us. We do not have any access to what they look like. In the scene, Austen implies that Marianne is the only one who can actually "see" or fully appreciate them, and she is outraged that no one else is giving them the attention that they deserve. The dismissal of Elinor's screens echoes Marianne's own grief and frustration, emotions that she does not want her sister to experience. She still thinks that Elinor has a chance of being united with Edward and she tells her "Dear, dear Elinor, don't mind them. Don't let them make *you* unhappy" (194). At the same moment that Elinor's screens are being evaluated, Marianne is being watched and judged. Her outburst about Elinor makes her appear nervous and fragile. John Dashwood says to Colonel Brandon "she has not such good health as her sister,—she is very nervous,—she has not Elinor's constitution;—and one must allow that there is something very trying to a young woman who *has been* a beauty in the loss of her personal attractions. You would not think it, perhaps, but Marianne was remarkably handsome a few months ago; quite as handsome as Elinor. Now you see it is all gone" (194). It is interesting to consider how Austen may have written parts of herself into both sisters in this scene. When the fragment of the novel "Elinor and Marianne" was first written during her time with Tom Lefroy, perhaps Austen experienced the depth of her emotions like Marianne although she may have wished to be more like Elinor. At the time she was revising "Elinor and Marianne" into *Sense and Sensibility*, she had accepted her position as an unmarried woman. The passing around of Elinor's screens, like the passing around of women's bodies as valuable or expendable commodities, underscores the realities and dangers of believing in an early passion that might not be returned. Elinor's screens originally painted at Norland, a place of happiness and hope and the place of her original love for Edward, in their new home on the Dashwood's wall framed and ornamented, they are fixed and dismissed. This is not the ending of the novel, where in a fictional world Elinor gets to be with her love, but it is the ending outside of the novel, when Austen is herself removed from the marriage market and relegated to the ranks of the unseen.

Elinor's painted fire screens operate on many levels in the novel. In the most literal sense, a fire screen protects a person from being burned. Metaphorically, a screen may shield one from being singed by romance, self-deception, disappointment, and betrayal. Screens also hide and shade people from scrutiny and observation; Elinor is able to protect herself to a point by struggling to hide her true emotions from others (Marianne can't do this). This dance of restraint and revelation echoes the complex composition of Jane Read's silhouettes, which follow the rules of portrait painting, but are also innovative creations, pastiche, hybrid forms that blend a variety of techniques to produce something new. In addition, screens are essential to the making of silhouettes. Silhouette artists used screens to trace a person's likeness through their shadow. Looking at Read's artwork alongside Austen's prose highlights what is visible and invisible in both genres. For both Janes what we can't see, what is only hinted at through outlines, becomes a metaphor for the writer and the artist herself; we will never gain full access to Austen or Read's experiences with romance and desire, but we can perhaps see traces of their past passions, triumphs, and heartbreaks in the shadows of their work.

Notes

1. Deidre Le Faye, ed., *Jane Austen's Letters, 4th ed.* (Oxford: Oxford University Press, 2011), 337.

2. Quoted in Sue McKechnie, "Read, Jane (McKechnie Section 6)," *Profiles of the Past,* 2014, http://www.profilesofthepast.org.uk/mckechnie/read-jane-mckechnie-section-6. *Profiles of the Past: 250 Years of British Portrait Silhouette History* (http://profilesofthepast.org.uk) is an excellent website with great information about silhouette artists, techniques, images, and current research.

3. For background on the history and artistic practice of silhouettes, see Emma Rutherford, *Silhouette: The Art of the Shadow* (New York: Rizzoli, 2009).

4. For more about Austen and silhouettes see Paula Byrne, *The Real Jane Austen: A Life in Small Things* (New York: Harper Collins, 2013), 13–27.

5. See McKechnie, Profiles of the Past, Section 6.

6. For more on Austen and James Stanier Clarke, see Laura Engel, *Austen, Actresses, and Accessories: Much Ado About Muffs* (London: Palgrave Macmillan, 2015), 57–67.

7. For more on John Opie and Jane Read, see Ada Earland, *John Opie and His Circle* (London: Hutchinson & Co., 1911), 99–114.

8. For more from Austen scholars about Jane and Tom Lefroy, see Joan Klingel Ray, "The One-Sided Romance of Jane Austen and Tom Lefroy," *Persuasions Online,* Vol. 28. No. 1 (Winter, 2007), http://www.jasna.org/persuasions/on-line/vol28no1/ray.htm; Linda Robinson Walker, "Jane Austen and Tom Lefroy: Stories," *Persuasions Online,* Vol. 27, No. 1 (Winter, 2006), http://www.jasna.org/persuasions/on-line/vol27no1/walker.htm; Marsha Huff "Becoming Jane: Sorting Fact From Fiction," JASNA, http://jasna.org/austen/screen/other/becoming-jane-sorting-fact-from-fiction/.

9. https://en.wikipedia.org/wiki/File:Jane_Beetham,_likely_1790s.jpg.

10. For more information about John Opie's "Portrait of a Lady in the Character of Cressida," see "Conserving for Display: John Opie's 'Portrait of a Lady in the Character of Cressida," The Tate Museum, London, https://www.tate.org.uk/about-us/projects/conserving-display-john-opies-portrait-lady-character-cressida.

11. http://www.profilesofthepast.org.uk/mckechnie/read-jane-mckechnie-section-6. Image no. 1557.

12. https://www.royalacademy.org.uk/art-artists/work-of-art/self-portrait-34.

13. https://commons.wikimedia.org/wiki/File:John_Opie_(1761-1807)_-_The_Angry_Father_(The_Discovery%E2%80%A6_Correspondence)_-_1885P2584_-_Birmingham_Museums_Trust.jpg.

14. Jane Austen, *Sense and Sensibility* (New York: Barnes & Noble Classics, 2004). Subsequent page references will be to this edition.

Chapter Fifteen

In Bed with Mr. Knightley

How Austen and Her Readers Understand Sexual Compatibility

Deborah Knuth Klenck and Ted Scheinman

In Margaret Drabble's early novel *The Waterfall*, the protagonist Jane Gray comments almost offhandedly,

> "How I dislike Jane Austen. How deeply I deplore her desperate wit . . . Emma got what she deserved, in marrying Mr. Knightley. What can it have been like, in bed with Mr. Knightley? Sorrow awaited that woman: she would have done better to steal Frank Churchill, if she could."[1]

Unlike Jane Gray, the two of us think that Jane Austen does let readers know that she has an idea of what it would be like, in bed with Mr. Knightley. Austen has left plentiful indications in her novels about which characters, and which personal qualities, promise a good time in bed. A smart but playful manner in conversation is one; a lack of selfishness is, self-evidently, another. And most of all, a good dancer makes a good lover. Henry Tilney makes this last association explicitly in his sustained joking conversation with Catherine Morland:

> "I consider a country-dance as an emblem of marriage. Fidelity and complaisance are the principal duties of both; and those men who do not chuse to dance or marry themselves, have no business with the partners or wives of their neighbours."[2]

When we "consider a country-dance"—for example, the Westons' ball at the Crown Inn—we find that a gallant and generous gesture indicates an auspicious lover. Mr. Knightley rescues Harriet Smith from the contemptible and contemptuous Eltons by asking her to dance; in doing so, he raises considerable animal spirits not only in his partner, but also in Emma, their witness:

> His dancing proved to be just what [Emma] had believed it, extremely good; . . . and [Harriet] bounded higher than ever, flew farther down the middle, and was in a continual course of smiles.[3]

Indeed, as Mr. Darcy observes, the prospect of a ball "is a subject which always makes a lady energetic."[4] And, though Sir William Lucas is not a generally reliable or perceptive source, we have no reason to disbelieve his comment on Darcy's first dance with Elizabeth: "'Such very superior dancing is not often seen" (*PP* 103). The pair's evident chemistry is clear not only to the very jealous Miss Bingley, but even to the most oblivious onlooker at the ball.

By contrast, one hardly has to read between the lines that describe Elizabeth's two "dances of mortification" with Mr. Collins to guess "what can it have been like, in bed" with Mr. Collins, who is "awkward and solemn, apologizing instead of attending, and often moving wrong without being aware of it"—a fair description of a bad lover in any age (*PP* 101). For her part, of course, Elizabeth is left in "shame and misery." The closest she gets to an erotic experience is when the dance is through: "The moment of her release from him was *extacy*" (*PP* 101; emphasis added).

One confirmation of the connection between dance and sex is the fact that many women who are "off the market," either as matrons or spinsters, do not themselves dance. Mrs. Weston, "capital in her country-dances," performs for an impromptu dance by the "young people" at the Coles' dinner party. And at her own ball at the Crown, the still relatively young Mrs. Weston's not dancing is a demure indication that she is pregnant (*E* 248, 354). A single woman on the dance floor, therefore, is quite explicitly on the market—and the dance, in turn, serves as a measure for the romantic compatibility that Austen's heroines (and their readers) so desire.

Accompanying dancing on the pianoforte can offer a semblance of participation to women who, for one reason or another, are "slighted by other men," as Mr. Darcy unkindly describes Elizabeth's situation at the assembly ball, though the pianist must avoid the "pedantic" manner of a Mary Bennet (*PP* 12; 27). In *Persuasion*, Captain Wentworth, still wounded by what he considers Anne Elliot's cowardly dissolving of their engagement eight years earlier, has made up his mind that, though "[i]t was now his object to marry[,] . . . he had a heart for any pleasing young woman who came in his way, excepting Anne Elliott."[5] When dancing at the Musgroves', he asks whether "Miss Elliot never danced?" (*P* 78). One of the Musgrove sisters somewhat thoughtlessly replies, "Oh! no, never; she has quite given up dancing," probably with no intention to confirm Anne's essential ineligibility for marriage (*P* 78). Wentworth, however, takes the description as evidence. Addressing Anne with distant politeness as "Madam," he observes that "[Anne's] seat" is at the pianoforte (*P* 78). Many pages elapse before Wentworth reconsiders these presumptions—a pointed illustration of how Austen's characters use dance as a proxy for sexual compatibility.

Pride and Prejudice uses dance most conspicuously as an indication for appropriate relationships. Before they have even met him, the Bennet daughters assess, with a little pun, Charles Bingley's reported eagerness for the ball at Meryton: "To be fond of dancing was a certain step towards falling in love" (*PP* 9). Mr. Bennet, subjected to a detailed account of Bingley's exploits at the ball, cries, "Oh! That he had sprained his ancle in the first dance!" (*PP* 13). Near the end of the novel, Mr. Bingley tells Elizabeth with atypical precision, "We have not met since the 26th of November, when we were all dancing together at Netherfield" (*PP* 290).

Mr. Darcy presents a glaring contrast with his friend, refusing introductions, claiming to disdain dancing itself. "Every savage can dance," he remarks; "[i]t is a compliment which I never pay to any place if I can avoid it" (*PP* 28). To be fair, Mr. Darcy's refusal to oblige "young ladies who are slighted by other men" by asking them to dance may not be simple bad manners, though his willingness to disdain the merely "tolerable" Elizabeth Bennet while the lady herself sits within earshot is deeply rude (*PP* 12).

But if we consider his instantaneous notoriety on entering the ballroom as "having ten thousand a year," we may find it possible to sympathize with this prominent target for single women and their rapacious mothers (*PP* 10, 12). More than once, we are told, Darcy considers himself "in some danger" from Elizabeth Bennet—of being "bewitched" by her (*PP* 57); after several evenings spent with her at Netherfield during Jane's illness, he "began to feel the danger of paying Elizabeth too much attention" (*PP* 64). Before putting up his guard, Darcy has gone so far as to flirt with Elizabeth in dancing terms. One evening at Netherfield, Miss Bingley varies her performance of Italian arias at the pianoforte with "a lively Scotch air," and he asks, "Do not you feel a great inclination, Miss Bennet, to seize such an opportunity of dancing a reel?" (*PP* 56). Elizabeth doesn't take this remark as flirtation, however, but as an invitation to "say 'Yes,' that [he] may have the pleasure of despising [her] taste"—an early example of how the subject of dancing contributes to the pair's misunderstanding of one another (*PP* 56).

The dance becomes an essential comic trope in Darcy and Elizabeth's relationship. The morning after the Meryton assembly, Charlotte mocks Elizabeth for Darcy's assessment that she is "only just *tolerable*" (*PP* 20). Mrs. Bennet stands up for her second daughter: "Another time, Lizzy, . . . I would not dance with *him*, if I were you" (*PP* 20). Elizabeth's reply is one of few instances where she seems to honor her mother's advice: "I believe, Ma'am, I may safely promise you *never* to dance with him" (*PP* 21): such a firm assertion invites or even teases the reader to guess the number of pages before this promise is broken (in the Cambridge edition, it's 80). The broken "promise *never*," Elizabeth's mock-solemn vow, calls to mind the Jerome Kern/Otto Harbach song "I won't dance! Don't ask me" from the Astaire/Rogers film *Roberta* (1935). Astaire turns down Rogers's character's invitation to dance:

> I won't dance! Don't ask me.
> I won't dance, Madame, with you.
> My heart won't let my feet do things they should do.[6]

It is a delightful paradox to set such lyrics to a dance tune, but there's more: the lines in fact claim that the suitor not only "won't dance"—he can't: holding his partner, he will do something else, something dancing stands for as a code in the eight immortal RKO Astaire/Rogers musicals—as it does in the novels of Jane Austen.

The incontrovertible connection between dancing and sex leads the perhaps sadder but wiser Mr. Bennet to admonish Kitty, after Lydia's disgrace: "Balls will be absolutely prohibited, unless you stand up with one of your sisters" (*PP* 330–31). The dangers of the dance are not merely illicit sex, of course; in Pope's "Rape of the Lock" (1714), the sylph Ariel marshals his invisible troops to protect the heroine Belinda in company, lest she "stain her honour or her new brocade."[7] The equivalence between loss of virginity and clothing comes up in *Pride and Prejudice* when Mrs. Bennet learns to her "amazement and horror" that her husband has no intention of buying Lydia a trousseau, "a privilege, without which her marriage would scarcely seem valid" (*PP* 343).

Social events like dances can damage a lady's reputation, if not her actual maidenhead, and, perhaps equally (or, to some, more) important, her gown may be spoiled. In *Northanger Abbey*, the dangers to her dress are uppermost in the mind of the heroine's chaperone Mrs. Allen at the crowded Upper Rooms at Bath:

> Mrs. Allen congratulated herself, as soon as they were seated, on having pre-served her gown from injury. "It would have been very shocking to have it torn," said she, "would not it?—It is such a delicate muslin. —For my part I have not seen any thing I like so well in the whole room, I assure you." (*NA* 14)

One suspects that the "great slit in [Lydia Bennet's] worked muslin gown" must have occurred at a ball at Brighton. It is an obvious cause for con-cern because Lydia worries about it in her otherwise thoughtless note to Mrs. Forster, breezily announcing that she has absconded with Wickham (*PP* 321). It's a very suggestive symbol, of course, this great slit. Austen was very likely sensitized to the image by *Tristram Shandy*, where placket holes (especially in nuns' habits) command considerable attention.[8] Whether or not Austen's readers appreciate its semiotics, she has already used the motif at the end of *Sense and Sensibility*, when the tongue-tied Edward Ferrars can barely pronounce the happy news that his former fiancée Lucy Steele is now married to his brother, leaving him free to propose to Elinor Dashwood. "He rose from his seat and walked to the window, apparently from not know-ing what to do; took up a pair of scissors that lay there, and while spoiling both them and their sheath by cutting the latter to pieces[,] he spoke . . . in an hurried voice."[9] An image akin to Lydia's slit gown comes up in David Lodge's academic satire *Nice Work* (1988), where a feminist literary critic teaches a fairly clueless businessman how a billboard advertises Silk Cut ciga-rettes—with a simple picture of a gash in a piece of expensive-looking red fabric. Having mastered his lesson, and slept with the teacher, he goes one better, whispering to her, "I love your silk cunt."[10]

Another, still more invidious, association with dancing is the possibility of incest. When, in *Mansfield Park*, the busybody Mrs. Norris prescribes to Sir Thomas Bertram the charity of fostering their niece Fanny Price, she dis-misses his anticipated worry: "You are thinking of your sons—but do you not know that of all things upon earth *that* is the least likely to happen; brought up, as they would be, always together like brothers and sisters? It is morally impossible."[11] At first, it seems that Mrs. Norris has been correct when, at the ball at Mansfield Park, Edmund Bertram, depressed about his prospects with Mary Crawford, finally gets around to the two dances he has reserved with his cousin Fanny:

> His mind was fagged, . . . "I am worn out with civility," said he. "I have been talking incessantly all night, and with nothing to say. But with you, Fanny, there may be peace. You will not want to be talked to. Let us have the luxury of silence." . . . [T]hey went down their two dances together with such sober tranquility as might satisfy any looker-on, that Sir Thomas had been bringing up no wife for his younger son. (*MP* 323–24)

In preparation for this ball, Fanny has been given two competing gold chains to wear with the amber-cross pendant from her brother William: like the slit in Lydia's gown, there is a sexual suggestion when the ornate necklace offered by the conspiring Crawfords "would by no means go through the ring of the cross," and Fanny is relieved to use instead the plain gold chain given by Edmund, "with delightful feelings, join[ing] the chain and the cross, the memorials of the two most beloved of her heart, those dearest tokens so formed for each other by every thing real and imaginary" (*MP* 314). A romance between the cousins is hardly "morally impossible" after all; indeed, if we are to judge from the metaphor of the chain, it is actually, in this case, the most moral of choices—and the most literally compatible.

The brother/sister dancing dilemma may be at its most teasing to the reader of *Emma*. After Mr. Knightley, who claims to disdain dancing, has broken his resolve at the ball at the Crown Inn for the forlorn Harriet Smith, Emma thanks her brother-in-law for this kindly action. He asks her about the next two dances,

> "Whom are you going to dance with?"
> She hesitated a moment, and then replied, "With you, if you will ask me."
> "Will you?" said he, offering his hand.
> "Indeed I will. You have shown that you can dance, and you know we are not really so much brother and sister as to make it at all improper" (*E* 358).

The chapter ends with Mr. Knightley's most suggestive reply, "Brother and sister! No, indeed" (*E* 358). This downright declaration anticipates another brief, no-nonsense, yet ironical statement: "I cannot make speeches, Emma . . . If I loved you less, I might be able to talk about it more"— a style of talk that one may take for an assurance that being "in bed with Mr. Knightley" would contrast well with sleeping with the speechifying Mr. Elton—or with Mr. Collins (*E* 469). After all, beginning a speech with "I cannot make speeches" is just as disingenuous as dancing to a tune called "I Won't Dance." Mr. Knightley has style in his sparing, well-chosen language, including the Augustan balance between "less" and "more." And readers have no cause to fear that conversational intercourse between Emma and Knightley would be less satisfying than the physical kind; throughout the novel, though Knightley doesn't speechify, he is endlessly, virtuosically teasing toward Emma, indicating an intimate knowledge of his future partner mingled with the sort of playful indulgence that promises to keep any marriage both frisky and firm.

Loquacity and male attractiveness are hardly mutually exclusive traits, of course. The self-consciously witty Henry Tilney proves that. And even Edward Ferrars, though habitually depressed for much of the novel, does have his verbal tours-de-force, most notably his Johnsonian contrast between plain speaking and the jargon of the picturesque, in his teasing conversation with Marianne on his first visit to Barton Cottage:

> "I have no knowledge in the picturesque, and I shall offend you by my ignorance and want of taste. . . . I shall call hills steep, which ought to be bold; surfaces strange and uncouth, which ought to be irregular and rugged; and distant objects out of sight, which ought only to be indistinct through the soft medium of a hazy atmosphere. . . . I know nothing of the picturesque" (*SS* 112).

This satisfying parodic set-piece is a perfect companion to Edward's nonverbal gesture, when faced with a nonjoking disclosure, with the embroidery scissors and their sheath.

It must be noted that Austen's characters include apparently compatible partners, whether in dance or conversation, who would nevertheless make for disastrous marriages. Mr. Wickham's attractiveness to Elizabeth (as with Miss Darcy) has to do with his person, his charm, and his ease in conversation—before she learns that such ease is insincere glibness, covering a crudely mercenary, predatory approach to women. The handsome John Willoughby, much like Wickham, has successfully seduced one poor girl, Colonel Brandon's ward Eliza, before he begins playing the part of "soulmate" to Marianne Dashwood; but, of course, he is consistently more interested in a woman's dowry than in her taste in poetry and the picturesque. The charming and rich, though plain, Henry Crawford, too, is a dangerous companion, despite his attractions, even to Fanny, as a speaker, a reader, and an actor. He acts the part of a selfless suitor to Fanny (and mentor to her brother), and takes on the additional part of a generous landowner concerned about his tenants with an aplomb to match his seductive performance as Frederick to Maria Crawford's Agatha in *Lovers' Vows*—that presages his actual seduction of Maria after her marriage to Mr. Rushworth. Dancing and banter can hardly be the sole factors as women assess their marital prospects.

In fact, a man's being *too* easy at charming is almost always a red flag in Austen; consider how many of her patrician heroes—Darcy, Ferrars, Knightley, Wentworth—are restrained in their speech and behavior in varying degrees, a decorousness that (Austen indicates) must be coupled with charm (within reason) and dance-floor gallantry (without too much *smoothness*).

Charm and dance-floor gallantry are by-words among Janeites at the country dances held annually at Jane Austen symposia across North America and the world. The tradition was popularized in twentieth-century America thanks in no small part to Jack Grey, the cofounder of JASNA, who was also a middle-school principal from Manhattan, an independent scholar, and a prolific Austen collector. In the collection of reminiscences and tributes given at the 1993 JASNA AGM in Lake Louise, just months after Jack's untimely death, Juliet McMaster reminded the company that Jack "was the first who laid on a ball and called for Regency dress" as an essential part of JASNA's annual get-togethers.[12] The tradition endures not only at AGMs, but at regional events around the United States and Canada, a tribute to Jack's deep understanding of the significance of dancing in Austen's novels, and today you will find Regency country dances being held at JASNA's annual meeting and at the Jane Austen Summer Program in Chapel Hill, North Carolina. If you're in the Asian subcontinent, you can even attend the costumed tea parties held by the Jane Austen Society of Pakistan.

In discussing Austen's novels with members of these various groups, we have found that Janeites, when they are among themselves, are an unblushing bunch, eager to find a partnerless dancer and spin a quadrille with them, regardless of either party's social class or even gender.

On the other hand, there is a positively prurient interest, among outsiders, about present-day Janeites. Many friends have plied us with variations on the question: *Do people hook up at Jane Austen conferences??* These quizzes can be tiresome, particularly given their unspoken premise that dressing up in Regency clothing is somehow centrally about sex. (It's not. It's mainly about books, and only a little bit about sex.) Yet one must grant that these outsiders are, in their way, asking a rather Austenian question—one that Janeites are eager to take up as they discuss the characters in the novels, and, occasionally, as they play matchmaker among the graduate students in attendance.

At a typical Janeite cotillion, the floor is rectangular or square, with room for at least two dozen couples to stand in two rows, facing each other over a distance of five or so paces. The action is graceful, even when performed by amateurs: as with line dancing, it's a collective effort, and best viewed—if you aren't dancing—from a balcony. Over the course of a Janeite ball, the company invariably becomes familiar with each of the antiquated group dances ("Mr. Beveridge's Maggot" is one of the standbys), helped in no small measure by the liberating effects of winepunch, and by a dance master at the head of the room, calling out the steps.

Whereas Austen codes her assessment of various characters' sexual aptitude, and various couples' sexual chemistry, present-day Janeites, when they meet and discuss these questions, are uncoded and quite direct. ("Had Lizzy married Mr. Collins," we were drily assured by one attendee at a symposium not long ago, "the match would not have borne fruit.") At JASNA's annual general meeting in Minneapolis in 2013, one of us (Ted) delivered the other's (Deborah's)[13] breakout talk, in which the question of Mr. Collins's sexual magnetism—or conspicuous lack thereof—was a central subject; indeed, the third section of the paper was a direct rebuttal of Ruth Perry's famous essay "Sleeping With Mr. Collins," in which Perry argues that readers are mistaken to think of Collins as physically undesirable: "If Austen does not imagine Charlotte Lucas's sexual disgust for Mr. Collins, neither does she imagine powerful physical attraction between her couples destined for marriage—not until *Persuasion* in any case."[14] Perry argues that modern readers fall into the trap of hating Collins because we project post-Romantic notions of love onto a pre-Romantic arrangement that was fundamentally practical. Indeed, this is the principal difference between Lizzy and her friend; Charlotte makes the difference explicit. "I am not romantic, you know," Charlotte says to Lizzy in explaining why she accepted Collins (and, frankly, tilted her cap at him) (*PP* 140). But Austen's narrator is clearly addressing an audience whom she expects to identify with Lizzy, and to agree with our heroine when she tells her sister Jane that "the woman who marries [Collins], cannot have a proper way of thinking" (*PP* 154). As recompense for losing a friend in Charlotte Lucas, Lizzy finds her devotion to Jane redoubled—and the narrator is careful to note how much Lizzy appreciates Jane's "delicacy," as compared with Charlotte's indelicate willingness to conjoin herself to this unworthy, and, we are convinced, physically repellent, suitor (*PP* 144).

After the talk, several scholars approached Ted to remark on Perry's curious thesis, and to heap disparagement on the smarmy cleric. "Your mother's right about Collins," one of them said; "she seems to have the proper ideas about Austen and sex."[15] Another was more direct. "Perhaps Ruth Perry should've married Mr. Collins and told us how it went."

As for Mr. Knightley, with his alternating teasing and reserve, his gallantry in "rescuing" Harriet Smith at the ball, and indeed his being much older than Emma, the Janeites nevertheless rank him quite highly on the scale of Austen's patrician heroes. While there is a discerning sub-coterie of Janeites who aver that Henry Tilney would have been the most fun, Knightley is often just behind Darcy and Captain Wentworth as objects of amorous Janeite affection. "I know he held [Emma] when she was a baby, and some people think that's creepy," one Janeite told Ted in 2014. "That might be. But also: how sexy is his sense of responsibility!"

Besides their irreverence for august academic hot takes—an irreverence that will serve any Janeite well—modern-day Janeites assess the characters' amorous compatibilities through their deep love of memes, those vernacular images that allow one (among many other things) to "ship" various characters—a fan-culture term for the practice of imagining that this or that pair of characters will end up (or at least sleep) together. Janeites' creation and passing-round of memes (not unlike the squibs and theatricals that Austen and her siblings wrote to and for one another) are particularly funny—and biting—when they apply twenty-first-century romantic expectations to Regency-era literature (a technique Austen herself, in the juvenilia and *Northanger Abbey*, had used to send up the gothic and lachrymose novels of the earlier eighteenth century), creating charmingly dissonant juxtapositions in tone. The comic possibilities of memes give Janeites a playful mode in which to address quite-serious questions about compatibility and romantic morality.

On Facebook pages such as "Pride and Prejudice" (19.3K members; closed membership) and the Jane Austen Fan Club (36.3K members; closed membership), or on Twitter accounts such as @DrunkAusten (abruptly and mysteriously terminated in August 2020, to the chagrin of its followers) and @JaneAustenBath, you will see (for example) how a smoldering still from Joe Wright's 2005 *Pride & Prejudice* inspires variations on the popular "this could be us but you playin'" meme. To participate in this particular meme format, someone posts a depiction of a happy-looking—or sometimes silly-looking—couple to show an unfaithful or unserious romantic partner what they might be missing. These memes are fun in their own right, but Janeites often take them further than the average memester (Figures 15.1–15.2). Casting Darcy and Lizzy in the "this could be us but you playin'" format, alone, is funny; when a Janeite places Wickham in the background, looking after Darcy and Lizzy with a hangdog expression, the meaning is

Figure 15.1. A most Austenian play on the "This could be us but you playin" meme. Ted Scheinman/Wikimedia.

Figure 15.2. Janeites even use memes to send up the relatively closed society of the novels. This meme is most certainly inspired by "Woman Relieved Soulmate Turned Out To Be In Same Socioeconomic Bracket," https://www.theonion. com/woman-relieved-soulmate-turned-out-to-be-in-same-socioe-1819578046.

deepened, offering a moral lesson about the happiness that people (or fictional characters) stand to lose when they don't bargain in good faith with their neighbors.

It might seem surprising to find Mr. Collins at the center of so many online Janeite debates. After all, he's one of the blander characters in the corpus, even if Austen's depiction of his distinct kind of banal unctuousness raises the character far beyond a mere type. Reading closer, though, one sees that Collins, in Austen fan culture, has become a stand-in for romantic settling of any kind—the sort of question that continues to bedevil lovers in any age. Recently, on the closed-membership "Pride and Prejudice" Facebook page, there was a long and lively thread sparked by a simple but provocative question from a Janeite named Andrea L.: "So, if Jane were not nearly 'engaged' would she have accepted Mr. Collins? Due to her good nature and all."[16] Scrolling past the reaction emojis—which ranged from shock (vacant stare, open mouth) to sadness (a face with a single tear)—one found a variety of competing and compelling answers. It was evident that many of these Janeites had considered the question before:

"I've always wrestled with this!!!!!" responded a Janeite named Kia L. "I'm afraid she would have!"[17]

"Lizzy would have done her best to prevent it," responded Allison G.[18]

Meghan B. argued that "Jane's too kind to know how to say no" while Ann M. commented simply, "I think she would have taken one for the team."[19]

Wendy C. disagreed with these assessments: "I don't think so; Lizzy and she have a whole discussion about love and marriage and how marriage without love equals their parents' marriage."[20]

For her part, Sally Jo S. wrote that "Despite his lackadaisical attitude, I think Mr. B[ennet] despised Collins too much and cared too much for his daughter to have allowed Jane to sacrifice herself that way."[21]

In a more gallant vein, Sunny J. wrote: "I vote nay. She may have almost been persuaded to but Bingley would have caught wind and snatched her away in time."[22]

From there, the conversation moved in an interesting direction: folks began "shipping" Mr. Collins and Mary Bennet. "I wish Lizzy had told Collins that she can't possibly marry him because her sister Mary likes him,"

Sunny J. wrote, seconded by Corinna L., Jay P., and many others.[23] The idea that the bookish, boring Mary would have found the cloying, boring clergyman a suitable mate is not new, but Janeites—in table talk or in cyberspace—are bringing such questions to ever-wider audiences across the globe, and offering nonacademic Janeites in particular an inviting seat at the table.

To the occasional mortification of certain graduate students at the larger Austen symposia, the Janeites' zeal for "shipping" fictional characters breaches containment and enters the real world, with powerful effects. While one of us (Deborah) is happily married, the other (Ted) has attended most of his Janeite balls as a singleton—a circumstance that can inspire certain notions of match-making and universal truth in the minds of the company. At JASNA in 2013, an attendee drew his attention to a winsome historical novelist with bouncy blonde ringlets and promptly pushed him in her direction. "She's been giving you the eye. Tell her she's the very image of Jane Bennet—that's your line!"[24] Later at the same ball, one of Ted's graduate school advisors arranged for him to book several dances with two ladies who were far too young, to the mortification of everyone save the advisor. Small moments like these bespeak the almost diasporic zeal to choreograph the younger generation into suitable couples. As zeals go, it's an understandable one: Janeites under the age of 40 tend to be a minority at the larger gatherings, doubly so for young or youngish men, and, besides the general (and not incorrect) sense that two people who enjoy Austen must surely enjoy each other, there is also (it seems to us) a further desire to see Janeism propagated in the next generation. The Janeites are hardly a wandering tribe—yet, as Mrs. Bennet can attest, the desire to see a future secured is a most natural thing for the stewards of any estate, real or literary.

Perhaps the most memorable bit of real-life "shipping" we've seen at Janeite meet-ups involved a couple at the UNC Jane Austen Summer Program in 2013, a pair of sixty-somethings dressed elegantly for the Saturday evening ball, long married and to all appearances still deeply in love. They told Ted they had a "routine" at these things:

"Sometimes we will separate before the ball, and observe one another from across the room—" the husband began.

His wife cut in with a stage whisper: "—and sometimes we dance with other people!" She raised her eyebrows. The husband merely giggled.

"She lends me out," he explained. "She won't tell you this, but I think it's because there are often so few men around, and she likes to see the women dancing."

"He's being very bad," the wife said. "The reason I have him dance with other people is so I can watch him. . . . It is thrilling to watch him charm the others."

"But we always end up together," the husband continued. "After we've spun the room with other people, that is."

This arrangement strikes us as a beautiful and rich way of enacting a course of Austenian romantic assessment: the man and wife separate from one another so that she can "ship" her man with various other women in the room, and they finish by "shipping" themselves with each other—that is, once the wife has been sufficiently "thrilled" by her mate's ability to please a select number of her Janeite sisters. In the same way, Emma is moved, more than she first recognizes, by Mr. Knightley's attentions to Harriet Smith on the dance floor. And for Emma, as for this couple with their amorous little routine, this observation of Knightley's gallant attentiveness is a strong sexual catalyst.

So—to return to the question that opened this essay—what *would* it have been like, in bed with Mr. Knightley? *Pretty good*, say many of the Janeites we've had the fortune to meet. These Janeites are deeply invested in the sexual energies of the characters in the novels, both as a literary exercise ("What trick is Austen playing on us here?") and as vicarious romance ("Which patrician nobleman would *you* find most bewitching?"). And when they're together, the Janeites take the logical next step of dramatizing these questions of sexual and romantic compatibility among their fellow conference-goers by setting them up together and feeding them romantic cues, more often than not plucked verbatim from the novels. Together, the heroines' assessments of possible mates and the frank (sometimes downright juicy) discussions of sex among Janeites in the present attest to the suggestive power of the sexual lacunae in the novels, where sex is never spoken of directly—but is hardly ever not spoken of.

Notes

1.   Margaret Drabble, *The Waterfall* (London: Weidenfeld and Nicholson, 1969; New York: Alfred A. Knopf), 65–66.

2.   Jane Austen, *Northanger Abbey*, ed. Barbara M. Benedict and Deirdre Le Faye (Cambridge University Press, 2006), 74. All quotations are taken from this edition and will appear in parenthetical citations with the abbreviation *NA*.

3. Jane Austen, *Emma,* ed. Richard Cronin and Dorothy McMillan (Cambridge University Press, 2005), 355. All quotations are taken from this edition and will appear in parenthetical citations with the abbreviation *E.*

4. Jane Austen, *Pride and Prejudice,* ed. Pat Rogers (Cambridge University Press, 2006), 26. All quotations are taken from this edition and will appear in parenthetical citations with the abbreviation *PP.*

5. Jane Austen, *Persuasion,* ed. Janet Todd and Antje Blank (Cambridge University Press, 2006), 66. All quotations are taken from this edition and will be cited parenthetically with the abbreviation *P.*

6. Otto Harbach, lyrics (revised by Dorothy Fields), for Jerome Kern's "I Won't Dance," cited in John Mueller, *Astaire Dancing: The Musical Films* (New York: Alfred A. Knopf, 1985), 71–72. For a performance of the full song, introduced by Astaire on the piano, see https://www.youtube.com/watch?v=6CTR3d2Ly80. Following his refusal to dance with Rogers, he goes into a furious solo tap routine, perhaps the equivalent of a cold shower.

7. Alexander Pope, "The Rape of the Lock," in *The Poems of Alexander Pope,* a one-volume version of the Twickenham edition, ed. John Butt (New Haven: Yale University Press, 1963), Canto II, 1.107.

8. For example, in Sterne's interpolated "Slawkenbergius's Tale," which begins his fourth volume, the abbess of Quedlingberg has come to Strasburg "to consult the university upon a case of conscience relating to [the sisters' of her convent] placket holes," neatly tying the bawdy symbol with Sterne's habitual anti-Roman Catholicism. (Laurence Sterne, *Tristram Shandy,* ed. Melvyn New and Joan New [University Presses of Florida, 1978, Vol. I, p. 301]). See Ruth Perry, "Words for Sex: The Verbal-Sexual Continuum in *Tristram Shandy*" in *Studies in the Novel,* 20, No. 1 (Spring, 1988): 27–42.

9. Jane Austen, *Sense and Sensibility,* ed. Edward Copeland (Cambridge University Press, 2006), 407. All quotations are taken from this edition and will be cited parenthetically with the acronym *SS.*

10. David Lodge, *Nice Work* (Harmondsworth, Penguin, 1988), 115, 289.

11. Jane Austen, *Mansfield Park,* ed. John Wiltshire (Cambridge University Press, 2005), 6–7. All quotations are taken from this edition and will be cited in the text with the acronym *MP.*

12. Juliet McMaster, "In Memoriam: Jack Grey: Tributes delivered at the JASNA 1993 Conference Lake Louise, Alberta, Canada, October 9, 1993" (privately printed pamphlet for participants), 6.

13. Deborah excused herself from the 2013 AGM on the grounds that both of her knees had recently been replaced.

14. Ruth Perry, "Sleeping with Mr. Collins," *Persuasions, The Jane Austen Journal,* 22 (Winter, 2000): 119–135; 133–34.

15. The talk was published as "Raptures and Rationality: Fifty Years of Reading *Pride and Prejudice*," in *Persuasions, the Jane Austen Journal,* 35 (Winter, 2013): 13–22.

16. Andrea L. "So, if Jane were not nearly 'engaged'," post in Pride and Prejudice Facebook group (private), September 28, 2020. https://www.facebook.com/groups/2204721688/posts/10157335197496689.

17. Kia L. "I've always wrestled with this!!!," Pride and Prejudice Facebook group (private), Monday, September 28, 2020.

18. Allison G. "Lizzy would have done her best," Pride and Prejudice Facebook group (private), Monday, September 28, 2020.

19. Meghan B., "Jane's too kind," Pride and Prejudice Facebook group (private), Monday, September 28, 2020. Ann M. "I think she would have taken one for the team," Pride and Prejudice Facebook group (private), Monday, September 28, 2020.

20. Wendy C., "I don't think so," Pride and Prejudice Facebook group (private), Monday, September 28, 2020.

21. Sally Jo S., "Despite his lackadaisical attitude," Pride and Prejudice Facebook group (private), Monday, September 28, 2020.

22. Sunny J., "I vote nay," Pride and Prejudice Facebook group (private), Monday, September 28, 2020.

23. Sunny J., "I wish Lizzy had told Collins," Pride and Prejudice Facebook group (private), Monday, September 28, 2020; Tricia S. and several others, Monday, September 28, 2020.

24. Reader, the historical novelist was already married.

Afterword

Sex, Romance, and Representation in Uzma Jalaluddin's *Ayesha at Last*

Juliette Wells

Fictional accounts of steamy love affairs with Jane Austen, erotic *Pride and Prejudice* sequels, and evangelical Christian romance novels loosely based on Austen's works: these were the main manifestations of sex and romance in the worlds of Austen's readers and fans that I mapped just over a decade ago in *Everybody's Jane: Austen in the Popular Imagination*. "Austen hybrids," I argued then, "are unmistakably an American phenomenon," although I acknowledged influential contributions by, among others, the Canadian comic artist Kate Beaton, the British novelist Helen Fielding, and the Canadian filmmaker Patricia Rozema.[1]

The contributors to *Jane Austen, Sex, and Romance: Engaging with Desire in the Novels and Beyond* compellingly demonstrate how much more there is to think about now with respect to Austen and sex, from both historical and contemporary perspectives. Laura Engel offers a new view of Austen's life and novels, especially *Sense and Sensibility*, via comparison with her all but forgotten contemporary, the portrait artist Jane Beetham Read. In addition to illuminating shadowy erotics in Austen, Engel's interpretation of Elinor Dashwood's fire screens makes an important contribution to the ever-evolving field of Austen and the arts.[2] Mary Ann O'Farrell argues, utterly convincingly, that teasing is sexy in *Pride and Prejudice* both before and after marriage, so much so that Georgiana Darcy receives an education in adult relationships simply by observing how her brother and his wife talk to each other in her presence. In a chapter that I plan to share with my undergraduate students, who hunger for nonheteronormative interpretations, Jade Higa attentively addresses "queer possibilities" in *Mansfield Park* and encourages all of Austen's readers to do the same.[3] In the kind of essay I wish all Austen-inspired creators would write, Diana Birchall takes us behind the scenes to explain the origins of her indelible, Bella Abzug–like Mrs. Elton. And I take my hat off to Devoney Looser for her indefatigable research into Austen erotica, which shows how much more there is to the story of this intriguing phenomenon.

The title and subtitle of this volume underwent several changes during its gestation; my own title here harks back to one of those earlier incarnations. The concept of representation, in the fullest sense of the word, is especially resonant today, in the midst of the Black Lives Matter movement and of continuing conversations about diversity within both Austen studies and Austen fandom.[4] Austenesque novels that focus on, or center, characters of color make a vital contribution to such conversations, and also to engaging new readers with Austen. I have written elsewhere about my first-year college students' delight in *Pride* (2018), Ibi Zoboi's YA "remix" of *Pride and Prejudice*, which elevates its young brown protagonists and acts as a love letter to its setting, multicultural Bushwick, Brooklyn.[5] Here, I will appreciatively examine Uzma Jalaluddin's witty, heartfelt *Ayesha at Last* (2018), promoted by its US publisher as a "modern-day Muslim *Pride and Prejudice* for a new generation of love," which is set in the author's home community of observant Muslim South Asians in Toronto.[6]

Like Austen before her, Jalaluddin acknowledges the real perils present in the world of her novel—Islamophobia, coercion of women, and hostility toward immigrants and refugees—while advocating that her characters, and her readers, "choose to live in a comedy, not a tragedy."[7] Jalaluddin's appealing, relatable central characters, Ayesha Shamsi and Khalid Mirza, reflect on, and in Khalid's case rethink, their commitments to religious observance and cultural customs.[8] By alternating chapters from Ayesha's and Khalid's points of view, Jalaluddin shows how each of them responds to their first-ever experiences of physical attraction and romantic love at the ages of twenty-seven and twenty-six, respectively. Jalaluddin's sympathetic, sensitive treatment of how both women and men live their singleness and sexuality in the context of committed faith is unique in Austen-inspired writing—and rare, too, in popular fiction aimed at a mainstream audience.[9]

For different reasons, both Ayesha and Khalid have long put their own desires behind their sense of duty to their families. Following her father's sudden death, Ayesha left India at age ten, along with her mother, brother, and grandparents. Initially dependent on the generosity of her uncle in Toronto, Ayesha and her immediate family have worked hard to establish themselves. A newly qualified high-school teacher, Ayesha moonlights as a spoken-word poet, a pursuit she loves but doesn't consider a reliable career.[10] While her very eligible cousin, twenty-year-old Hafsa, amasses marriage proposals for the fun of it, Ayesha reflects ruefully that she has "never even held someone's hand." Her best friend Clara, a white Canadian originally from Newfoundland, asks her "When do you get to be happy?", to which Ayesha responds matter-of-factly, "My family is counting on me to set a good example to Hafsa. . . . All that other stuff can wait" (3). Only Ayesha's Shakespeare-quoting grandfather, "a retired English professor from Osmania University in Hyderabad, India," encourages her to remember about love and romance (25). Elaine McGirr, reflecting on her own efforts to manage motherhood and career, asks whether Austen's decision not to marry Harris Bigg Wither was "a positive choice to keep her own needs and wants central, rather than having to rebalance her life in favor of a husband and children?" The compelling question that drives *Ayesha at Last* is not whether Ayesha will find love (or have sex) "at last" but rather how she will ultimately find a joyful new balance, both personal and professional, that will for the first time take into account what she wants and needs.

Unlike Ayesha, Khalid was born in Canada, a few years after his family emigrated from Hyderabad. He and his wealthy, domineering mother (who calls Lady Catherine de Bourgh to mind) have recently moved from western Toronto to Ayesha's neighborhood in eastern Toronto, which is full of "brown and black faces that reflected his own" (8–9). Khalid's reason for remaining unmarried is, like Ayesha's, rooted in family duty, though different in kind: he has never questioned his mother's belief that "Western ideas of romantic love are utter nonsense"; he finds it "comforting" to trust her to arrange his marriage, through which he will join, he thinks, "an unbroken chain that honored tradition and ensured family peace and stability" (2–4). In the meantime, Khalid is careful to keep his distance from women, observing a "no-touch rule" at work and exercising self-discipline in the form of "cold showers" (14). As the narrator trenchantly observes, "There wasn't much more that a twenty-six-year-old virgin-by-choice could do, really" (12).

The novel opens with Khalid hoping to catch a glimpse of a "beautiful" young woman with "a dreamy smile" and skin of a "golden burnished copper," whom he has often seen leaving her house across the street in the morning. Jalaluddin immediately makes clear both Khalid's attraction to this unknown woman—Ayesha, as we subsequently learn—and his effort to resist that attraction: "*It is not appropriate to stare at women, no matter how interesting their purple hijabs*, Khalid reminded himself" (1). It is important to note that Khalid is not ashamed of his interest in looking at Ayesha. Rather, by stopping himself from staring, he deliberately places respectful behavior over his pleasure in gazing at her.

When the two subsequently encounter each other, at an open-mic night where Ayesha performs, she responds to his physical presence as well. First, though, she notices his haughty attitude and conservative self-presentation:

> He looked bored and aloof, and the clothes he was wearing caught her attention. He was dressed in a long white robe and kufi skullcap, his beard well past acceptable hipster levels. Their eyes met briefly. A tiny spark of electricity passed between them.
>
> Ayesha looked away, and then back again.
>
> He was a good-looking man, she acknowledged. Large brown eyes in a pale face, sensual mouth pressed into a severe line. His dark beard was thick and long, accentuating a square jaw and sharp cheekbones. The white robe, so stark against the sea of tight jeans and T-shirts, hinted at broad shoulders and a powerful chest. He kept his gaze on the table in front of him, finely sculpted brows furrowed.
>
> He was not the sort of man Ayesha usually looked at. He looked a bit like a priest in a strip club, she thought with a smile. He looked up at her again, eyes dark as they observed her expression. She shivered, though the lounge was warm. (39)

Unlike Khalid, who is well aware of why he enjoys seeing his beautiful neighbor, Ayesha does not yet identify what she is feeling as attraction. Thus she does not stop herself from observing him. In conveying Ayesha's corporeal reactions to Khalid, Jalaluddin matches the "keen attention," as Stephanie Oppenheim argues, that Austen pays to Jane Fairfax's body in *Emma*.

Ayesha is distracted from examining her sensations, however, by the insult Khalid shortly afterwards makes in her hearing. Looking distrustingly at the nonalcoholic drink in front of her—his "face betrayed his doubts about the Shirley Temple's virginity"—he mutters disapprovingly about "the type of Muslim who frequents bars" (40). Ayesha reacts not by laughing off the slight among her friends, à la Elizabeth Bennet, but instead by confronting it head-on during her performance. "Who did that bearded fundy think he was?" she fumes to herself, before launching into a powerful poem against prejudice, which includes the lines:

> What do you see when you think of me,
> A figure cloaked in mystery
> With eyes downcast and hair covered,

An oppressed woman yet to be discovered? . . .
You fail to see
The dignified persona
Of a woman wrapped in maturity.
The scarf on my head
Does not cover my brain. . . .
What do I see when I think of you?
I see another human being
Who doesn't have a clue (42–43)

Ayesha delivers the last lines while looking straight at Khalid. Her message is plain: though a fellow Muslim, Khalid has jumped to conclusions about her as readily as an ignorant Westerner who assumes a hijab to be a symbol of subjugation.

Self-respect and respect for others are core values for both Ayesha and Khalid, as they gradually discover once many misunderstandings, including a Shakespeare-inspired mistaken identity, are resolved. Jalaluddin makes clear that the pair's attraction, on its own, is insufficient to bring them together: they must also learn to appreciate each other's qualities of character. Their process of doing so is gradual, as Maria Clara Pivato Biajoli has astutely pointed out is true of Elizabeth and Darcy but not typical of fan-authored fiction. Ayesha comes to realize both Khalid's handsomeness and his goodness as she "glanc[es] at Khalid's face in profile. He had long eyelashes and beautiful skin, big hands and thick fingers. She felt safe and comfortable beside him. *You are good and kind and wholly unexpected*, she thought with surprise" (127).

Jalaluddin writes especially movingly about how Khalid and Ayesha each respond to a brief physical encounter, which takes place after her grandmother has taught him, an enthusiastic cook, how to make the perfect parathas (flatbread). Ayesha, unintentionally, is the initiator:

[S]he noticed he had flour in his beard, and she reached out and absently brushed it away. His beard was like spun cotton, and her hand lingered.

He clasped her wrist to stop her, and their eyes met—hers wide in sudden realization, his steady. Ayesha blushed bright red, embarrassed at violating their unspoken no-touch rule. He looked at her for a long moment, then gently, reluctantly dropped her hand. . . .

She shouldn't have touched him; she couldn't believe that she had. Yet her hands on his face felt natural and right. She could still feel the gentle pressure on her wrist from his warm hand, the heat in his eyes. (143)

This unusual intimacy of touch and gaze smolders precisely because Ayesha and Khalid trust and appreciate the other's customary self-restraint—and because Jalaluddin narrates the scene so simply and directly. As Nora Nachumi rightly argues of Austen's novels, "[s]exual tension . . . often is generated by the disparity between the protagonists' private, or internal experience and how they must appear and behave in the public realm." Judy Tyrer too champions in *Ever, Jane* what she calls "the more subtle forms of romance and erotica," such as "the slight brushing of the fingers over a man's ungloved hand while handing him a recent book of poetry." In a very different register, Christien Garcia brings our attention to the erotics of Austen's depiction of hands in *Sense and Sensibility*.

Further in keeping with *Pride and Prejudice*, Ayesha and Khalid each let go of hardened beliefs for the sake of self-development, rather than to deserve or win back the other. Khalid expresses in a pivotal letter his awareness of his own "tendency towards judgment" that affected his first impression of Ayesha. "I have come to realize," he writes, that "you are a loyal, intelligent, outspoken person who has made great sacrifices for the people you love and the principles you live by. That is the definition of faith in my mind" (273). Knowing Ayesha has changed Khalid's conception of marriage too, he tells his friend and coworker Amir: "After I met Ayesha, I realized there were many paths to love and happiness, and they didn't all involve arranged marriage" (243). He even reconsiders his longstanding habit of wearing a full beard and clothing that signals his commitment to Islam—or, in Amir's words, makes him look like a "socially awkward religious nut" (314). After this "makeover" is complete, Khalid confesses to Ayesha's friend Clara, "I think I held on to the robe for too long. Just like I held on to some other things" (326).

In her affecting second proposal scene, Jalaluddin underscores Khalid's transformation as well as Ayesha's autonomy. Like Darcy, Khalid offers marriage only after seeking, and receiving, encouragement to do so—which Ayesha offers, more boldly than Elizabeth, by directly stating her wishes. "I was lost for so long, but you helped me see myself," Ayesha tells Khalid. "I know what I want now. I want to travel the world. I want to paint pictures with my words. But most of all, I want *you*." In return, he thanks her for showing him that "faith [is] a wide road" and for cultivating his compassion, before concluding, "I need you in my life, Ayesha. My heart is yours to take" (342). By establishing a strong bond of mutual understanding, respect, and attraction between Ayesha and Khalid, Jalaluddin leaves her readers in no doubt that they will enjoy a happy and satisfying marriage. Indeed, the couple confirms Deborah Knuth Klenck and Ted Scheinman's trenchant claim that, in Austen's novels, a "smart but playful manner in conversation" and "a lack of selfishness" combine to ensure conjugal delight.

Jalaluddin thought-provokingly juxtaposes the egalitarian nature of Ayesha and Khalid's partnership with the imbalanced relationships endured by two other couples, which demonstrate how the gender double standard persists regardless of ethnicity and religion. Clara (the Charlotte Lucas character) is frustrated by her boyfriend Rob's reluctance to commit. Inspired by Ayesha's story of how the Prophet Muhammad's wife, a successful businesswoman, proposed to him, Clara decides to send Rob a rishta—a formal offer—via Khalid, which Rob, bemused, accepts. For Hafsa, Ayesha's nubile cousin, Jalaluddin devises a chilling update of Wickham's seduction of Lydia Bennet, via ultra-gorgeous Tarek Khan, who not only defrauds Ayesha's mosque but also uploads nude pictures of Hafsa, without her consent, to a website that sells pictures of so-called "unveiled hotties" (291). Tarek fully bears out Margaret Dunlap's point, apropos of the Lydia Bennet "sex tape" in *The Lizzie Bennet Diaries,* about the enduring power of "men like Wickham who are both handsome and white, or—lacking those advantages—rich and powerful."

This brief exploration of *Ayesha at Last* can hardly do justice to the novel's strengths and subtleties. Particularly deserving of fuller attention is Jalaluddin's nuanced treatment of arranged marriage throughout her novel, notably in the subplot involving the post-scandal life of Khalid's sister Zareena (a recognizable, but significantly different, version of Georgiana Darcy).

Jalaluddin's multilayered reworking of *Pride and Prejudice* is especially impressive given that she did not originally conceive her romantic comedy as Austenesque. She began writing, she recalls in a letter to readers appended to the US edition of *Ayesha at Last,* "when diverse, representational stories were few and far between, particularly the joyful, romantic types featuring South Asians and Muslims" (n.p.). By her own account, she had worked on her draft for quite a while before noticing that her characters resembled Austen's. In an April 2021 interview with Amanda Diehl for *BookPage* promoting her second novel, *Hana Khan Carries On*, Jalaluddin emphasizes the purposeful use she made of that "happy accident": "Part of the reason why I decided to turn my head toward Jane Austen in my first book was because I was a little bit scared that people wouldn't know how to deal with my story." Indeed, as Diehl notes, "Jalaluddin's concerns were justified. Even with the Austen hook, *Ayesha at Last* was rejected countless times by publishers who didn't know how to sell a novel that featured characters and storylines outside of the industry's narrowly defined expectations for a Muslim romance."[11]

By anchoring her love story in *Pride and Prejudice*, Jalaluddin extends a warm invitation to a broad audience to reconsider any prejudices and unexamined assumptions they might have about observant Muslims in the West. In this respect, Jalaluddin's project is wholly distinct from those of fan fiction writers who, as Marilyn Francus argues, share "a desire for the modern world to be Austen's world" and who make an "effort to avoid or circumvent modernity and overwrite it with Austen." At the same time, Jalaluddin offers an affirming mirror to fellow members of her own faith community by depicting characters who are fully as witty, sexy, and romantic as Austen's. And Jalaluddin makes a strikingly unusual contribution to Austen adaptation, by highlighting the power—and the empowerment—of deliberate restraint. In this sense, Jalaluddin's take on Austen is much truer to the spirit of the original novels than Rachel Brownstein asserts is typical of present-day adaptation, with its "kinky sub-plots," "sexy shots" and other "adult" content. Looser claims that the "supposedly shocking newness" of sexualized Austen adaptations has been "used to sell these texts to readers, by claiming that they were making old-fashioned Austen stories into new-fangled bawdy fiction." Jalaluddin persuasively shows an alternative way of engaging present-day readers, by sensitively depicting the fulfillment of self-possession, as experienced by characters that represent identities and communities seldom seen in mainstream popular fiction. In the words of the imam of Ayesha's mosque, "[t]here are many paths to love" (291).

Notes

1. Juliette Wells, *Everybody's Jane: Austen in the Popular Imagination* (New York: Bloomsbury Academic [formerly Continuum], 2011), 178.

2. See, most recently, Anna Battigelli, ed., *Art and Artifact in Austen* (Newark, DE: University of Delaware Press, 2020) and Joe Bray and Hannah Moss, eds, *The Edinburgh Companion to Jane Austen and the Arts* (Edinburgh: University of Edinburgh, forthcoming).

3. I address undergraduate students' perspectives on gender in Austen in Juliette Wells, "Race, Privilege, and Relatability: A Practical Guide for College and Secondary Instructors," in *The Routledge Companion to Jane Austen*, ed. Cheryl A. Wilson and Maria H. Frawley (Milton Park, UK: 2021), 547–58.

4. See, in particular, the "Race and the Regency" lecture series sponsored by *JA & Co.* at the University of North Carolina, https://www.janeaustenandco.org/recorded-events; and *Beyond the Bit of Ivory: Jane Austen and Diversity*, special issue of *Persuasions On-Line* 41.2 (summer 2021), ed. Danielle Christmas and Susan Allen Ford, https://jasna.org/publications-2/persuasions-online/volume-41-no-2/.

5. Ibi Zoboi, *Pride* (New York: Balzer + Bray, 2018); Juliette Wells, "'*Pride and Prejudice*, Here and Now': Reflecting on a First-Year College Seminar," in *Beyond the Bit of Ivory*, https://jasna.org/publications-2/persuasions-online/volume-41-no-2/wells/.

6. Uzma Jalaluddin, *Ayesha at Last* (2018; New York: Berkeley, 2019), back cover. Subsequent page references will be to this title.

7. This phrasing is from the end of Jalaluddin's letter to US readers; in the novel, Ayesha's grandfather expresses the same sentiment in slightly different form.

8. On the concept of relatability in connection with teaching Austen at the undergraduate level, see Wells, "Race, Privilege, and Relatability" and Wells, "'*Pride and Prejudice*, Here and Now.'"

9. On how American Evangelical romance novelists have asserted common ground between the "purity" culture of today and the ideology of Austen's era, see Juliette Wells, "True Love Waits: Austen and the Christian Romance in the Contemporary U.S.," in *Global Jane Austen*, special issue of *Persuasions On-Line*, ed. Susan Allen Ford and Inger Sigrun Brodey, http://www.jasna.org/persuasions/on-line/vol28no2/wells.htm. On singleness, Christian faith, and Austen fandom from an American woman's perspective, see Juliette Wells, "Seeking Austen, from Abroad: Lori Smith's Memoir *A Walk with Jane Austen* (2007)," in *Transnational Literature* 1.2 (May 2009), http://fhrc.flinders.edu.au/transnational/home.html.

10. Austenesque novelists have long reimagined Mary Bennet as a writer: see Juliette Wells, "The Afterlives of Mary Bennet." *Sensibilities* 47 (2013): 122–36; and Camilla Nelson, "The Mary Bennet Makeover: Postfeminist Media Culture and the Rewriting of Jane Austen's Neglected Female Character," in *Persuasions On-Line* 40.2 (spring 2020), http://jasna.org/publications-2/persuasions-online/volume-40-no-2/nelson/. A more recent phenomenon, the choice to reinvent Elizabeth Bennet as a writer and/or a teacher of literature, is frequently—and inspiringly—made by writers of color who are creating characters of color. In addition to Jalaluddin's poet-teacher Ayesha, Zuri Benitez in Zoboi's *Pride* is an aspiring poet, and Alys Binat, the present-day Pakistani version of Elizabeth Bennet in Soniah Kamal's *Unmarriageable* (2019), teaches literature and advocates for the inclusion of South Asian women writers on her syllabi.

11. Amanda Diehl, "Uzma Jalaluddin: A new spin on a classic recipe," *BookPage,* April 2021, https://bookpage.com/interviews/26146-uzma-jalaluddin-romance#.YJVcQmZKhTY. The title character of *Hana Khan*

Carries On (New York: Berkeley, 2021) is an Austen fan rather than an updated version of an Austen heroine: Hana claims *Persuasion* as her favorite novel (278). Muslim Austen fans deserve more critical attention: see, for example, memoirist Huma Qureshi's description of her younger self as reading "Jane Austen obsessively, always a little disappointed that Marianne didn't get to be with Willoughby." Huma Qureshi, "Destined for an arranged marriage, I chose to follow my heart," *The Guardian,* 6 February 2021, https://www.theguardian.com/lifeandstyle/2021/feb/06/destined-for-an-arranged-marriage-i-chose-to-follow-my-heart.

Contributors

Maria Clara Pivato Biajoli is professor of English literature and English language at Federal University of Alfenas, Brazil. She has a PhD in Literary Theory and History (State University of Campinas, Brazil, 2017), and wrote a dissertation about Jane Austen's current popularity and the Austenmania phenomenon through an analysis of fan fiction. She has presented her research at conferences in several countries outside of Brazil, including England, the United States, Portugal, and Colombia, and has essays published in Brazilian academic journals and in *Persuasions Online,* the official journal of the Jane Austen Society of North America. Her current work includes Austen's reception in Brazil and translations of her novels into Portuguese.

Diana Birchall is retired from Warner Bros where she was a story analyst and book expert for many years. She is the author of Austen-related novels such as *Mrs. Darcy's Dilemma* and *The Bride of Northanger,* as well as many stories and plays. She has also written a scholarly biography of her grandmother, Onoto Watanna, the first Asian American novelist.

Rachel M. Brownstein, Professor Emerita at Brooklyn College and The Graduate Center, CUNY, is the author of *Becoming a Heroine: Reading about Women in Novels* (1982) and *Why Jane Austen?* (2011), as well as *Tragic Muse: Rachel of the Comédie-Française* (1993). Her new book, *American Born,* is forthcoming from The University of Chicago Press in 2023.

Margaret Dunlap served as a writer, director, and coexecutive producer of *The Lizzie Bennet Diaries,* the Emmy-winning transmedia adaptation of Jane Austen's *Pride and Prejudice*—dubbed "the best Austen adaptation around" by *The Guardian*—and cocreated the groundbreaking interactive series *Welcome to Sanditon.* Since then, she's written for numerous television series including *Dark Crystal: Age of Resistance, Marvel Rising: Heart of Iron,* and *Bladerunner: Black Lotus.* Find her on the web at www.margaretdunlap.com or on Twitter as @spyscribe.

Laura Engel is professor in the English department at Duquesne University where she specializes in eighteenth-century British literature and theatre. She is the author of *Women, Performance and the Material of Memory: The Archival Tourist* (Palgrave, 2019), *Fashioning Celebrity: Eighteenth-Century British Actresses and Strategies for Image Making* (Ohio State University Press, 2011), *Austen, Actresses and Accessories:*

Much Ado About Muffs (Palgrave Pivot, 2014), and coeditor of *Stage Mothers: Women, Work and the Theater, 1660–1830* (Bucknell University Press, 2015). She recently cocurated an exhibition "Artful Nature: Fashion and the Theater, 1770–1830," at the Lewis Walpole Library and is working on a new project entitled "The Art of The Actress in the Eighteenth Century" for the Cambridge University Press Elements Series.

Marilyn Francus, professor of English at West Virginia University, is the author of *The Converting Imagination: Linguistic Theory and Swift's Satiric Prose* and *Monstrous Motherhood: 18th-Century Culture and the Ideology of Domesticity.* She edited *The Burney Journal* (2006–2021), which is dedicated to the works of Frances Burney, one of Jane Austen's major influences. Marilyn has published articles on Jane Austen and popular culture, female conduct codes, and motherhood, and is currently working on the origins of the mommy wars. Marilyn was the Jane Austen Society of North America's international fellow in Chawton, UK, in 2015 and chair of JASNA's International Visitor Program from 2015 to 2022.

Christien Garcia is a University of Toronto Arts and Science Postdoctoral Fellow at the Centre for Comparative Literature. His research looks to literature and visual culture to explore questions about the political meanings and limits of sex. He is also a candidate at the Toronto Institute of Psychoanalysis, where he has practiced as a therapist in training since 2020.

Jade Higa is a faculty member of the English Department at 'Iolani School in Hawai'i where she teaches 9th graders as well as Asian American Literature and Creative Non-Fiction for 11th and 12th graders. She is interested in the intersection of eighteenth-century literature and queer studies, and she has published on Horace Walpole's *Mysterious Mother* and Charlotte Charke's *Narrative*.

Deborah Knuth Klenck taught satire, poetry, and fiction of the long eighteenth century for 42 years at Colgate University, both on campus and during seven semesters in London. She speaks at regional and international Jane Austen Society conferences and has been an annual guest at the Jane Austen Summer Program at the University of North Carolina, Chapel Hill, since 2014. Now Professor Emerita, she writes on literary pedagogy and on the works of Alexander Pope, Samuel Johnson, Barbara Pym, and especially Jane Austen.

Devoney Looser is Regents Professor of English at Arizona State University. She is the author or editor of nine books, including *The Making of Jane Austen,* named a *Publishers Weekly* Best Summer Book/Nonfiction, and *The Daily Jane Austen: A Year in Quotes.* Her essays have appeared in *The Atlantic,* the *New York Times, Salon, Slate, The TLS, Entertainment Weekly,* and *The Washington Post.* A Guggenheim Fellow and National Endowment for the Humanities Public Scholar, Looser's next book is a biography, *Sister Novelists: The Trailblazing Porter Sisters, Who Paved the Way for Austen and the Brontës* out from Bloomsbury in 2022.

Elaine McGirr is professor of eighteenth-century studies in the Department of Theatre, University of Bristol. Her recent publications include *Partial Histories: A Reappraisal of Colley Cibber* (Palgrave 2016) and *Stage Mothers: Women, Work, and the Theatre* (Bucknell 2014) and articles on Richardson, Aphra Behn, Shakespearean adaptation, eighteenth-century comedies, private theatricals, celebrity, and the authority of actresses. Her current project, "The Age of the Actress," recovers the careers of eighteenth-century actresses and the plays that made them famous.

Nora Nachumi is associate professor of English and coordinator of the minor in Women's Studies at Yeshiva University. She is the author of *Acting Like a Lady: British Women Novelists and the Eighteenth-Century Stage* and coeditor of this volume and of *Making Stars: Biography and Celebrity in Eighteenth-Century Britain,* with Stephanie Oppenheim and Kristina Straub, respectively. Recent work includes two pieces cowritten with Stephanie Oppenheim: "Was It Good for You?: Sex, Love and Austen" and "*Lady Susan* and *Love & Friendship*: Laughter, Satire, and the Impact of Form." She is currently at work on a biography of the eighteenth-century actress Elizabeth Farren.

Mary Ann O'Farrell is associate professor of English at Texas A&M University, specializing in Austen and James, the novel of manners, and representations of the body. Author of *Telling Complexions: The Nineteenth-Century English Novel and the Blush* and editor of *Virtual Gender: Fantasies of Subjectivity and Embodiment,* she has published numerous articles and book chapters in such venues as *PMLA, The Henry James Review,* the English Institute collection on *Compassion,* and *Janeites.* Her work on Jane Austen has been discussed in a range of media, including the *Atlantic* and the *New York Times.* She is currently completing a book about Austen's appearances in contemporary popular culture and political discourse.

Stephanie Oppenheim is associate professor of English at Borough of Manhattan Community College, the City University of New York. She has published articles on pedagogy, gender, and British literature, including "'I have traveled so little': Jane Austen's Women on the Road," "Already Twice Removed: Teaching Gender in British Literature," and, with Nora Nachumi, "Sex, Love and Austen: Was It Good for You?" and "*Lady Susan* and *Love & Friendship*: Laughter, Satire, and the Impact of Form."

Ted Scheinman is a senior editor at Smithsonian magazine and a contributing editor at the *Los Angeles Review of Books.* His reporting and essays have appeared in the *Chronicle of Higher Education,* the *New Republic,* the *New York Times,* the *Paris Review,* and elsewhere. His first book, *Camp Austen: My Life as an Accidental Jane Austen Superfan,* appeared via Farrar, Straus & Giroux in 2018.

Judy Tyrer began her career in educational gaming in 1977 working for Control Data Corporation as part of their PLATO project. She moved from there to UNIX operating system where she worked in clustered UNIX for customers such as IBM, HP, SCO, and DEC. Once clusters found their market, Judy moved back to games, using her programming skills as a network engineer for Ubisoft and her management skills as Lead Engineer for Sony Online Entertainment and Linden Lab. She is now living her dream as CEO of 3 Turn Productions LLC, makers of *Ever, Jane: The Virtual World of Jane Austen.*

Juliette Wells is professor of literary studies at Goucher College in Baltimore, Maryland. She is the author of two histories of Austen's readers, both published by Bloomsbury Academic—*Reading Austen in America* (2017) and *Everybody's Jane: Austen in the Popular Imagination* (2011)—and is working on a third, tentatively titled *Americans for Austen.* For Penguin Classics, she created 200th-anniversary reader-friendly annotated editions of *Persuasion* (2017) and *Emma* (2015). She has written widely on Austen and her cultural legacy: most recently, her "Intimate Portraiture and the Accomplished Woman Artist in *Emma*" appeared in *Art and Artifact in Jane Austen* (2020). Her forthcoming essays include "'He has great pleasure in seeing the performances of other people': Austen's Men and the Arts," in *The Edinburgh Companion to Jane Austen and the Arts*; and "'Here's harmony!': Music and Gender in Kirke Mechem's *Pride & Prejudice* (2019) and Jonathan Dove's *Mansfield Park* (2011)," in *Women and Music in Georgian Britain.*

Index

Page numbers in italics indicate illustrations.

Garcia, Christien, 7, 47–55, 248
Garson, Greer, 155
Gay, Penny, 44n1
Geater, Charlotte, 81n46
genre, 64, 159; "fix-it," 87, 94; romantic comedy, 87, 94
Glosson, Sarah, 230n90
Goode, Mike, 66, 67
Grahame-Smith, Seth, 62. *See also Pride and Prejudice and Zombies*
Grange, Amanda, 62, 104
Granson, Lily, 88
Grant, Hugh, 139
Green, Hank, 196n1
Greenfeld, Sayre, 89
Grey, Jack, 234

Haker, Ann, 69
Hale, Shannon, 66, 74n4, 88–89
Hall, Lynda A., 117n41
Halperin, David, 49
Harris, Rosemary, 156
Harry Potter fan fiction, 64, 65, 67, 69, 123
Haywood, Eliza, 156
Heckerling, Amy, 136, 154–55
Hellekson, Karen, 72
Heller, Joseph, 201
Herendeen, Ann, 199
Herr, Joelle, 202
Heydt-Stevenson, Jill, 4, 106
Heyer, Georgette, 86
Heywood, Eliza, 106
Higa, Jade, 6–7, 30–44, 243–44
Hills, Matthew, 102
Holt, Desiree, 204
Hopkins, Lisa, 88, 146–47

Inchbald, Elizabeth, 36

Jack and Alice (Austen juvenilia), 209
Jalaluddin, Uzma, 10, 244–50, 252n12

James, E. L., 205, 207
James, Henry, 158
Jane Austen Fan Fiction (JAFF) Index, 76n14
Jane Austen Kama Sutra (Herr's novel), 202
Jane Austen Society of Australia, 82n53
Jane Austen Society of North America (JASNA), 5, 12n30, 82n53, 123, 234–35, 239
Jane Austen Society of Pakistan, 234
Jane Austen's Guide to Pornography (Dawson's play), 203–4
"Jane-o-mania," 158
Janeites, 5, 123, 158, 205, 234–39
Janeites.com, 124
Jenkins, Henry, 4, 70–73, 75n10
Jenkins, Richard, 96–97
Jing, Elise, 81n47
Johnson, Claudia L., 2, 79n32, 96
Johnson, Samuel, 121
Jordan, Elaine, 44n1
Justice, George, 5

Kamal, Soniah, 251n10
Kauer, Deborah, 92
Keaton, Kate, 243
Kemp, Will, 29n3
Kern, Jerome, 230
Kiley, Rachel, 187, 193, 196n4
Kimball, Roger, 55n2
Kinski, Nastasia, 211
Kipling, Rudyard, 71
Kirkham, Margaret, 126
Knight, Edward, 216
Knuth Klenck, Deborah, 10, 227–40, 249
Koda, Harold, 41
Koetzebue, August von, 36, 40, 162–72

Langton, Simon, 143–44